AN INTRODUCTION TO
ISLAMIC FAITH AND THOUGHT

HOW TO LIVE AS A MUSLIM SERIES

AN INTRODUCTION TO ISLAMIC FAITH AND THOUGHT

Ali Ünal

New Jersey

Published by Tughra Books
335 Clifton Avenue
Clifton, New Jersey, 07011, USA

www.tughrabooks.com

Library of Congress Cataloging-in-Publication Data

Unal, Ali.
  An introduction to Islamic faith and thought / Ali Unal.
      p. cm. -- (How to live as a Muslim series ; 1)
  Includes bibliographical references and index.
  ISBN 978-1-59784-210-5 (pbk. : alk. paper) 1. Islam. 2. Islam--Doctrines.
I. Title.
  BP161.3.U53 2009
  297--dc22

                                                              2009008388

Printed by
National Book Network

CONTENTS

INTRODUCTION

Despite its centuries of close contact and co-existence with other cultures, Islam remains somehow alien and "other" to many. Having played a significant part in the colonized Muslim world's struggle to throw off its colonial masters and resume its rightful place in the world, Islam inevitably became associated in the popular mind with politics and ideology. More recently, it has become associated with backwardness and being reactionary as Muslims strive to rediscover their spiritual and cultural heritage and to live accordingly. Many people, always ready for simplistic answers to and explanations of an impossibly complex issue, latch on to such obvious associations and "truths" and probe no further.

This book does not deal with such matters. Rather, it is an attempt to peel away the layers of what we think we know about Islam to reveal what Islam says about itself, and to explain the pillars of the Islamic faith. It discusses Islamic thought, how we fit into it, and what God expects of us. It explains why Prophets were sent to guide us to the truth, why the Qur'an is the best guide for this journey, and how and why God equipped us to make this journey.

When faced with a Prophetic Message, as promised in: *For We have sent a Messenger to every community* (16:36), a new stage is reached in each person's life journey, both as a member of a community as well as an individual, and certain questions must be answered before it can resume: Do I accept this Message and do my best to redirect my life so that I may realize its ultimate goal? Do I reject it and do what I can to block its spreading to others? Or do I remain indifferent and continue to live as I have been doing?

During 610–23, the Arab community of Makka reached a turning point and had to make a decision. In 610, God raised one of their own as a Prophet and told him to begin preaching the very same Message that had been revealed in the past to other communities. This man, Muhammad, upon him be peace and blessings, had such an excellent reputation among his people for honesty and morality that he was known by all as *al-Amin* (the Trustworthy). Accepting his Divine appointment and striving to realize it until his peaceful death twenty-three years later, surrounded by his family members and an expanding community of grief-stricken followers, Muhammad, upon him be peace and blessings, brought his people—and many others—to their crossroads with the Divine. He then told them to use their God-given free will to choose what course they would follow during the rest of the years allotted to them.

The core beliefs of Islam are beyond dispute. The Qur'an was revealed in Arabic through a Messenger who was born and lived among his people. Thus his words, actions, and views could not become the stuff of legend or hearsay. As Arabic remains a living language, the inherent dangers of mistranslation and cultural misunderstanding cannot arise. In addition, Islam has never experienced the loss of its Sacred Scripture, the uncertainty of having more than one official version, or the issue of what to do with apocryphal and non-canonical writings. What Islam and its Messenger stand for are perfectly clear and readily understandable.

One consequence of such self-assurance and doctrinal soundness is Islam's continued ability to provide logical and reasonable answers to modern questions. Islam does not ask for suspended belief or blind faith, or appeal to "Divine mystery," when discussing such matters. Rather, it provides the basic framework within which answers are to be sought, as well as the methodologies by which to deduce acceptable answers from the core principles when necessary, and then leaves the person or community free to decide how best to apply it so that the desired goal is achieved.

The decision that we make at this crossroads will determine how we spend our remaining years on this planet. If we accept the Message, everything changes. Our personal goals are subsumed into those of the Message. We relate to ourselves, family members and other people, animals and nature, and even to life itself in totally new ways. No longer are we blinded by the artificial constructs handed down over the generations: gender and racial bias, tribalism and nationalism, feelings of superiority and inferiority, physical and economic exploitation of the weak, and so on.

While we make choices every day, many of us remain on the fence when it comes to making a spiritual choice. We seek to postpone it until we are older, until our situation changes, until it "feels right." But life contains two certainties against which such procrastination cannot defend itself: death and that delaying such an important decision is never rewarded.

CHAPTER 1

Islam as the Universal Religion and
the Religion of Perfect Harmony

ISLAM AS THE UNIVERSAL RELIGION AND
THE RELIGION OF PERFECT HARMONY

The Qur'an uses *din*, usually translated as "religion," in different contexts with various meanings, of which the most important and common are: judging, rewarding, punishing (1:4, 51:6, 82:18-19, 37:53, 56:86); way, law, constitution (12:76); penal law (24:2); the collection of moral, spiritual, and worldly principles, system, way of conduct (33:5, 40:26); servanthood, obedience (16:52); and peace and order (8:39).

GENERAL ISLAMIC BELIEFS

With Islam, God perfected the religion He revealed and chose for humanity (5:3). Literally, Islam means submission, peace, and salvation. In its most fundamental aspect, Islam is epitomized in the most frequently recited of all Qur'anic phrases, the *Basmala*—In the name of God, the All-Merciful (*ar-Rahman*), the All-Compassionate (*ar-Rahim*). Both words are related to the quality of *rahma* (mercy and compassion). God manifests Himself through His absolute, all-inclusive Mercy and Compassion, and Islam is founded upon that affirmation. The Qur'an calls Prophet Muhammad's mission a mercy for all the worlds.

Tawhid (Monotheism)

Islam is uncompromisingly monotheistic, for its theology begins and ends with God's Unity *(tawhid)*. Given this, the universe is seen as an integral whole of interrelated and cooperative parts in which a splendid coordination, harmony, and order is displayed both throughout the universe and within each living organism.

This harmony and order come from the Unity of the One Who created them and Who is absolute, without partner, peer, or like. The universe operates according to the laws God established for it, and therefore is literally *muslim*—absolutely submitted to God. Thus its operations are stable, orderly, and harmonious.

Humanity

God created the universe so that He could be known and recognized in all His Names and Attributes, and so His creation includes one creature with free will: humanity. Of all creatures, only humanity can manifest the Divine Names the All-Willing, All-Knowing, and All-Speaking in the most comprehensive level. God then endowed us with the knowledge of things ("names"), and made us His vicegerent on the earth to inhabit and improve it according to His laws. As having free will means that one must choose, each person's life consists of choosing between what is right and wrong.

God endowed humanity with three principal faculties fundamental to our survival and carrying out our function as His vicegerent: an appetite for such things as the opposite sex, offspring, livelihood, and possessions; anger or forcefulness in defense and struggle; and reason or intellect. Since we are tested in this worldly life and are free to choose, God did not restrict these faculties.

According to Islam, our individual and collective happiness lies in disciplining our faculties so that we may produce a harmonious and peaceful individual and social life. If they remain undisciplined, they may drive people to immorality, illicit sexual relationships, unlawful livelihoods, tyranny, injustice, deception, falsehood, and other vices. To prevent the ensuing chaos and suffering, we must submit to an authority that guides and regulates our collective affairs. Since one person will not accept the authority of another, humanity needs a universal intellect, a guidance from beyond human reason and experience, to whose authority all may assent freely. That guidance is the religion revealed and perfected by God through His Prophets: Islam.

Prophets

All Prophets came with the same essentials of belief: belief in God's Existence and Unity, the world's final destruction, Resurrection and Judgment, Prophethood and all Prophets without distinction, all Divine Scriptures, angels, and Divine Destiny and Decree (including human free will). They called people to worship the One God, preached and promoted moral virtue, and condemned vice. Differences in particular rules and injunctions were connected with the economic and political relationships existing at that time, and because all Prophets prior to Prophet Muhammad, upon him be peace and blessings, were sent to their own people and for their own time. Prophet Muhammad, upon him be peace and blessings, was sent as the heir to all previous Prophets and therefore to the whole of humanity regardless of time or place. Thus to be a Muslim means believing in all previous Prophets and the original previous Scriptures.

A Prophet, one purified of sin and vice and having a deep relation with God, guides people to truth and sets a perfect example for them to follow. Such people have the following essential characteristics: absolute and complete truthfulness, trustworthiness, and communication of the Divine Message; the highest intellectual capacity, wisdom, and profound insight; sinlessness; and no mental or physical defects. Just as the sun attracts the planets by the invisible force of gravitation, Prophets attract people by the force of their profound relation with God, certain miracles, and the sheer nobility of their person, purpose, and character.

Faith or belief

Faith or belief, the essence of religion, is not just a simple brief affirmation based on imitation. Rather, it has degrees and stages of expansion or development, just as a tree's seed gradually is tranformed into a fully grown, fruit-bearing tree. Belief contains so many truths pertaining to God's Names and the realities contained in the universe that the most perfect human science, knowledge, and virtue is belief as well as knowledge of God originating in belief based on argument and investigation. Such belief has as many degrees and grades of manifestation as the number of Divine Names. Those who attain the degree of certainty of belief coming from direct observation of the truths on which belief is based (*ayn al-yaqin*) can study the universe as a kind of Divine Scripture.

The Qur'an, the universe, and humanity are three manifestations of one truth. Therefore, in principle, there can be no contradiction or incompatibility between Qur'anic truths (from the Divine Attribute of Speech) and truths derived from the objective study of its counterpart, the created universe (from the Divine Attributes of Power and Will). An Islamic civilization true to its authentic, original impulse contains no contradiction between science (the objective study of the natural world) and religion (the set of God's laws for the life of humanity which guides humanity to happiness in both worlds and enables it to obtain God's approval and good pleasure). True belief is not based on blind imitation, but rather should appeal to our reason and heart, and combine reason's affirmation and the heart's inward experience and submission.

Another degree of belief is known as certainty coming from the direct experience of its truths (*haqq al-yaqin*). This depends on regular worship and reflection, and those who possess it can challenge the world. So, Muslims' foremost duty is to acquire this degree of belief and try, in full sincerity and purely to please God, to communicate it to others.

> The highest aim of creation and its most sublime result is belief in God. The most exalted rank of humanity is the knowledge of God. The most radiant happiness and sweetest bounty is the love of God contained within the knowledge of God; the purest joy for the human spirit and the purest delight for a person's heart is the spiritual pleasure contained within the love of God.[1]

Worship

Belief engenders different kinds of worship, such as responding to explicit injunctions (e.g., the Prescribed Prayers, fasting during the month of Ramadan, the Prescribed Purifying Alms-giving, and pilgrimage to the Ka'ba) and avoiding prohibitions (e.g., killing, usury, fornication and adultery, violation of filial responsibilities, taking any intoxicants, gambling, and deception). Those seeking to strengthen their belief and attain higher ranks of perfection should be careful of their heart's and intellect's "acts" (e.g., contemplation, reflection, invocation, recitation of God's Names, self-criticism, perseverance, patience, thankfulness, self-discipline, and perfect reliance upon God). Moral virtues are the fruits of religious life. As Prophet Muhammad, upon him be peace and blessings, said: "I have been sent to perfect good character."[2]

Islam also regulates our collective life. By means of belief and worship, as well as its intellectual, moral, and spiritual principles, Islam educates us in the best possible way. In addition, its socio-economic principles establish an ideal society free of dissension, corruption, anarchy, and terror, one that allows everyone to obtain happiness both in this world and in the Hereafter.

The Good Life

Many Western intellectuals and their counterparts in the Muslim world assert that serving God or living a religious life is a compensatory device contrived to console people for their own weaknesses and defects. But such people, even though armed with science, technology, and the illusions of freedom from belief and servanthood to a Supreme Being as well as of their own existence as powerful beings, abase themselves before anyone or anything, regardless of how low, if they consider it in their self-interest to do so.

Sincere believers do not follow this path of self-degradation. Dignified servants of God, they reject any worship of that which is not God, even if it is something of the greatest benefit. Though modest and gentle in their nature and bearing, they "lower" themselves voluntarily before others only to the degree that their Creator permits. Though aware of their weakness and neediness before God, they rely upon their One Master's Wealth and Power and so are independent of others. They act and strive purely for God's sake and good pleasure, and to be equipped with virtue.

Students of the Qur'an see that everything in the universe glorifies, mentions, and praises God to an infinite degree. Though weak enough to be defeated by a microbe and driven to distress and despair by the least grief and anxiety, they can rise to such exalted ranks as to be beloved friends of God (10:62).

The life of religion and serving God accepts right, not force, as the point of support in social life. It proclaims that the aim of both individual and collective life is to attain virtue and God's approval instead of realizing selfish interests, and mutual assistance instead of conflict. It orders that a community's internal unity should be through ties of religion, profession, and country, not through racism and negative nationalism. It works to erect a barrier against worldly desires and encourages us to strive for perfection by urging the soul to sublime goals. Right calls for unity, virtue brings solidarity, and mutual assistance means helping each other. Religion secures fellow-feeling, and attraction. Self-discipline and urging the soul to virtue brings happiness in this world and the next.

Why the Muslim world went into decline

According to Said Nursi, Muslims are required to be *muslim* (submitted to God) in all of their attributes and actions, but fail always to be so in practical life. It is the same with non-Muslims, for not all of their attributes and actions necessarily originate in unbelief or transgression. Thus non-Muslims who acquire Muslim attributes and conform to Islamic principles can defeat Muslims who neglect to practice Islam.

God has established two kinds of laws: the religion (issuing from His Attribute of Speech and governing our religious life) and the so-called laws of nature (issuing from His Attribute of Will and governing creation and life). The reward or punishment for following or ignoring them is given at different times. In the first case, this usually is given in the afterlife; in the second case, this usually is given in this world.

The Qur'an constantly draws our attention to natural phenomena, the subject matter of science, and urges us to study them. Throughout the first five centuries of Islam, Muslims united science with religion, the intellect with the heart, and the material with the spiritual. Later on, however, Europe took the lead in science due to its unconscious obedience to the Divine laws of nature, and thus was able to dominate the Muslim world, which no longer practiced Islam's religious and scientific aspects.

HUMANITY IN ITS RELATIONSHIP WITH RELIGION

Immediately after our birth, we have no conscious knowledge of ourselves or our surrounding environment. Yet we are not aliens, but rather beings who are fit to survive here. For example, each person's body is made up of the same elements that exist in nature. The building blocks making up the earth's mineral, vegetable, and animal elements also constitute the sperm and the egg that, when joined, initiate our earthly life. Yet no one knows how this inanimate matter is transformed into living forms. We can say only that it is a direct gift of the Creator. Thus we are children of nature and aware of ourselves as creatures made by the Creator. This awareness makes us conscious of the second aspect of our being: our heavenly aspect.

Typically, children are born into a welcoming environment and know the embrace of parents and a wider family of relatives. Moreover, they are immediately provided with the most perfect nourishment: a mother's milk. As they grow, children experience the world as a fully ordered environment of sight and sound, heat and light

and rainfall, and an enormous diversity of plants, fruits, and ani
mals. All of these enable children to exercise and develop the senses,
feelings, and intellect implanted within them by the Creator.

Likewise, their bodies function without their conscious effort
or decision. Each person receives a minutely arranged and coordinated physical body as a gift from the Creator when He bestows
life, so that his or her life may be supported and mature. Very little of what we have can be said to be our own doing. In fact, without the Creator's help, we could not even manage our own bodies
and therefore would die.

The One Who created the universe and subjected it to our
stewardship is also the One Who created us. Given this, it makes
perfect sense to consider what our responsibility is and, considering all that we have been given, to reflect on how we will answer
for ourselves and for what has been placed in our care. Human responsibility before the Creator is voluntary, whereas all non-human creatures perform their duties without reflection but also
without defect.

The apparent efficiency of modern technology obscures our
relative impotence and vulnerability. We cannot create even a leaf
or a fly, although we are free to tamper with God's creation to the
extent He wills. We have no dominion over our body's operations,
such as its hunger or thirst, or the world. We cannot determine
our parents, our time and place of birth and death, or our phy-
sique or physical structure. We have to use the natural world to
sustain and enlarge our lives. The One Who subjected nature to us
also implanted within us the necessary intellectual faculties by
which we can use nature. Our intellect is capable of obtaining
some knowledge of nature's orderly operations and then formulat-
ing laws based upon the observed uniformity and reliability. These
laws are our imperfect, human intimations of the supreme laws
created and used by the Supreme Being to create the universe.

The quality of being human comes from our immaterial and
spiritual aspects, not from our natural and material aspects. The

spirit and intellect do not originate in the physical body, for the spirit's departure from a dead body reduces that body to something that will decompose into the soil. The body remains for a while, but all of its former senses are now absent. This means that the spirit uses the body, and that only life gives the body any meaning.

This body–spirit relation can be understood somewhat by the following analogy: A factory, no matter how complex, sophisticated, and excellent, has no more value than a pile of mechanical junk if there is no electricity to operate it. This does not mean that the spirit is everything in and of itself and that the body is junk; rather, the spirit needs matter or a corporeal form to express its powers and functions.

A fruit tree's future life is encapsulated in its seed, and a tree is basically worth as much as the value of the fruit it yields. In the same way, each person's life history is recorded and is of value only in proportion to the number of good deeds done and the level of virtue attained. Again, just as a tree increases by means of the seeds in its fruit, we prosper by our good deeds, the weight and consequence of which one day will be revealed to us.

We scatter our deeds in this world and harvest the results in the next world. Given this, the All-Majestic, All-Powerful, All-Wise Creator, Who brings us into existence from non-existence and Who brings us to life by breathing the "spirit" into our bodies fashioned from nature's clay, will resurrect us after we decompose into the ground. For Him, doing so is as easy as bringing day after night, spring after winter, and making what appears to be dry wood at the end of autumn yield grapes the following summer.

In addition to all of this, we have three principal drives: desire, anger, and intellect. We desire or lust after the opposite sex, and love our children and worldly possessions. We direct our anger at what stands in our way, and by using it can defend ourselves. Our intellect enables us to make right decisions. The Creator does not restrain these drives, but rather requires us to seek perfection through self-discipline so that we do not misuse them.

It is this struggle that determines our humanity, for without it we would have no purpose and would be the same as all other non-human creatures.

Human beings mature spiritually and intellectually; they have been equipped with the necessary ingredient for this process: free will. The other creatures, without free will, live lives that are wholly determined within nature, for without free will they have no way to keep themselves within the correct limits. If we ignore these limits as human beings, we may usurp the property of others or seek illicit sexual relations, or use our intellect to deceive others.

This is why our powers must be held in check. Our intellect was given to us to be used with wisdom, and our desire and anger to be used lawfully and in moderation. Moreover, since we are social beings we must restrain ourselves, or else wrongdoing, injustice, exploitation, disorder, and corruption will occur.

But what is lawful and right, moderate and wise? Who decides the criteria, and how will they be accepted by people? Who am I? Where do I come from? What is my final destination? What does death demand from me? Who is my guide on this journey, beginning from clay and passing through the stages of a sperm drop, a blood clot, and a lump of flesh, another creation where the spirit is breathed into my body, and finally reaching the grave and through there to the Hereafter? In all of these questions lie the essential problem of human life.

It is rare for even two or three people to agree on the truth of a matter. If the rich and powerful define truth, their truth will exclude or disadvantage the poor and vice versa. Truth cannot be decided by majority vote, for truth is truth regardless of how many people vote for it. Truth is—and can only be determined by—the Ultimate Truth, another name for God, Who created humanity and the universe. Our task is to discover that truth and abide by it.

Of course there are some universal truths, such as honesty, generosity, altruism, truthfulness, helpfulness, and compassion. These are essentially reflections of our true nature given us by the Creator.

Created by the One, Who is the All-Wise, the All-Generous, the All-Compassionate, every person has an innate inclination toward these virtues. Therefore, they are confirmed and established by Islam, which was revealed by God through His Prophets to show humanity how to resolve all of its psychological and social problems.

While constant change is observed in nature, there is an underlying aspect of permanence in everything. For instance, a seed germinates underground and grows into a tree without the laws of germination and growth changing. Likewise the essential nature and purposes of all people, regardless of any external material or other changes in their lifestyles, as well as their impact on our lives and environment have remained unchanged since the creation of Adam and Eve. All of us share certain general conditions of life and value: we are born, mature, marry, have children, and die; we have some degree of will and common desires; we share certain values, such as honesty, kindness, justice, courage, and so on.

Thus all Prophets sent by God were sent with the same message concerning God's Absolute Oneness and Absolute Transcendence: He does not beget nor is He begotten, for He is Eternally Self-Existent. Each created being naturally depends on his or her Creator. Only the Creator is Self-Existent, unique and single, and not composite, subject to change, or contained by time or space. Belief in such a Divine Being constitutes the primary foundation of the Divine Religion preached by all Prophets. Its other pillars are belief in the Resurrection, all Prophets without distinction, angels, Divine Scriptures, and Divine Destiny (including human free will). Through sincere faith and worship, as well as adherence to the Prophets' pristine teachings, we can attain the highest degree of elevation, even becoming worthy of heaven.

Those who do not use their free will to discipline themselves face the danger of enslavement by their passions. Such lack of self-discipline causes us to wrong others, for the goal of such behavior is to satisfy our desires. Since the Divine Religion does not allow such wrongdoing, those who pursue it try to corrupt religion in order to justify their whims and fancies. This causes disorder, oppression, unending conflict, and destruction. God wills mercy for His creation, not oppression or injustice, and that they live in peace so that justice prevails. However, history relates that the followers of earlier Prophets split into opposing factions and tampered with the religion to serve a given sect's local cultural preference or interest.

All previous Prophets were sent to restore the Divine Religion to its original purity by purging the innovations and deviations added by its adherents. This is why Prophet Muhammad was sent after Jesus to preach the same pillars of faith. God revealed to him the Qur'an, which contains the eternal principles for our individual and collective life. Since God decrees that the Qur'an is absolutely and permanently preserved, Prophet Muhammad, upon him be peace and blessings, is the last Messenger.

Islam honors the religious experience of those who came before its revelation because Islam confirms and completes what is true in those religions. Given this, Muslims say that Prophet Abraham and all other Prophets were Muslim. Such an outlook explains why Islamic civilization, from its very beginnings, was and remains tolerant, plural, and inclusive. It has always been this way, except for the rarest of exceptions.

WE NEED GOD AND RELIGION MORE THAN EVER BEFORE

Although modern technology has blinded us to some fundamental human limitations so that we consider ourselves omnipotent, self-sufficient, and self-existent or possessors of unlimited power, in reality we are weak, frail, needy, and destitute. Although we cannot create a leaf or a gnat, or even a molecule of water, our entrapment by the spell of modern technology makes us loathe to admit this. We are content to ascribe all natural events, from sunrise and sunset to the movements of atoms, to nominal natural laws that function without our intervention. Even our bodies work independently of us, for we cannot prevent ourselves from sleeping, becoming hungry or thirsty, or dying as a result of an encounter with a microscopic creature.

We always are accompanied by sorrows arising from past misfortunes and by worries about the future. Fear, love, and expectations are inseparable from our existence, while such things as youth and beauty, of which we are very fond, leave without saying goodbye. We greatly fear and are overwhelmed unexpectedly by misfortune, old age, and death. Countless requirements must be maintained if we are to go on living, yet we have total control over none of them. We may be injured, accidents may end our hopes, and disease and unexpected events always threaten and block our way to happiness. We endure earthquakes, storms, floods, fires, and other natural catastrophes. Both the vast variety of phenomena and our awareness of our own frailty make our own weakness and helplessness quite clear.

Despite our claims to have dominated nature and conquered space, we have more need of religion than our ancestors ever did. We may not be worshipping fetishes as they did, such as trees, animals, rivers, fire, rain, and heavenly bodies, but, according to Erich Fromm, millions of us have our own fetishes: national heroes, movie stars, politicians, sports figures, musicians, and many, many others.[3]

Furthermore, millions practice such modern religions as transcendental meditation, necromancy, Satanism, and spirit worship in the hope of satisfying that which cannot be satisfied with scientific and technological advances. Others seek fulfilment in stadiums, nightclubs, casinos, jobs, and trade unions. They transform such places into places of devotion because they cannot suppress their need to worship. Inevitably, those who do not believe in and worship the One God become the slaves of numerous deities.

ISLAM, HUMANITY AND NATURE

Everyone talks so much about the danger of war and environmental pollution that *peace* and *ecology* have become quite fashionable words. However, those who are expected to diagnose these problems wish to remove them through the further conquest and domination of nature.

This problem has arisen because the humanity–nature equilibrium has been destroyed by the modern materialistic conception of, and corrupt attitude toward, humanity and nature. Most people are reluctant to perceive that social peace and peace with nature is possible only through peace with the spiritual order. To be at peace with the earth one must be at peace with his or her heavenly self, and this is impossible if one is not at peace with Heaven.

The dangers caused by our domination of nature are well known, despite new measures taken to protect it. Nature is no longer considered sacred, as it was in the medieval era, and so has lost its meaning. The resulting void caused by the disappearance of this indispensable aspect of human existence continues to exist within our souls and manifests itself in many ways, sometimes violently and desperately.

This domination of nature is largely responsible for many problems, among them urban sprawl and congestion, the exhaustion of natural resources, the destruction of natural beauty, and the abnormal rise in mental illnesses. This, together with giving our animalistic tendencies complete freedom, has made the problem of war so crucial.

Islam contains an elaborate hierarchy of knowledge integrated by the principle of Divine Unity (*tawhid*). This hierarchy includes juridical, social, and theological sciences, as well as spiritual and metaphysical ones, all of which derive their principles from the Qur'an. Elaborate philosophical, natural, and mathematical sciences, each originating from one of God's Beautiful Names, also developed.

For example, the Name the All-Healing shines on medicine; geometry and engineering depend on the Names the All-Just, All-Shaping, and All-Harmonizing; and philosophy reflects the Name the All-Wise. Each level of knowledge portrays nature in a particular light. Jurists and theologians consider knowledge to be the background for human action, philosophers and scientists see it as a domain to be analyzed and understood, and metaphysicians view it as the object of contemplation and the mirror reflecting supra-sensible realities.

Muslim scholars have no tradition of separating the study of nature from knowing God. Thus, many Muslim scientists, such as Ibn Sina, Nasiruddin at-Tusi, and Jabir ibn al-Hayyan, were also practicing Muslims with deep spiritual devotion.[4] Muslims always have considered observing and contemplating nature very important aspects of their spiritual life.

Furthermore, Muslims have maintained an intimate connection between science and other fields of Islamic studies. This connection is found in the Qur'an itself, for as the Divine Scripture of Islam it corresponds to the macrocosmic revelation (the universe). Thus Islam is also the name of the Divine system of the universe. The Book of Islam is "the revealed and recorded Qur'an (*al-Qur'an at-tadwini*)" and the entire universe is the "Qur'an of creation (*al-Qur'an at-takwini*)."

Humanity is also a Divine Book that corresponds to the Qur'an and the universe. Given this, *ayat* designates a Qur'anic verse, events taking place within our souls, and all phenomena occurring within nature. Human life is so interrelated with natural phenomena that those who can discern them can draw correct conclusions about human social life. In other words, the laws of history can be deduced from the laws of nature. For example:

> Your Lord is God, Who created the heavens and the earth in six days. He was then established on the Supreme Throne, covering day with night, which pursues it urgently—and the sun, moon, and stars subservient, by His command. Verily, His are the creation and the command. Blessed be God, the Lord of all being. Call on your Lord, humbly and secretly. He loves not transgressors. Do not do corruption in the land after it has been set right. Call upon Him in awe and eagerly. Surely the grace of God is nigh to the good-doers. It is He Who

> looses the winds, bearing good tidings before His grace, till, when they are charged with heavy clouds, We drive them to a dead land and use them to send down water and bring forth all fruits [from the soil]. Even so, We shall bring forth the dead. Hopefully you will remember. And the good land's vegetation comes forth by the leave of its Lord, and the corrupt [land's vegetation] comes forth but scantily. Even so We turn about signs for a people who are thankful. (7:54–58)

These verses apparently discuss natural phenomena yet mention the Resurrection and prayer's importance. Corruption in the land is forbidden, and we are told that God commands everything and has no partners either in creation or command. Thus, the main principles of faith (belief in God's Oneness and the Resurrection) are emphasized while we are reminded of our function or duty: as God's vicegerent, we are to pray, establish justice, and avoid corrupting and transgressing the Divine law.

Other inner meanings are hinted at. For example, day and night symbolize happy moments and misfortunes respectively, which alternate in both a person's and a nation's life. Rain, the symbol of Divine Grace, is mentioned as the grace of God, which is close to those who do good. The winds bearing the good tidings of rain correspond to the pioneers or leaders of a religious revival, and their message is likened to heavy clouds of rain.

Hearts without faith and minds without good judgment and sound reasoning resemble dead lands that need rain to be made fruitful. Just as a fertile land's vegetation emerges by its Lord's leave, hearts and minds ready for the Divine Message are the sources from which faith, knowledge, and virtues radiate. However, there always will be some desert-like minds and hearts that do not receive enough rain to produce any vegetation and so do not benefit from this grace.

Finally, these verses console believers living as small oppressed minorities amidst a corrupt, wrong-doing community with the good tidings that victory is near as long as they keep striving for God's cause and seeking help in patience and prayer.

Thus Revelation is inseparable from the cosmic revelation, which is also a book of God. By refusing to separate humanity from nature, Islam preserves an integral view of the universe and sees the flow of Divine grace in the arteries of the cosmic and natural order. As we seek to transcend nature from its very bosom, nature can be an aid in this process, provided that we learn to contemplate it as a mirror reflecting a higher reality:

> In the creation of the heavens and the earth and in the alternation of night and day there are signs for people with minds, who remember God and mention His Name, standing and sitting and on their sides, and reflect upon the creation of the heavens and the earth: "Our Lord, You have not created this for vanity. Glory be to You! Guard us against the punishment of the Fire. (3:190-91)

Humanity is located at the axis and center of the cosmic milieu. By being taught the names of all things, we receive the keys to knowledge of all things and so gain dominion over them. However, we receive this power only in our capacity of serving as God's vicegerent *(khalifa)* on the earth, not as a rebel against Heaven.

In fact, humanity is the channel of grace for nature, for our active participation in the spiritual world causes light to enter the world of nature. Due to our intimate connection with nature, our inner state is reflected in the external order. Thus, when our inner being turns to darkness and chaos, nature turns from harmony and beauty to disequilibrium and disorder. We see ourselves reflected in nature, and penetrate into nature's inner meaning by delving into our own inner depths. Those who live on the surface of their being can study nature as something to be manipulated and dominated, while those who turn toward the inner dimension of their existence can recognize nature as a symbol and come to understand it in the real sense.

This concept of humanity and nature, as well as the presence of a "metaphysical" doctrine and a hierarchy of knowledge, enabled Islam to develop many sciences that were influential in the

West's own development of science and yet did not disturb Islam's intellectual edifice. Someone like Ibn Sina could be a physician and peripatetic philosopher and yet expound his "Oriental philosophy" that sought knowledge through illumination. A Nasiruddin at-Tusi could be the leading mathematician and astronomer of his day as well as the author of an outstanding treatise on Islamic spiritual life. Jabir ibn al-Hayyan's emphasis on Islamic spirituality did not prevent him from founding algebra and chemistry. And Ibn Jarir at-Tabari,[5] one of the most outstanding figures in Islamic jurisprudence, history, and Qur'anic interpretation, wrote about the winds' fertilizing clouds so that rain would fall. Ibrahim Haqqi of Erzurum, a well-known seventeenth-century spiritual master, was a brilliant astronomer, mathematician, and physician.

There are many more such examples, but these are enough to show that Islam's hierarchy of knowledge and its possession of a "metaphysical" dimension have satisfied its followers' intellectual needs. And so they never sought to satisfy their thirst for causality outside of religion, as happened in the modern West.

Islam is the universal order, the integral religion of harmony, and the unique system that harmonizes the physical with the metaphysical, the rational with the ideal, and the corporeal with the spiritual. Each dimension of our earthly life has its own place within Islam's matrix and thus can perform its own function, enable us to be at peace with the dimensions of our existence and our community and nature, and to gain happiness in both worlds.

CHAPTER 2

_____

God's Existence and Oneness

GOD'S EXISTENCE AND ONENESS

Of all the religions existing today, Islam is the one that places the greatest stress on Divine Unity (*tawhid*) and is purely monotheistic. All others, whether God-revealed or esentially polytheistic, unfortunately have been darkened to a certain extent.

THE UNIVERSE AND GOD'S EXISTENCE

The existence of God is too evident to need any arguments. Some scholars even have stated that God is more manifest than any other being, but that those who lack insight cannot see Him. Others have said that He is concealed from direct perception because of the intensity of His Self-manifestation.

However, the great influence of positivist and materialist schools of thought on science and on all people of recent centuries makes it necessary to discuss this most manifest truth. As this now-prevalent "scientific" worldview reduces existence to what can be perceived directly, it blinds itself to those invisible dimensions of existence that are far vaster than the visible.

Let us reflect on one simple historical fact: Since the beginning of human life, the overwhelming majority of humanity has believed that God exists. This belief alone is enough to establish God's existence. Those who do not believe cannot claim to be smarter than those who do. Among past and present-day believers are innovative scientists, scholars, researchers and, most importantly, Prophets, who are the experts in the field. In addition, people usually confuse the non-acceptance of something's existence with the acceptance of its non-existence. While the former is only a negation or a rejection, the latter is a judgment that requires proof. No one has ever proven God's non-existence, for to do so is impossible, whereas countless arguments prove His existence. This point may be clarified through the following comparison.

Suppose there is a large palace with a thousand entrances, 999 of which are open and one of which appears to be closed. No one could reasonably claim that the palace cannot be entered. Unbelievers are like those who, in order to assert that the palace cannot be entered, confine their (and others') attention only to the door that is seemingly closed. The doors to God's existence are open to everybody, provided that they sincerely intend to enter through them.

The most important factor leading many, especially those under the spell of materialistic science and its worldview, to fix their eyes on the apparently closed door is causality. Belief in causality leads to the vicious chain of cause and effect, for each cause is also an effect. Moreover, the effect is totally different from the cause. All things and effects are usually so full of art and beneficial purposes that even if all causes gathered they would be unable to produce one single thing, let alone their simple immediate causes.

In order for a cause to produce an effect, it has to be able to produce the whole universe in which that effect takes place, for that effect cannot exist without the whole universe. Nor can they exist separately. The universe is a whole entity, each part of which is interrelated with the others. For example, in order for a single apple to come into existence, the sun, air, water, soil, and the seed of the apple tree should be coordinated in proper measures. This requires the existence of One with all-encompassing knowledge, will and power, One Who has absolute dominion over all things simultaneously. Materialist scientists imagine powerless, dependent, and ignorant causes to be responsible for the existence of beings and things, and thus fancy them to possess absolute qualities. In this way they are implying (tacitly believing) that each of those causes possesses qualities that only can be attributed to God.

However, the latest discoveries of modern science, like the universe's unity and its parts' inseparability, exclude the possibility of all the explanations put forward by materialistic science. They demonstrate that all entities, whether in nature or in the laws and causes attributed to them, are devoid of power and knowledge. They are contingent, transient, and dependent beings. But the properties attributed to any of these entities need infinite qualities like absolute power and knowledge.

This shows that belief in the notion of causality is by no means necessarily linked with "objective" study or "neutral" scientific investigation. It is no more than a personal opinion. Moreover, it is an opinion that is irrational and devoid of sense.

When we study the universe, we see that all beings utterly refute the false claims of materialist and atheistic reasoning through their order, mutual relationship, and duties. They affirm that they are nothing but the property and creatures of a Single Creator. Each rejects the false notions of chance and causality, ascribes all other beings to its own Creator, and proves that the Creator has no partners. Indeed, when the Creator's Unity is known and understood correctly, it becomes clear that nothing requires that causes should possess any power. Thus they cannot be partners to the Creator, for it is impossible for them to be so.

The universe is a document for believers to use. The Qur'an informs us that believing in God is to assent with one's heart to the Creator with all His Attributes supported by the universe's testimony. The true affirmation of God's Unity is a judgment, a confirmation, an assent, and an acceptance that can find its Owner present with all things. It sees in all things a path leading to its Owner, and regards nothing as an obstacle to His Presence. If this were not the case, it would be necessary to tear and cast aside the universe in order to find Him, which is impossible for us.

The universe has been made in the form of an intelligible book so as to make known its Author. The book, which addresses humanity, seeks to make humanity read the book and its parts, and respond with worship and thanks to its Author's Will. Humanity attains to that worship by uncovering the order in the Book of the Universe through scientific study and displaying the functioning of the universe's beings and workings.

The universe is not passive or neutral. We cannot interpret it as we wish, for there is only one correct way of looking at the world, one universal worldview. This view is taught to us in the Qur'an as well as in the Book of the Universe by our Creator, and it contains no fragmentation or conflict, only harmony, assistance, peace, and compassion.

The materialist scientific worldview is based on radical fragmentation, for it views nature as a mechanism with no inherent value and meaning. It isolates an object by cutting off its connections with the rest of the world, and studies it within its immediate environment.

But our perception of ourselves tells us that we are meaningful and part of the whole universe, and that everything must have a meaning and be part of the universe. Materialist science has left the subject—humanity—out of the universe and, insofar as this science is taking over, people feel that they have no place in this world. Thus they are isolated and live lives without meaning, except in a very limited, egoistic sense. People are alienated from their environment and from themselves.

The universe is an inseparable whole. Indeed, the unity observed in its totality, including humanity, is so clear that no one can deny it. Thus the materialistic approach to the scientific method has to be reconsidered. This method is reductionist, for it reduces everything to fragments and then attributes each fragment to causes. But in reality, all things are interconnected and interdependent, for it is impossible to attribute anything, however small, to causes that are themselves transient and contingent. Since whatever is responsible for one thing must be responsible for everything, we cannot have one thing without the whole.

Why can we ascribe a thing to its antecedents in time but not to its neighbors in space? Why should a thing be able to produce another thing just because it happened before? All modern scientists know that space and time are fully equivalent and unified into a four-dimensional continuum in which both "here" and "there" and "before" and "after" are relative. In this four-dimensional space, the temporal sequence is converted into a simultaneous co-existence, the side-by-side existence of all things. Thus causality appears to be an idea limited to a prejudiced experience of the world.

Causality does have some meaning. Opposites are mingled in this world: truth with falsehood, light with darkness, good with evil, white with black, and so on. Since people have ingrained inclinations toward both good and evil, they are tested in this world to determine whether they will use their free will and other faculties in the way of truth and good or otherwise.

Divine Wisdom requires that the veil of causes and laws be drawn before Divine Power's operations. If God had willed, He could train the planets with His "Hands" in a way observable by us or let visible angels administer them. Then we would not be speaking of the laws of causes involved, such as gravitation. Or, in order to communicate His Commandments, God could speak to each person directly without sending any Prophets, or could write His Name with stars in the sky in order to compel us to believe in His Existence and Oneness. But in this case, humanity's earthly existence would not be an arena of trial that pushes us to new developments and discoveries in science and technology, thereby enabling us to remove one more veil from the meaning of existence.

Like a mirror's two sides, existence has two aspects or dimensions: one visible and material, known as the Realm of Opposites and (in most cases) Imperfections, and the transparent, pure, and perfect spiritual realm. The material dimension must—and does—contain events and phenomena that appear disagreeable to us. Those who cannot perceive the Divine Wisdom behind all things may even criticize the Almighty for those disagreeable events and phenomena. To prevent that, God uses natural laws and causes to veil His acts. For example, so that we do not criticize God or His Angel of Death for the loss of our beloved ones or our own death, God places diseases and natural disasters (among other "agents" or "causes") between Himself and death.

On account of this world of testing and trial's essential imperfection, we encounter and suffer from many deficiencies and shortcomings. In absolute terms, every event and phenomenon is good and beautiful in itself or in its consequences. Whatever God Almighty does or decrees is good, beautiful, and just. Injustice, ugliness, and evil are only apparent or superficial and arise from humanity's errors and abuses. For example, although a court may pass an unjust sentence on you, you should know that Destiny permits that judgment because of a crime that has been left concealed. Whatever befalls us is usually the result of self-wronging, an evil that we ourselves have done, or because God wills to promote us to higher moral and spiritual ranks through any misfortune happening to us, as is the case with the Prophets. However, those who lack the necessary sound reasoning and judgment to understand the Divine Wisdom behind events and phenomena may impute directly to God the apparent ugliness or evil, imperfections and shortcomings, experienced in worldly life, even though God is absolutely free of any defect or imperfection.

Therefore, so that people do not ascribe any ugliness or evil to God, His Glory and Grandeur require that natural causes and laws be a veil before His acts, while belief in His Unity demands that those causes and laws should not be ascribed to any kind of creative power.

If God Almighty acted in the world directly, and not through causes and laws, we would be unable to develop scientific knowledge or live even an instant of a happy life free of fear and anxiety. We can observe and study patterns in phenomena thanks to God's acting from behind natural causes and laws. Otherwise, each event would be a miracle. The regularity within the flux and mutability of events and phenomena makes them comprehensible to us, and so awakens within us the desire to wonder and reflect, which is a principal factor in establishing science. For the same reason, we are able to plan and arrange our future affairs to some degree. Just consider how life would be if we did not know whether the sun would rise tomorrow!

God Almighty owns absolute Beauty and Perfection. He also owns a holy, transcendent love, which He manifests by displaying His Beauty and Perfection. For Beauty and Perfection are loved because of themselves. So, the universe where His Beauty and Perfection are manifested is a theater of love. If He manifested His Names and Attributes directly, without the "medium" of causes and laws, we could not endure them. He manifests them as He does and by degrees within the confines of time and space so that we can connect with them, reflect on them, and perceive them. The gradual manifestation of Divine Names and Attributes is also a reason for our curiosity and wonder about them.

THE CONCEPT OF DEITY AND GOD ALMIGHTY

God Almighty should be considered from five perspectives. One is His "Essence" as Divine Being (*Dhat* in Islamic terminology), which only He can know. A Prophetic Tradition says: "Do not reflect on God's 'Essence'; instead, reflect on His works and acts."[1] God has no partners, likes or resemblance, as pointed to by the verse: *There is nothing like or compared unto Him* (42:11). The second perspective is His Essential, "Innate" Qualities as God, which are the Attributes' source. The third perspective is His Attributes, which are of three kinds: Essential Attributes (e.g., Existence, Having No Beginning, Eternal Permanence, Oneness, Being Unlike the Created, Self-Subsistence); Positive Attributes (Life, Knowledge, Power, Speech, Will, Hearing, Seeing, Creating); and innumerable "Negative" Attributes, summed up as "God is absolutely free from any defect and shortcoming."

The Attributes are the sources of the Names: Life gives rise to the All-Living, Knowledge to the All-Knowing, and Power to the All-Powerful. The Names are the sources of the acts: giving life has its source in the All-Living, and knowing everything down to the smallest detail or thing originates in the All-Knowing. God is "known" through His acts, Names, and Attributes. Whatever exists in the universe, in the material and immaterial worlds, is the result of the Names' and Attributes' manifestations: Universal and individual provision points to His Name the All-Providing, and the All-Healing is the source of remedies and patient recovery. Philosophy has its source in Wisdom, and so on. The acts, Names, and Attributes are the "links" between God and the created, or the "reflectors" with which to have knowledge of God.

Although we try to know or recognize God by His acts, Names, and Attributes, we must not think of Him in terms of associating likeness or comparison unto Him, for nothing resembls Him. He is absolutely One, Single, and totally different from all that exists or has the potential to exist. In this sense, His Oneness is not in terms of number. To have some knowledge of Him through His acts, Names, and Attributes, some comparisons are permissible. This is pointed to in the verse: *To God applies the most sublime attributes* (16:60).

Some of God's Names are as follows:

- *Allah*: Translated as God, Allah is the proper Name of the Divine Being Who creates and administers His creatures, individually and as a whole, Who provides, brings up, sustains, protects, guides each and all, Who causes to perish and revives each and all, Who rewards or punishes, and so on. All His Attributes are Attributes of absolute perfection, and He is absolutely free from any and all defects. He is Unique and Single, having no like or resemblance and nothing is comparable to Him. He is absolutely beyond any human conception. He is the Unique, Single Being with the exclusive right to be worshipped and to be made the sole aim of life. He is loved in and of Himself. Everything is dependent on Him and subsists through Him. Every truth has its source in Him. Knowledge of God (in the sense of the Arabic *'ilm*) is impossible in respect of His Being or Essence (*Dhat*). Because there is none like or comparable unto Him, it is therefore impossible to grasp or comprehend His Essence. However, we can recognize God or have some knowledge of Him (in the sense of the Arabic *ma'rifah*) through His works, acts, Names, Attributes and Essential Qualities (*shu'un*). Awareness of His works (what we see in the world, His creation) leads us to become aware of His acts, and that awareness leads us to His Names and Attributes which, in turn, lead us to His Essential Qualities, and thence to an awareness of the One Who has these Qualities.

- *(Al-)'Adl*: The All-Just
- *(Al-)'Afuww*: The All-Pardoning (Who overlooks the faults of His servants); The One Who grants remission; The One Who excuses much
- *(Al-)Ahad*: The Unique One (Who is beyond all kinds of human conceptions of Him and absolutely free from having any partners, likes, parents, sons or daughters)
- *(Al-)Ahir*: The Last (Whom there is none that will outlive)
- *(Al-)'Alim*: The All-Knowing
- *(Al-)'Aliyy*: The All-Exalted
- *(Al-)Amin*: The One in Whom Refuge is Sought
- *(Al-)'Atuf*: The All-Affectionate
- *(Al-)Awwal*: The First (Whom there is none that precedes)
- *(Al-)'Aziz*: The All-Glorious with irresistible might (Whom none can prevent from doing what He wills)
- *(Al-)Baqi*: The All-Permanent
- *(Al-)Bari*: The All-Holy Creator (Who is absolutely free from having any partners and Who makes every being perfect and different from others)
- *(Al-)Basir*: The All-Seeing
- *(Al-)Batin*: The All-Inward (Who encompasses the whole existence from within in His Knowledge, and there is none that is more penetrating than Him)
- *(Ad-)Dayyan*: The Supreme Ruler and All-Requiting (of good and evil)
- *(Al-)Fard*: The All-Independent, Single One (free from having any equals or likes in His Essence and Attributes)
- *(Al-)Fatir*: The All-Originating (with a unique individuality)
- *(Al-)Fattah*: The One Who judges between people with truth and separates
- *(Al-)Ghaniyy*: The All-Wealthy and Self-Sufficient
- *(Al-)Habib*: The All-Loving and Loved
- *(Al-)Hadi*: The All-Guiding
- *(Al-)Hafiz*: The All-Preserving and Keeper of records
- *(Al-)Hakim*: The All-Wise (in Whose every act and decree there are many instances of wisdom)
- *(Al-)Halim*: The All-Clement (showing no haste to punish the errors of His servants)

- *(Al-)Hamid*: The All-Praiseworthy (as the Lord Who creates, provides, and rears)
- *(Al-)Hannan*: The All-Kind and Caring
- *(Al-)Haqq*: The Ultimate Truth and Ever-Constant
- *(Al-)Hayy*: The All-Living
- *(Al-)Jabbar*: The All-Compelling of supreme majesty (Who subdues wrong and restores right)
- *(Al-)Jalil*: The All-Majestic
- *(Al-)Jamil*: The All-Gracious and All-Beautiful
- *(Al-)Jawad*: The All-Generous
- *(Al-)Kabir*: The All-Great
- *(Al-)Kafi*: The All-Sufficing
- *(Al-)Karim*: The All-Munificent
- *(Al-)Khabir*: The All-Aware
- *(Al-)Khaliq*: The Creator (Who determines measure for everything and brings it into existence out of nothing)
- *(Al-)Latif*: The All-Subtle (penetrating into the most minute dimensions of all things); the All-Favoring
- *(Al-)Mahmud*: The All-Praised
- *(Al-)Malik*: The Sovereign
- *(Al-)Mannan*: The All-Bounteous and Favoring
- *(Al-)Ma'ruf*: The One Known (with His works); the All-Recognized
- *(Al-)Mubin*: The One from Whom nothing is hidden and Who makes all truth manifest
- *(Al-)Mughni*: The All-Enriching
- *(Al-)Muhaymin*: The All-Watchful Guardian
- *(Al-)Muhit*: The All-Encompassing
- *(Al-)Muhsin*: The All-Benevolent
- *(Al-)Muhyi*: The One Who revives, Who gives life to the dead
- *(Al-)Mu'in*: The All-Helping and Supplying
- *(Al-)Mu'izz*: The All-Exalting and Honoring
- *(Al-)Mujib*: The All-Answering (of prayers) and Meeting (of needs)
- *(Al-)Mu'min*: The Supreme Author of safety and security Who bestows faith and removes all doubt
- *(Al-)Mumit*: The One Causing to Die; the All-Dealer of death
- *(Al-)Mundhir*: The All-Informing and Warning
- *(Al-)Murid*: The All-Willing
- *(Al-)Musawwir*: The All-Fashioning
- *(Al-)Mutakabbir*: The One Who has exclusive right to all greatness

- *(Al-)Mu'ti*: The All-Granting
- *(An-)Nur*: The All-Light
- *(Al-)Qaim*: The All-Observing and Controlling
- *(Al-)Qadir*: The All-Powerful
- *(Al-)Qahhar*: The All-Overwhelming (with absolute sway over all that exists)
- *(Al-)Qarib*: The All-Near
- *(Al-)Qawiyy*: The All-Strong
- *(Al-)Qayyum*: The Self-Subsisting (by Whom all subsist)
- *(Al-)Quddus*: the All-Holy and All-Pure (Who is absolutely free of any defect and keeps the universe clean)
- *(Ar-)Rabb*: The Lord (God as the Creator, Provider, Trainer, Upbringer, and Director of all creatures)
- *(Ar-)Rahim*: The All-Compassionate (Who has particular compassion for each of His creatures in their maintenance, and for His believing servants, especially in the other world)
- *(Ar-)Rahman*: The All-Merciful (Who has mercy on the whole existence and provides for all without making a distinction between believers and unbelievers)
- *(Ar-)Rauf*: The All-Pitying
- *(Ar-)Razzaq*: The All-Providing
- *(As-)Sabur*: The All-Patient (Whom no haste induces to rush into an action)
- *(As-)Salam*: The Supreme Author of peace and salvation
- *(As-)Samad*: The Eternally-Besought-of-All (Himself being needy of nothing)
- *(As-)Sami'*: The All-Hearing
- *(As-)Sani'*: The Maker
- *(As-)Sattar*: The All-Veiling (of His servants' shortcomings and sins)
- *(Ash-)Shafi*: The All-Healing
- *(Ash-)Shahid*: The All-Witnessing
- *(Ash-)Shakur*: The All-Responsive (to the gratitude of His creatures)
- *(As-)Subhan*: The All-Glorified
- *(As-)Sultan*: The Absolute, Eternal Authority
- *(At-)Tawwab*: The One Who accepts repentance and returns it with liberal forgiveness and additional reward
- *(Al-)Wadud*: The All-Tender and Excusing; The All-Loving and All-Beloved
- *(Al-)Wahhab*: The All-Bestowing
- *(Al-)Wahid*: The One (having no partners and equals; One Who manifests all His Names upon the whole of the universe, or a species, or on a whole)

- *(Al-)Wakil*: The One to rely on and to Whom affairs should be entrusted
- *(Al-)Waliyy*: The Guardian, the Protecting Friend (to rely on)
- *(Al-)Warith*: The One Who survives all beings and inherits them
- *(Al-)Wasi'*: The All-Embracing (in His Mercy)
- *(Az-)Zahir*:The All-Outward (Who encompasses the whole of existence from the outside, and there is none that encompasses Him)[2]

TAWHID (GOD'S ONENESS)

All religions revealed to the Prophets have the same essence. Over time, however, the original message was misinterpreted, mixed with superstition, and degenerated into magical practices and meaningless rituals. The concept of God, the very core of religion, was debased by anthropormorphism, deifying angels, associating others with God, considering Prophets or godly people as incarnations of God, and personifying His Attributes through separate deities.

Prophet Muhammad, upon him be peace and blessings, rejected such theological trends and restored the concept of God as the only Creator, Sustainer, and Master of all creation to its pristine purity. Thus, as John Davenport puts it:

> Among many excellencies of which the Qur'an may justly boast are two eminently conspicuous: the one being the tone of awe and reverence which it always observes when speaking of, or referring to, the Deity, to Whom it never attributes human frailties and passions; the other the total absence throughout it of all impure, immoral and indecent ideas, expressions, narratives, etc., blemishes, which, it is much to be regretted, are of too frequent occurrence in the Jewish scriptures.[3]

Tawhid, Divine Unity and/or Oneness, is clearly observed throughout the universe. If we look at ourselves and our environment, we easily discern that everything depends upon this principle. For example, our bodily parts cooperate with each other. Each cell is so connected with the whole body that the One Who created it must be He Who created the body. Likewise, each element constituting the universe is interrelated and in harmony with each other element and the universe as a whole.

Given this, the only logical conclusion is that the same Creator Who created the particles created the universe, and that the motion of subatomic particles is the same as that observed in the solar system. Everything originates from "one" and returns to "one": *God originates creation and then reproduces it, and He will bring it forth anew* (10:34). A tree, for instance, grows out of a seed or a stone and finally results in a seed or a stone. This strict obedience to the One Who established that order explains why the universe is so orderly and harmonious. As the Creator, One, All-Omnipotent and All-Knowing, operates it directly, how could it be otherwise?

As the Qur'an reminds us:

> Each god would have taken off what he created, and some of them would have risen up over others. Had there been gods in the earth and the heaven other than God, they both would have been in disorder. (21:22)

Tawhid is the highest concept of deity that God revealed to us through His Prophets, among whom were Moses, Jesus, and Muhammad, upon them be peace. Over time, people deviated from the pure teachings after their Prophets died. Turning to polytheism or idolatry, they relied upon their own faulty reasoning, false perceptions, and biased interpretations to satisfy their lusts. Such a course is impossible with a *tawhid*-based system, for this requires that they obey only the One Supreme God's commandments.

'Ali ibn Abi Talib[4] is reported to have said:

> The foremost in religion is God's knowledge, the perfection of His knowledge is to testify to Him, the perfection of testifying to Him is to believe in His Oneness, the perfection of believing in His Oneness is to regard Him as pure, and the perfection of His purity is to deny all kinds of negative attributes about Him.

He is infinite and eternal, self-existent and self-sufficient. As stated in the Qur'an:

> He, God, the Unique One, needy of nothing and Everlasting Refuge; He begets not, nor is He begotten; and there is none like unto Him (112:1–4). There is nothing like or compared unto Him (42:11). Vision perceives Him not, and He perceives all vision; and He (alone) is the All-Hearing and All-Seeing (6:103).

In the words of 'Ali:

> He is Being but not through the phenomenon of coming into being. He exists but not from non-existence. He is with everything but not by physical nearness. He is different from everything but not by physical separation. He acts but without the accompaniment of movements and instruments. He is the One, only such that there is none with whom He keeps company or whom He misses in his absence.[5]

God's Attributes cannot be transferred or present in another, since they are infinite. One who cannot keep himself alive cannot give life to others. One who cannot protect his own power cannot govern the vast universe. The more one reflects, the clearer it becomes that all divine powers and attributes must exist in only that one particular Being.

Literally, *tawhid* means "unification" (making something one) or "asserting oneness." It comes from the Arabic verb *wahhada* (to unite, unify, or consolidate). However, when used in reference to God, it means realizing and maintaining God's Unity in all of our actions that directly or indirectly relate to Him. It is the belief that God is One, without partner in His dominion and His actions, without similitude in His Essence and Attributes, and without rival in His Divinity and in worship. These three categories are commonly referred to by the following titles: *Tawhid ar-Rububiyya* (Maintaining the Unity of Lordship), *Tawhid al-Asma was-Sifat* (Maintaining the Unity of God's Names and Attributes), and *Tawhid al-'Ibada* (Maintaining the Unity of God's Worship).

Tawhid ar-Rububiyya is based upon the fundamental concept that God alone caused all things to exist when there was nothing, He sustains and maintains creation without any need from it or for it, and He is the sole Lord of the universe and its inhabitants without any real challenge to His sovereignty. In Arabic, the word used to describe this quality is *Rububiyya,* which is derived from the root *Rabb* (Lord). According to this category, since God is the only real power in existence, it is He Who has given all things the power to move and to change. Nothing happens in creation except what He allows to happen. In recognition of this reality, Prophet Muhammad, upon him be God's peace and blessings, often would repeat the exclamatory phrase *La hawla wa la quwwata illa bi'llah* (There is neither strength, nor power, save with God).

Tawhid al-Asma was-Sifat has four aspects. In order to maintain the unity of God's Names and Attributes in the first aspect, God must be referred to according to how He and His Prophet have described Him and called Him. The second aspect involves referring to God as He has referred to Himself, without giving Him any new names or attributes. In the third aspect, God is referred to without giving Him the attributes of His creation. For example, He cannot be said to rest or sleep, for this would give Him some of the attributes belonging to His creation. Nor can He be portrayed as "repenting" for His "bad thoughts," for this is what people do after they realize their errors. The attributes of hearing and seeing are among human attributes, but are without comparison in their perfection when attributed to the Divine Being. In other words, God does not need eyes and ears to possess these attributes. The fourth aspect requires that no person can be given the attributes of God in their perfection.

In spite of the wide implications of the first two categories, firm belief in them alone is not sufficient to fulfill the Islamic requirements of *tawhid. Tawhid ar-Rububiyya* and *Tawhid al-Asma was-Sifat* must be accompanied by their complement, *Tawhid al-'Ibada,* in order for *tawhid* to be considered complete according to Islam.

It requires that all forms of worship must be directed only to God, because He alone deserves worship and can grant benefit to created beings as a result of His worship. Furthermore, there is no need for any intermediary between humanity and God. God emphasized the importance of directing worship to Him alone by pointing out that this was the main purpose for creating jinn and humanity, and the essence of the Message brought by all Prophets.

SHIRK (ASSOCIATION OF PARTNERS WITH GOD)

Consequently, the gravest sin is *shirk* (the worship of others instead of God or along with God). In *Sura al-Fatiha*, which every Muslim recites in his or her prayers at least seventeen times daily, verse four reads: *You alone do we worship and from You alone do we seek help*, a clear statement that all forms of worship should be directed only to the One Who can respond: God.

The study of *tawhid* cannot be considered complete without a careful analysis of its opposite: *shirk*. *Shirk* literally means partnership, sharing, or associating. In Islamic terms, however, it refers to assigning partners to God in whatever form it may take.

KINDS OF ASSOCIATING PARTNERS WITH GOD (SHIRK)

One may associate partners with God in His *Rububiyya*, *Asma was-Sifat*, and *'Ibada*.

Shirk in ar-Rububiyya

This kind of *shirk* refers either to the belief that others share in God's Lordship over creation as His equal or near equal, or that there exists no Lord over creation at all. In the first case, *shirk* by association, this means that a main God or Supreme Being over creation is recognized; however, His dominion is shared by lesser deities, spirits, mortals, heavenly bodies, or earthly objects. According to Islam, all such systems are polytheistic. In the second case, *shirk* by negation, various philosophies and ideologies almost amount to an explicit or implicit denial of God's Existence. For example, pantheism and monism fall into this category.

Shirk in al-Asma was-Sifat

This includes both the common pagan practice of giving God the attributes of His creation as well as the act of giving created beings God's Names and Attributes in their absolute meaning particular to God. In the first case, *shirk* by humanization, God is given the form and qualities of human beings and animals. Due to humanity's superiority over animals, the human form is more commonly used by idolaters to represent God in creation. Consequently, the image of the Creator is often painted, molded, or carved in the shape of human beings possessing the physical features of those who worship them. In the second case, *shirk* by deification, created beings or things are given or claim God's Names or His Attributes in their absolute meaning particular to God.

Shirk in al-'Ibada

This means to direct acts of worship to other than God, and to seek the reward for worship from the creation instead of the Creator. This category also has two main aspects, as follows:

Ash-Shirk al-Akbar (Major Shirk): This occurs when any act of worship is directed to that which is not God. It represents the most obvious form of idolatry, which God sent all Prophets to call upon humanity to abandon. This concept is supported by: *Surely We have sent to every nation a Messenger ordering, worship God and avoid Taghut* (false gods) (16:36).

Taghut actually means anything that demands worship and is worshipped along with God or instead of God. Much emphasis has been placed on such evil, for it contradicts the very purpose of creation as expressed in God's statement: *I have not created jinn or humanity except to worship Me* (51:56).

Major *shirk* represents one of the two worst acts of rebellion against the Lord of the Universe, the other being unbelief. So, it is the ultimate sin that cancels all of a person's good deeds and guarantees its perpetrator eternal damnation in Hell. Consequently, false religion is based primarily upon this type of *shirk*.

Ash-Shirk al-Asghar (Minor Shirk): God's Messenger said: "The thing I fear for you the most is the minor *shirk* (*ash-shirk al-asghar*)." The Companions asked: "O Messenger of God, what is minor *shirk*?" He replied: "Showing off *(ar-riya')*, for God will say on the Day of Resurrection when people are receiving their rewards: 'Go to those for whom you were showing off in the material world and see if you can find any reward from them.'" He also declared: "O people, beware of secret *shirk!*" The people asked: "O Messenger of God, what is secret *shirk*?" He replied: "When a person gets up to pray and strives to beautify his prayer because people are looking at him, that is secret *shirk*."[6]

IMPLICATIONS OF *TAWHID*

Monotheists, those who maintain *tawhid,* cannot be narrow-minded. Their belief in One God, Creator of the heavens and the earth, Master of the east and the west, and Sustainer of the universe, leads them to view everything as belonging to the same Lord, to Whom they belong as well. Thus they consider nothing as alien. Their sympathy, love, and service are not confined to any particular race, color, or group, and they come to understand the Prophetic saying: "O servants of God, be brothers/sisters as God orders you!"[7]

Monotheism produces the highest degree of self-respect and self-esteem in people. Monotheists know that only God has true power, can benefit or harm them, fulfill their needs, cause them to die, or wield authority and influence. This conviction makes them indifferent to and independent and fearless of all powers other than those of God. They never bow in homage to any of God's creatures.

Monotheists, although humble and mild, never abase themselves by bowing before anyone or anything except God. They never aim at any worldly advantage by their worship. They seek only to please God and obtain His approval.

Monotheists, although naturally weak and powerless as human beings, become powerful enough through their Lord's Power to resist the whole world. They are virtuous and altruistic, for their purpose is to gain God's approval by working for His good pleasure. Boisterous pride in power and wealth can have no room in their hearts, for they know that whatever they possess is bestowed by God, and that God can take away as easily as He can give.

Monotheists know that the only way to success and salvation is to acquire a pure soul and righteous behavior. They have perfect faith in God, Who is above all need, related to none, absolutely just, and without partner in His exercise of Divine Power. Given this belief, they understand that they can succeed only through right living and just action, for no influence or underhanded activity can save them from ruin.

Monotheists do not become hopeless and disappointed. Their firm faith in God, Master of all treasures of the earth and the heavens, and Possessor of limitless grace and bounty and infinite power, imparts to their hearts extraordinary consolation, fills them with satisfaction, and keeps them filled with hope. In this world they might meet with rejection at all doors, nothing might serve their ends, and all means might desert them. But faith in and dependence on God, which never leave them, give them the strength to go on struggling. Such profound confidence can come only from belief in the One God. Such belief produces great determination, patient perseverance, and trust in God. When they decide to devote their resources to fulfilling the Divine Commands to secure God's good pleasure and approval, they are sure that they have the Lord of the Universe's support and backing.

Many polytheists and atheists, on the other hand, have small hearts and depend on limited powers. Thus their troubles and the resulting despair soon overwhelm them and, frequently, they commit suicide. Professor Joad's testimony is explicit on this point:

> For the first time in history there is coming to maturity a generation of men and women [in the West of the 1950s] who have no religion, and feel no need for one. They are content to ignore it. Also they are very unhappy, the suicide rate is abnormally high.[8]

As opposed to this, a non-Muslim historian who is not sympathetic to Islam, writes the following about *tawhid*:

> In this uncompromising monotheism, with its simple, enthusiastic faith in the supreme rule of a transcendental being, lies the chief strength of Islam. Its adherents enjoy a consciousness of contentment and resignation unknown among followers of most creeds. Suicide is rare in Muslim lands.[9]

Monotheism inspires bravery, for it defeats the two factors that make people cowards: fear of death and love of safety, and the belief that someone other than God can somehow be bribed into forgiving their sins. Belief in the Islamic creedal statement that "there is no deity but God" purges the mind of these ideas. The first idea loses its influence when people realize that their lives, property, and everything else really belong to God, for this makes them willing to sacrifice whatever they have for God's approval. The second idea is defeated when people realize that there is no power other than God that creates, causes to die, rewards, punishes, and forgives. Also, no one can die before his or her appointed time, even if all of the world's forces were to combine to make it so. Nothing can bring death forward or push it backward even one instant. This firm belief in One God and dependence upon Him makes monotheists the bravest of people.

Monotheism creates an attitude of peace and contentment, purges the mind of subtle passions and jealousy, envy and greed, and prevents one from resorting to base and unfair means to achieve success. Monotheists understand that God holds their wealth; that He bestows honor, power, reputation, and authority as He wills and subjects them to His Will; and that their duty is only to endeavor and struggle fairly. They know that success and failure depend upon His Grace, for no power can block His Will to give or not to give. They also know that they must strive to deserve His Grace. But many of those who do not believe in God consider success and failure to be the result of their own efforts or by the help of earthly powers, and do not take God's Grace and Will into consideration. Therefore they remain slaves to cupidity and envy, and use bribery, flattery, conspiracy, and other base and unfair means to achieve success.

Monotheists know that God is aware of everything, whether hidden or open, and is nearer to them than their jugular vein. If they sin in secret even under the cover of night, God knows it. He knows our unformed thoughts and intentions, even those of which we ourselves are unaware. We can hide things from people, but not from God. We can evade everyone, but not God's grasp. The firmer our belief in this respect, the more observant we will be of His Commands. This is why the first and most important condition for being a Muslim is to have firm and sincere faith in God's Oneness.

This is also the most important and fundamental principle of the Prophet's teachings, as well as Islam's bedrock and the mainspring of its power. All other beliefs, commands, and laws of Islam stand firm on this foundation. Lastly, we quote the remarks of Dr. Laura Veccia Vaglieri, a famous Italian Orientalist, concerning the universal spirit of Islamic monotheism:[10]

> The Prophet, with a voice which was inspired by a deep communion with his Maker, preached the purest monotheism to the worshippers of fetish and the followers of a corrupted Christianity and Judaism. He put himself in open conflict with those regressive tendencies of mankind which lead to the association of other beings with the Creator.
>
> In order to lead men to a belief in one God, he did not delude them with happenings which deviate from the normal course of nature. Rather, he simply invited them, without asking them to leave the realm of reality, to consider the

Universe and its laws, Being confident of the resultant belief in the one and indispensable God, he simply let men read in the book of life.

Thanks to Islam, paganism in its various forms was defeated. The concept of the Universe, the practices of religion, and the customs of social life were each liberated from all the monstrosities which had degraded them, and human minds were made free of prejudice. Man finally realized his dignity.

CHAPTER 3

The Invisible Realm of Existence

THE INVISIBLE REALM OF EXISTENCE

B elief in the invisible realm of existence and the beings inhabiting it is another essential of Islamic faith. Since our sensory powers are limited, it is not wise to deny outright the existence of realms beyond our senses. Also, we know so little about existence that what we do know is considerably less than what we do not. Our sciences are still in their "childhood," and the future will witness dazzling scientific discoveries and developments.

Sciences are supported by theories and develop through trial-and-error investigation of those theories. Numerous "established" facts were once considered false, and many other "established" facts are now known to be incorrect. We accept unquestionably, and without any scientific basis, the existence of many things. Since the beginning of time, most people have believed in the existence of the spirit and angels, jinn and Satan. So, it would seem to be more scientific to allow their existence in theory and then investigate it. Denying their existence is unscientific, insofar as such a judgment or conclusion must be based on concrete proof. No one can prove and therefore scientifically claim the non-existence of the invisible realm of existence.

Many physical qualities, such as heat and cold, and such abstract qualities as beauty and charm, and feelings of joy, sorrow, and love, can be experienced directly and measured to some degree. Materialists attribute these to some biochemical processes in the brain, and some scientists (like psychologists and psychiatrists) still try to explain them by natural or physical laws. However, our non-physical side (namely, our feelings, beliefs, potentialities, desires, and so on that vary enormously from individual to individual, although everyone has the same material elements) is too profound to be explained by physics, chemistry, or biology.

ANGELS AND OTHER INVISIBLE BEINGS

Angels are purely spirit beings that represent the purely good aspect in existence, while Satan and his descendants represent the purely evil aspect. God is One and Infinite, without opposite. All other beings and existents have an opposite. Since we have two opposite aspects in our nature, one inclined toward good and the other toward evil, angels reflect this good aspect while Satan reflects the evil one. Angels invite us to our purely spiritual or "angelic" aspect, while Satan tries to seduce us through tempting us to do evil. The resulting struggle in each individual, and in the universe as a whole, has been ongoing since the beginning of existence. Everyone feels a stimulus toward good and evil at the same time. The former comes from the angels or our unpolluted spirit; the latter comes from Satan collaborating with our carnal self, which represents our animal aspect.

We accept the existence of natural laws and forces unquestionably, and even go so far as to attribute to them all phenomena in the universe. We ascribe a tiny seed's growth into a huge, elaborate tree to the law of germination and growth in that seed, and the universe's incredible balance to the laws of gravitation and repulsion. But we ignore the absolute will, knowledge, power, and wisdom necessary for the universe's very existence, operation, and balance. The One Who has absolute Will, Knowledge, Power, and Wisdom has such powerful invisible beings as winds or gales, and others much more powerful than natural forces or laws. These beings are angels.

In addition to religious scholars, almost all Muslim philosophers and even all Oriental philosophers agree on the existence of angels and all kinds of spirit beings, despite differences in naming them. All Prophets, numbering 124,000 in reliable religious sources, unanimously report the existence of angels, spirit beings, jinn, and Satan. All saints and religious scholars agree on this invisible realm's existence. We hardly need to say that two specialists in a matter are preferable to thousands of non-specialists. In addition, it is an established fact that once a matter is confirmed by two people, its denial by thousands carries no weight. Furthermore, all people of religion and followers of almost all religions unanimously accept the existence of these beings.

All Divine Scriptures record the existence of spirit beings and the human spirit, and the story of Satan and his intrigues to seduce us exist in all of them. Above all, can one doubt the report of the Qur'an and the testimony and experiences of Prophet Muhammad, upon him be peace and blessings? The proofs of the Qur'an's Divine authorship, Prophethood's mission, and the Prophethood of Muhammad and all other Prophets, upon them be peace, also prove the invisible realm's existence and thus the existence of the spirit, angels, jinn, and Satan.

The best and most rational way of establishing the existence of such beings is expounded by Islam, described by the Qur'an, and was seen by the Prophet, upon him be peace and blessings, during his Ascension through the heavens. The Qur'an explains the meaning of angelic existence so reasonably that anyone can understand it. It relates that we are a community responsible for carrying out the Divine Commandments issuing from the Divine Attribute of Speech, and that angels are a community whose "working class" carries out the Divine Laws of nature issuing from the Attribute of Will. They are God's honored servants who do whatever He commands. The existence of angels and other spirit beings can be established by proving the existence of an individual angel, because denying them amounts to denying the species. Thus, accepting the individual requires accepting the species.

A consensus has formed, especially among followers of religions, that there have always been some who can see and converse with angels, jinn, Satan, and other spirit beings. Therefore, we can conclude that religious belief in the existence of such beings is based on the experiences which the Prophets and other godly persons have had with them. Such accounts have been narrated by reliable sources.

LIFE IN OTHER PLACES AND ANGELS

Science is still unable to explain what life really is. This world is the arena where God manifests His Will from behind the veil of what we experience and describe as "natural causes," but life is the result of the direct manifestation of His Name, the All-Living. So, as long as science insists on its positivist, even materialist, viewpoint, it will never penetrate the mystery of what life is.

Scientists restrict the concept of life to the conditions that obtain on or beneath the outer surface of our planet. Therefore, when they have looked for extra-terrestrial life, what they have looked for is conditions which are the same as or similar or closely corresponding to the conditions in which life is evident on the surface of the earth. But surely, if they had retained sufficient sense of the absolute wonder of life (and that absolute wonder is an aspect of life's being a direct manifestation of the All-Living), they should not have ruled out forms and conditions of life which are at present beyond their understanding. In their view, the arguments put forward by Bediüzzaman Said Nursi for the existence of angels and other spirit beings may not be worthy of consideration. However, the latest discoveries in deep sea biology may persuade them to review Nursi's arguments. Said Nursi wrote at the beginning of the 1930s:

> Reality and the wisdom (purposiveness) in the existence of the universe require that the heavens should have conscious inhabitants of their own as does the earth. These inhabitants of many different kinds are called angels and spirit beings in the language of religion.
>
> It is true that reality requires the existence of angels and other spirit beings because the earth, although insignificant in size compared with the heavens, is continually being filled with and emptied of conscious beings. This clearly indicates that the heavens. . . are filled with living beings who are the perfect class of living creatures. These beings are conscious and have

perception, and they are the light of existence; they are the angels, who, like the jinn and humankind, are the observers of the universal palace of creation and students of this book of the universe and heralds for their Lord's kingdom.

The perfection of existence is through life. Moreover, life is the real basis and the light of existence, and consciousness, in turn, is the light of life. Since life and consciousness are so important, and a perfect harmony evidently prevails over the whole creation, and again since the universe displays a firm cohesion, and as this small ever-rotating sphere of ours is full of countless living and intelligent beings, so it is equally certain that those heavenly (realms) should have conscious, living beings particular to themselves. Just as the fish live in water, so those spirit beings may exist in the heat of the sun. Fire does not consume light, rather, light becomes brighter because of fire. We observe that the Eternal Power creates countless living beings from inert, solid substances and transforms the densest matter into subtle living compounds by life. Thus It radiates the light of life everywhere in great abundance and furnishes most things with the light of consciousness. From this we can conclude that the All-Powerful, All-Wise One would certainly not leave without life and consciousness more refined, subtle forms of matter like light and ether, which are close to and fitting for the spirit; indeed, He creates animate and conscious beings in great number from light, darkness, ether, air and even from meanings and words. As He creates numerous species of animals, He also creates from such subtle and higher forms of matter numerous different spirit creatures. One kind. . . are the angels, others are the varieties of spirit beings and jinn.[1]

Half a century after Said Nursi wrote this, nearly three hundred animal species, almost all them previously unknown, have been discovered living around hydrothermal vents which form when sea water leaking through the ocean floor at spreading ridges is heated by the underlying magma and rushes into the cold ocean. Verena Tunnicliffe writes:

All life requires energy, nearly all life on earth looks to the sun as the source. But solar energy is not the only kind of energy available on the earth. Consider the energy that drives the

movement and eruption of the planet's crust. When you look
at an active volcano, you are witnessing the escape of heat that
has been produced by radioactive decay in the earth's interior
and is finally reaching the surface. Why should there not be
biological communities associated with the same nuclear energy that moves continents and makes mountains? And why
could not whole communities be fuelled by chemical, rather
than, solar energy?

. . . Most of us associate the escape of heat from the interior
of the earth with violent events and unstable physical conditions, with extreme high temperatures and the release of toxic
gases—circumstances that are hardly conducive to life. The
notion that biological communities might spring up in a geo-
logically active environment seemed fantastic. And until recently, few organisms were known to survive without a direct or
indirect way to tap the sun's energy. But such communities do
exist, and they represent one of the most startling discoveries
of twentieth-century biology. They live in the deep ocean,
under conditions that are both severe and variable.[2]

This "startling" discovery of biology contains clues to some
other realities, which the sciences should consider. The Prophet
Muhammad, upon him be peace and blessings, states that angels are
created from "light." We read in the Qur'an that God created humanity from dried earth, from wet clay and from an extract of clay.
According to the Qur'an, humanity has been made a *khalifa* on the
earth. *Khalifa* means, literally, one who succeeds. Many interpreters
of the Qur'an have concluded from this that the jinn once ruled the
earth and they were succeeded by men.

Starting from the clues above, it should be possible to do for-
mal studies to determine the worth of conclusions such as these:

During the gradual creation of the universe, God Almighty
spread one kind of existence through another having different, particular characters according to the conditions of each realm of existence, compounding and interweaving. He also created living beings in every phase of creation appropriate for each phase. Thus,
He has numerous kinds of creatures such as angels, that are created from "light (*nur*)," and the jinn, created from "smokeless fire"

or something like energy (55:15). While He inhabited the heavens, the pure realms of material existence, with angels, He settled the jinn on the earth. He also created plants, animals and humans on the earth. He adorned every part and phase of the universe with creatures, among them living ones, that are appropriate for that part and phase.

THE CHARACTERISTICS OF ANGELS

Angels are created from what the Qur'an calls nur.[3] We cannot exactly know whether *nur* is light or something like light. The Qur'anic word for angel is *malak*. According to its root form, *malak* means "messenger," "deputy," "envoy," "superintendent," and "powerful one." The root meaning also implies descent from a high place. Angels are beings who build relations between the meta-cosmic world and the material one, convey God's commands, direct the acts and lives of beings (with God's permission), and conduct their worship in their own realms.

Having refined or subtle bodies of *nur*, angels move very rapidly and permeate or penetrate all realms of existence. They place themselves in our eyelids or in the bodies of other beings to observe God's works through our or their eyes. They also descend into the hearts of Prophets and other beloved servants of God to bring them inspiration.

Some animals, like honeybees, act according to Divine inspiration, although science asserts that all animals are directed by instincts. But science cannot explain what an instinct is and how it occurs. Scientists are trying to discover how migrating birds find their way, and how young eels hatched in the rivers of Europe find their way to the ocean, which is their native water. Even if we attribute this to information coded in their DNA, this information is assuredly from God, Who knows everything, controls the universe, and assigns angels to direct the lives of such creatures.

Everything that exists, either as an individual or as a species, has a collective identity and performs a unique, universal function. Each flower displays a superlative design and symmetry and recites, in the tongue of its being, the Names of the Creator manifested on it; the entire earth performs a universal duty of glorification as though it were a single flower; and the heavens praise and glorify the Majestic Maker of the universe through their suns, moons, and stars. Even inert material bodies, although outwardly inanimate and unconscious, perform a vital function in praising God. Angels represent these immaterial bodies in the world of the inner dimensions of things, and express their praise. In return, these immaterial bodies are the angels' dwellings and "mosques" in this world.

There are various classes of angels. One class is engaged in constant worship; another worships by working also. These working angels have functions that resemble human occupations, like shepherds or farmers. In other words, the earth's surface is like a general farm, and an appointed angel oversees all of its animal species by the command of the All-Majestic Creator, by His permission and Power, and for His sake.

The earth's surface is also an arable field where all plants are sown. Another angel is appointed to oversee all of them in the name of Almighty God and by His Power. Lower ranking angels worship and glorify Almighty God by supervising particular plant species. Archangel Michael, upon him be peace, is the head of all these angels.

Angels who function as shepherds or farmers bear no resemblance to human shepherds or farmers, for their supervision is purely for God's sake, in His name, and by His Power and command. They observe the manifestations of God's Lordship in the species they are assigned to supervise, study the manifestations of Divine Power and Mercy in it, communicate Divine commands to it through some sort of inspiration, and somehow arrange its voluntary actions.

Their supervision of plants, in particular, consists of representing in the angelic tongue the plants' glorification in the tongue of their being. In other words, they proclaim in the angelic tongue the praises and exaltations that all plants offer to the Majestic Creator through their lives. These angels also regulate and employ the plants' faculties correctly and direct them toward certain ends. Angels perform such services through their partial willpower and a kind of worship and adoration. They do not originate or create their acts, for everything bears a seal particular to the Creator of all things, meaning that only God creates. In short, whatever angels do is worship, and it is therefore not like the ordinary acts of human beings.

The Majestic Maker of this huge palace of creation employs four kinds or classes of laborers: angels and other spirit beings; inanimate things and vegetable creations, which are quite important servants of God working without wages; animals, which serve unconsciously in return for a small wage of food and pleasure; and humanity, which works in awareness of the Majestic Creator's purposes. Men and women learn from everything, and supervise lower-ranking servants in return for wages in the form of rewards here and in the Hereafter.

The first class consists of angels. These beings are never promoted for what they do, for each has a fixed, determined rank and receives a particular pleasure from the work itself, as well as a radiance from worship. That is, their reward is found in their service. Just as we are nourished by and derive pleasure from air and water, as well as light and food, angels are nourished by and receive pleasure from the "lights" of remembrance and glorification, worship and knowledge, and love of God. Since they are created of *nur*, *nur* sustains them. Even fragrant scents, which are close to *nur*, are a sort of enjoyable nourishment for them. Indeed, pure spirits take pleasure in sweet scents.

From their jobs performed at the command of the One Whom they worship, their actions for His sake, their service rendered in His name, their supervision through His View, their honor gained through connection with Him, their "refreshment" found in studying His Kingdom's material and immaterial dimensions, and their satisfaction in observing His Grace and Majesty's manifestations, angels receive such elevated bliss that we cannot even begin to comprehend it. In addition, only they can perceive this bliss.

Angels do not sin or disobey, for they do not have an evil-commanding soul that must be resisted. They have fixed stations, and so are neither promoted nor abased. They are also free of such negative qualities as envy, rancor, and enmity, and from all lusts and animal appetites found in human beings and jinn. They have no gender, do not eat or drink, and do not feel hunger, thirst, or tiredness. Praise, worship, recitation of God's Names, and glorification of Him are their nourishment, as are light and sweet fragrances.

Besides those deputed to represent and supervise various species on the earth and present their worship to God, there are four Archangels and other angels having special nearness to God. There are other groups of angels known as *Mala'-i A'la* (the Highest Council), *Nadiy-i A'la* (the Highest Assembly), and *Rafiq-i A'la* (the Highest Company), as well as angels appointed to Paradise and Hell. Angels who record a person's deeds are called *Kiramun Katibun* (the Noble Recorders), and 360 angels are responsible for each believer's life. They guard their charges, especially during infancy and old age, pray for them, and ask God to forgive them. Other angels help believers during times of war, attend assemblies that praise and glorify God, as well as study meetings held for God's sake and to benefit people.

God Almighty is powerful over everything. Even though He can guard everyone by Himself, He may appoint angels to guard His servants. To earn such a guardianship and the company of angels, one has to willingly do what is good and establish a close relation with God Almighty. One must have strong belief in God and all other pillars of faith, never abandon regular worship and prayer, lead a disciplined life, and refrain from forbidden things or sinful acts.

Belief in angels has many benefits. For example, it provides us with some sort of peace and removes our loneliness. The inspiration breathed by angels exhilarates us, enlightens us intellectually, and opens new horizons of knowledge and thought. Awareness of the continuous company of angels also helps us abstain from sin and improper behavior.[4]

THE CHARACTERISTICS OF JINN

The word *jinn* literally means something hidden or veiled from sight. As mentioned earlier, jinn are a species of invisible beings. A short Qur'anic chapter is named after them, and in it we learn that a band of jinn listened to Prophet Muhammad, upon him be peace and blessings, and some became believers (72:1–2, 11).

From this, we understand that jinn are conscious beings charged with Divine obligations. They were created before Adam and Eve and were responsible for cultivating and improving the world. Although God later superseded them with us, He did not exempt them from religious obligations.

The Qur'an states that jinn are created from smokeless fire (55:15). In another verse, it clarifies that this fire is scorching and penetrates as deep as the inner part of the body (15:27).

Like angels, jinn move extremely fast and are not bound by the time and space constraints within which we normally move. However, since the spirit is more active and faster than jinn, a person who lives at the level of the spirit's life and who can transcend what we know as limits of matter and the confines of time and space, can be quicker and more active than them. For example, the Qur'an relates that when Prophet Solomon, upon him be peace, asked those around him who could bring the throne of the Queen of Saba' (Yemen), one jinn answered that he could bring it before the meeting ended and Prophet Solomon stood up. However, a man with special knowledge from God replied: "I can bring it to you quicker than the blink of an eye," and he did so (27:38–40).

Nothing is difficult for God Almighty. It is as easy for Him to create the universe as it is for Him to create a tiny particle. He has provided human beings, jinn, and angels with the power and strength appropriate for their functions or duties. As He uses angels to supervise the movements of celestial bodies, He allows humanity to rule the earth, dominate matter, build civilizations, and produce technology.

Power and strength are not limited to the physical world, nor are they proportional to bodily size. We see that immaterial things are far more powerful than huge physical entities. For example, our memory is far more spacious and comprehensive than a large room. Our hands can touch a very near object, but our eyes can travel long distances in an instant, and our imagination can transcend time and space all at once. Winds can uproot trees and demolish large buildings. A young, thin plant shoot can split rocks and reach the sunlight. The power of energy, whose existence is known through its effect, is apparent to everybody. All of this shows that something's power is not proportional to its physical size; rather, the immaterial world dominates the physical world, and immaterial entities are far more powerful than material ones.

ANGELS AND JINN IN THIS WORLD

Angels and jinn can assume a form and appear in this world in the form of any being. Here, we observe movement from the visible to the invisible: water evaporates and disappears into the atmosphere, solid matter becomes a liquid or a gas (steam), and matter becomes energy (nuclear fission). Likewise, we observe movement from the invisible to the visible: gases become fluids, evaporated water becomes rain (as well as snow or hail), and energy becomes matter. Similarly, intangible thoughts and meanings in our minds can appear in the tangible form of letters and words in essays and books.

In an analogous way, such invisible beings as angels, jinn, and other spirit entities are clothed in some material substance, such as air or ether, and then become visible. According to Imam Shibli, if God wills, He allows them to assume a form when they utter any of His Names, for this functions like a key or a visa enabling them to assume a form and become visible in this world. If they try to do so without God's permission, by relying upon their own abilities, they are torn into pieces and perish.

When Gabriel came to Prophet Muhammad, upon him be peace and blessings, with Revelation or God's Messages, he rarely appeared in his original form. Rather, he usually came as a warrior, a traveler, or a Companion named Dihya. Once he came as a traveler dressed in white and, in order to instruct the Companions in religion, asked the Prophet such questions as: What is belief? What is Islam? What is *ihsan* (perfect goodness or excellence or perfection of virtue)? When is the Day of Judgment?[5]

Jinn also can appear as snakes, scorpions, cattle, donkeys, birds, and other animals. When the Prophet, upon him be peace and blessings, took the oath of allegiance from the jinn in the valley of Batn al-Nakhla, he wanted them to appear to his community either in their own form or in other agreeable forms, not in the forms of such harmful animals as dogs and scorpions. He warned his community: "When you see any vermin in your house, tell it three times: 'For God's sake, leave this place,' for it may be a friendly jinn. If it does not leave, it is not a jinn."

The jinn who gave allegiance to God's Messenger promised him: "If your community recites the *Basmala* (In the Name of God, the All-Merciful, the All-Compassionate) before anything they do and cover their dishes, we will not touch their food or their drink." Another Tradition says: "[After you relieve yourselves] do not clean yourselves with bones and dried pieces of dung, for they are among the foods of your jinn brothers."[6]

JINN AND HUMAN BEINGS

Some people have an innate ability to go into a trance and contact beings from the invisible realms of existence. However, it should not be forgotten that whether these are angels or jinn, invisible beings have their own conditions of life and are bound to certain limits and principles. For this reason, one who gets in touch with jinn should be careful, for one may easily fall under their influence and become their plaything.

Sins and uncleanliness invite the influence of evil spirits and unbelieving jinn. People of a susceptible nature, those who tend to be melancholy, and those who lead a dissipated and undisciplined life are their primary targets. Evil spirits usually reside in places for dumping garbage or other dirty places, public baths, bathrooms, and nests of vermin.[7]

Jinn can penetrate a body even deeper than X-rays. They can reach into a being's veins and the central points of the brain. They seem to be like lasers, which are used in everything from computers to nuclear weaponry, from medicine to communication and police investigations, and removing obstructions in our veins and arteries. So, when we consider that Satan and all jinn are created from a smokeless fire that penetrates deep into the body, like radiation or radioactive energy, we can understand the meaning of the Prophetic Tradition: "Satan moves where the blood moves."[8]

Although science does not yet accept the existence of invisible beings and restricts itself to the material world, we think it is worth considering the possibility that evil spirits play some part in such mental illnesses as schizophrenia. We constantly hear of cases that those who suffer from mental illness, epilepsy, or even cancer recover by reciting certain prayers. Such cases are serious and significant, and should not be denied or dismissed by attributing them to "suggestion" or "auto-suggestion." When science breaks the thick shell in which it has confined itself and accepts the existence of the metaphysical realm and the influence of metaphysical forces, its practitioners will be able to remove many obstructions, make far greater advances, and make fewer mistakes.

The Qur'an states that God bestowed upon the House of Abraham the Scripture, Wisdom, and a mighty kingdom (4:54). This mighty kingdom manifested itself most brilliantly through the Prophets David and Solomon, upon them be peace. Prophet Solomon ruled not only a part of humanity, but also jinn and devils, birds and winds:

God subdued unto him devils, some of whom dove for pearls and did other work (21:82). Solomon had armies of jinn and birds, and he employed jinn in many jobs: *They made for him what he willed: synagogues, fortresses, basins like wells and boilers built into the ground* (34:13); and: *Wind was also subdued to him; its morning course was a month's journey and the evening course also a month's journey* (34:12).

SATAN AND HIS WHISPERING

The jinn we know as Satan was created from (some sort of) fire. Before his obedience and sincerity were tested through Adam, he had been in the company of angels. Unlike angels, however, who cannot rebel against God (66:6), Satan (called Iblis prior to his test) was free to choose his own path of conduct. When God tested him and the angels by commanding them to prostrate before Adam, the seeds of his conceit and disobedience blossomed and swallowed him. He replied in his vanity: *I am better than him. You created me from fire, while You created him from clay* (38:76).

Satan was created for important purposes. Since God has free will, He also gave us free will so that we could know good from evil and choose between them. In addition, God gave us great potentials. It is our development of these potentials and the struggle to choose between good and evil that cause us to experience a constant battle in our inner world. Just as God sends hawks upon sparrows so that the latter will develop their potential to escape, He created Satan and allowed him to tempt us so that our resistance to temptation will raise us spiritually and strengthen our willpower. Just as hunger stimulates human beings and animals to further exertion and discovery of new ways to be satisfied, and fear inspires new defenses, so Satan's temptations cause us to develop our potentials and guard against sin.

There is an infinitely long line of spiritual evolution between the ranks of the greatest Prophets and saints down to those of people like Pharaoh and Nimrod. Therefore, it cannot be claimed that the creation of Satan is evil. Although Satan is evil and serves various important purposes, God's creation involves the whole universe and should be understood in relation to the results, not only with respect to the acts themselves. Whatever God does or creates is good and beautiful in itself or in its effects. For example, rain and fire are very useful, but they also can cause great harm when abused. Therefore, one cannot claim that the creation of water and fire is not totally good. It is the same with the creation of Satan. The main purpose for his existence is to cause us to develop our potential, strengthen our willpower by resisting his temptations, and then rise to higher spiritual ranks.

Evil thoughts, fancies, and ideas that occur to us involuntarily are usually the result of Satan's whispering. Like a battery's two poles, there are two central points or poles in the human heart (by "heart" we mean the seat or center of spiritual intellect). One receives angelic inspiration, and the other is vulnerable to Satan's whispering.

Satan attacks humans from their four sides (7:16–17). Especially when believers deepen their belief and devotion, and if they are scrupulous and delicate in feeling, Satan attacks them more. He does not busy himself much with those who follow him voluntarily and indulge in all that is transitory, but usually seeks out those sincere, devout believers trying to rise to higher spiritual ranks. He whispers new, original ideas to sinful unbelievers in the name of unbelief, and teaches them how to struggle against true religion and those who follow it (6:121).

Satan does everything he can to seduce us. He approaches us from the left and tries, working on our animal aspect and our feelings and faculties, to lead us into all sorts of sin and evil. When he approaches us from the front, he causes us to despair of our future, whispers that the Day of Judgment will never come, and that whatever religion says about the Hereafter is mere fiction. He also suggests that religion is outdated and obsolete, and thus of no use for those who are living now or who will live in the future. When he comes upon us from behind, he tries to make us deny Prophethood and other essentials of belief, like God's Existence and Unity, Divine Scriptures and angels. Through his whispers and suggestions, Satan tries to sever completely our contact with religion and lead us into sin.

Satan approaches devout, practicing believers from their right to tempt them to ego and pride in their virtues and good deeds. He whispers that they are wonderful believers, and gradually causes them to fall through conceit and the desire to be praised for their good deeds. This is a perilous temptation for believers, and so they must be incessantly alert to Satan's coming upon them from their right.

In fact, Qur'an 4:76 tells us that the guile of Satan is ever feeble. It resembles a cobweb that appears while you are walking between two walls. It does not cause you to stop, and you should not give it any importance. He suggests or whispers and presents sinful acts in a "falsely ornamented wrapper," so believers must never accept his "gifts."

To free ourselves from Satan's evil suggestions, we should remove ourselves from the attractive fields of Satan and sin. Heedlessness and neglect of worship are invitations to Satan's "arrows." The Qur'an declares: *Whose sight is dim to the remembrance of the All-Merciful, We assign unto him a devil who becomes his comrade* (43:36). Remembrance of the All-Merciful, noble or sacred phenomena, and a devout religious life protect us from Satan's attacks. Again, the Qur'an advises:

> If a suggestion from Satan occurs to you, seek refuge in God. He is All-Healing, All-Knowing. Those who fear God and ward off (evil), when a passing notion from Satan troubles them, they remember, and behold! they see. (7:200-1)

Satan sometimes tries to tempt us through obscene scenes. He causes us to obsess over illicit pleasures. On such occasions, we should try to persuade ourselves that any illicit pleasure will result in fits of remorse and may endanger our afterlife or even our mortal life. We should not forget that the life of this world is but a passing plaything, a comforting illusion, and that the true life is that of the Hereafter.[9]

SPELLS AND SORCERY

Those who deny spells and sorcery do so either because they do not believe in anything related to metaphysics or what they suppose to be connected with religion, or because they are unaware of realities beyond the physical realm.

Most of us have heard of or even seen many such cases. As the Prophet, upon him be peace and blessings, declared that the evil eye is an undeniable fact, sorcery is also an undeniable reality.[10] The Qur'an speaks about (and severely condemns) the sorcery practiced to cause a rift between spouses. According to the Qur'an and Islam, sorcery and casting spells are as sinful as unbelief (2:102).

While breaking a spell is a good, meritorious deed, it must not be adopted and practiced as a profession. Although our Prophet, upon him be peace and blessings, met with jinn, preached Islam to them, and took their allegiance, he never explained how to contact them or how to cast or break a spell. However, he taught how jinn approach us and seek to control us, how we can protect ourselves against their evil, and how to ward off and be saved from the evil eye.

The safest way to protect ourselves against evil spirits is to have a strong loyalty to God and His Messenger, upon him be peace and blessings. This requires following the principles of Islam strictly. In addition, we should never give up praying, for prayer is a weapon against hostility, protects us from harm, and helps us to attain our goals. Prayer does not mean to ignore and neglect material means in attaining goals. Rather, applying them is included in prayer. As we pray for ourselves, we also must request those who we believe to be near to God to pray for us. The Companions frequently asked the Prophet to pray for them.

Some people go to exorcists. Although a few people might know how to drive out evil spirits, such activity is usually quite dangerous, for most exorcists deceive people. Also, an exorcist must be very careful about his or her religious obligations, refrain from sin, and be an upright person who knows how to exorcise somebody.

Believers should not go to those psychiatrists or doctors who restrict themselves to the narrow confines of matter. Materialist psychiatrists who do not believe in the spirit and spirit beings may advise patients suffering from spiritual dissatisfaction or possessed by evil spirits to indulge themselves in pleasure and amusement. This is like advising a thirsty person to quench his or her thirst with salty sea water.

God's Messenger, upon him be peace and blessings, mentioned that special prayers should be recited to protect oneself against the evils of Satan and other unbelieving jinn. The Verse of the Throne (2:255) is one of them. We also read that: *If a stimulus from Satan occurs to you, seek refuge in God immediately* (41:36). That is, say: "I seek refuge in God from Satan, the accursed."

As reported by 'A'isha, the Mother of Believers and one of the Prophet's wives, God's Messenger recited *Sura al-Falaq* and *Sura an-Nas* three times every morning and evening, and then breathed into his joined palms and rubbed them against the parts of his body he could reach.[11] He recited these *sura*s also to be preserved against spells and sorcery.[12] He also recited three times every morning and evening: "In the Name of God, Whom nothing on the earth and in the heavens can harm as against His Name. He is the All-Hearing, the All-Knowing."[13] This recitation and the following one are among the prayers advised for protection against paralysis: "I seek refuge in all of God's words from all devils and vermin and from all evil eyes."[14] Imam al-Ghazzali advises us to protect ourselves against spells, charms, and evil spirits by reciting: "In the Name of God, the All-Merciful, the All-Compassionate" once, "God is the Greatest" ten times, *The magician will not be successful wherever he appears* (20:69), and *from the evil of blowers upon knots* (113:4). Another imam advises us to recite these two verses nineteen times after each sip of liquid (e.g., water, tea, or soup).[15]

THE SPIRIT: ITS EXISTENCE AND IDENTITY

The spirit is from the world of Divine Commands

There are many other worlds than those we commonly think of, such as those of plants, animals, human beings, and of the world of jinn. Our visible, material world addresses itself to our senses. From tiny particles to galaxies, this world is the realm where God Almighty gives life, fashions, renews, changes, and causes things to die. Science concerns itself with these phenomena.

Above this visible, material world is the immaterial world of Divine Laws or Commands. To learn something about this world, consider how a book, a tree, or a human being comes into existence. The main part of a book's existence is its meaning. Regardless of how excellent the printing machine is or how much paper we have, a book cannot exist without meaning. In the case of a tree, the essence of life and the law of germination and growth (with which it is endowed) stimulates its seed to germinate underground and grow into a tree. We can observe the entire growth process with our own eyes. If this invisible essence and these unobservable laws did not exist, there would be no plants.

We derive the existence of such laws from the almost never-changing repetition of these processes. Likewise, by observing the "natural" phenomena around us, we derive the existence of many other laws, such as gravitation and repulsion, and the freezing and vaporization of water.

Like these laws, the spirit is also a law issuing from the world of Divine Laws or Commands. This is stated in the Qur'an: *Say: "The spirit is of my Lord's Command"* (17:85) But it is unique in one way: it is a living, conscious law. If the spirit were stripped of life and consciousness, it would be "regular" law; if "regular" laws were given life and consciousness, each one would become a spirit.

Science cannot define or perceive the spirit

While matter or anything in the material world is composed of atoms, and atoms are made up of more minute particles, the spirit is a simple, non-compound entity. We cannot see it, but we can know it through its manifestations in this world. Although we accept its existence and observe its manifestations, we cannot know its nature. Such ignorance, however, does not mean that it does not exist.

We see with our eyes, as they are our instruments of sight. The main center of sight is located in the brain. But the brain does not see. You do not say: "My brain sees"; rather, you say: "I see." It is the individual who sees or hears or senses. But what is this "I"? Is it something composed of a brain, a heart, and other organs and limbs? Why can we not move when we die, although all our organs and limbs are there? Does a factory operate by itself, or does something else (i.e., electrical energy) cause it to work? Any defect or error in a factory that causes a disconnect between it and its electrical energy can reduce a once highly productive and invaluable factory to a heap of junk. Is such a relation at all comparable to that between the spirit and the body?

When the body's connection with the spirit is cut by death, the body is reduced to something that must be disposed of quickly, before it begins to rot and decompose.

The spirit is not an electrical power, but rather a conscious, powerful thing that learns, thinks, senses and reasons. It develops continually, usually in parallel with the body's physical development, as well as mentally and spiritually through learning and reflection, belief and worship. The spirit determines each individual's character, nature, or identity. As a result, although all human begins are substantially made of the same elements, each individual is unique.

The spirit commands our inner faculties

According to the Qur'an, God has given a particular nature to each creature: *All that is in the heavens and the earth submits to Him, willingly or unwillingly, and they will be returned to Him* (3:83); and *Glorify the Name of your Lord, the Most High, Who has created (all things) and well proportioned (them); Who has assigned for each a particular form and a particular way to follow and ordained their destinies, and guided (them)* (87:1–3).

Whatever exists in the universe, including the human body, acts according to the primordial nature (*fitra*) God Almighty assigned to it. This is why we observe determinism in how the universe operates. The primordial nature of things does not deceive. For example, since God orders the earth to revolve around its own axis as well as the sun, it always does so. A seed says in the tongue of its being or primordial nature: "I will germinate underground in proper conditions and grow into a plant," and it does what it says. Water declares that it freezes at 0°C and vaporizes at 100°C, and does what it declares.

Similarly, the human conscience, as long as it remains sound, does not lie. If it is not deluded by the carnal soul or harmful desires, it deeply feels the existence of God and finds peace through believing in and worshipping Him. Thus, the spirit directs or commands our conscience and other faculties. It seeks the world from which it came, and yearns for its Creator. Unless it is stunted and spoiled by sin, it will find the Creator and attain true happiness in Him.

The spirit has deep relations with the past and the future

Animals have no concept of time, for their God-given primordial nature causes them to live only for the present, without feeling any pain for the past or anxiety for the future. On the other hand, we are deeply influenced by such pain and anxiety, for our spirit is a conscious, sentient entity. The spirit is never satisfied with this mortal, fleeting world, and our accomplishments or possessions (e.g., money, status, satisfied desires) cannot make it content. Rather, especially when considered for their own sakes or for that of the carnal soul alone, such things only increase its dissatisfaction and unhappiness, for the spirit finds rest only through belief, worship, and remembrance of God.

Every person feels a strong desire for eternity. This desire cannot come from the physical dimension of our existence, for our mortality precludes any feeling of and desire for eternity. This desire for eternity originates in the eternal dimension of our existence, which is inhabited by our spirit. Our spirit causes us to lament: "I am mortal but do not desire what is mortal. I am impotent but do not desire what is impotent. What I desire is an eternal beloved (who will never desert me), and I yearn for an eternal world."

The spirit needs our body in this world

The spirit, a non-compound entity issuing from the world of Divine Commands, must use material means to be manifested and function in this world. As the body cannot contact the world of meanings and immaterial forms, the spirit cannot contact this world if there is no human heart, brain, or other bodily organs and limbs to mediate. The spirit functions through the body's nerves, cells, and other elements. Therefore, if one or more bodily system or organ goes awry, the spirit's relation with them is disconnected and can no longer command it. If the failure or "illness" causing this disconnection severs the spirit's relation with the entire body, what we call death occurs.

Although such psychoanalysts as Freud offered various explanations for dreams, dreams cannot only be the subconscious mind's jumbled activities. Almost everyone has had dreams that have given news of some future events and have come true. Many scientific or technological discoveries have been made because of true dreams. So, dreams point to the existence of something within us that can see in a different way while we are sleeping. This something is the spirit.

The spirit manifests itself mostly on a person's face and our spirit makes us unique

Truly, our face is a window opened on our inner world, for its features disclose our character. Psychologists assert that almost all of our movements, even coughing, reveal our character. The face's ability to reveal one's character, abilities, and personality resulted in physiognomy, the art of judging character from facial features. The spirit determines these features.

Our body's cells are renewed continuously. Every day, millions of cells die and are replaced. Biologists say that all bodily cells are renewed every six months. Despite this continuous renewal, the main features of every individual remain unchanged. We recognize individuals from their unchanging facial features, and each individual can be detected or recognized even from their DNA, hair and fingerprints. The cells of a finger change, due to renewal or injury and bruising, but its prints never changes. Each individual's unique spirit makes these distinguishing features stable.

Our moral, spiritual, and intellectual differences have nothing to do with our physical structure

Our body experiences ceaseless change throughout its existence. This change is directed toward physical growth and development until a certain period, gradually becoming stronger and more perfect. When this growth stops at a certain point, decay begins. Unlike our body which is decaying, we can grow continuously in learning and development. Our moral, spiritual, and intellectual education does not depend on our bodily changes.

It is not the physical body which receives education

Although we are composed of the same substantial, physical or material elements, we are morally and intellectually unique. Which part of us receives this moral and intellectual education, and which part is trained physically? Does physical training have any relation to learning or moral and intellectual education? Are physically well-developed people smarter and more moral than others?

If physical training or development does not affect our scientific, moral, and intellectual level, why should we not accept the spirit's existence? How can we attribute learning and moral and intellectual education to some biochemical processes in the brain? Are those processes quicker in some people? Are some smarter because they have quicker processes, or are the processes quicker because some study and thus become smarter? What relation do these processes have with our spiritual and moral education and development? How can we explain the differences regular worship makes to one's face?

Our physical changes engender no parallel changes in our character, morality, or thinking. How can we explain this, other than by admitting that the spirit exists and is the center of thinking and feeling, choosing and deciding, learning and forming opinions and preferences, and is the cause of unique characters?

Our spirit feels and believes or denies

All people have innumerable, complex feelings: love and hate, happiness and sadness, hope and despair, ambition and the ability to imagine, relief and boredom, and so on. We like and dislike, appreciate and disregard, experience fear and timidity as well as courage and enthusiasm. We repent, become excited, and long for various things. If we look through a dictionary, we find hundreds of words that express human feelings. Moreover, we do not all "feel" the same way. We may reflect on what is going on around us, the beauty of creation, develop ourselves through learning, compare and reason, and thus believe in the Creator of all things. Worshipping and following His commandments causes us to develop morally and spiritually, until finally we are perfected. How can we explain such phenomena other than by admitting that each human being has a conscious spirit? Can we attribute them to chemical processes in the brain?

Are we only physical bodies?

If we are only a physical entity of blood and bones, flesh and tissues, and attribute all our movements to biochemical processes in the brain, why should we obey any laws? We have established that our physical body is renewed every six months. Therefore, if we are tried for a murder we committed a year ago, will it be unreasonable and unjust to punish us if we are composed of only a physical body, which is renewed every six months?

How can anyone be merely a physical entity? Can their movements, feelings, thoughts, beliefs, and decisions be the results of the brain's biochemical processes? Such assertions are untenable. The main part of our being is our living and conscious spirit. This part of our body feels, thinks, believes, wills, decides, and uses the body to enact its decisions.

The spirit is the basis of human life

God acts in this world through causes. However, there are many other worlds or realms: the world of ideas, symbols or immaterial forms, the inner dimensions of things, and spirits, where God acts directly and where matter and causes do not exist. The spirit is breathed into the embryo directly, making it a direct manifestation of the Divine Name the All-Living, and therefore the basis of human life. Like natural laws, which issue from the same realm as the spirit, the spirit is invisible and known through its manifestations.

In this world, matter is refined in favor of life. A lifeless body, regardless of size, such as a mountain, is lonely, passive, and static. But life enables a bee to interact with almost the entire world so that it can say: "This world is my garden, and flowers are my business partners." The smaller a living body is, the more active, astonishing, and powerful life becomes. Compare a bee, a fly, or even a micro-organism with an elephant. The more refined matter is, the more active and powerful the body becomes. For example, wood produces flame and carbon when it burns, and water vaporizes when heated. We come across electrical energy in the atomic and subatomic worlds. We cannot see it, but we are aware of its presence and power though its manifestations.

This means that existence is not limited only to this world; rather, this world is only the apparent, mutable, and unstable dimension of existence. Behind it lies the pure, invisible dimension that uses matter to be seen and known. As the spirit belongs to that dimension, it is therefore pure and invisible.

Our spirit has its own cover

When the spirit leaves the body at death, it retains this cover, which is like a body's "negative." It is called by many names: the envelope of light, the person's ethereal figure, energetic form, second body, astral body, double (of that person), and phantom.[16]

CHAPTER 4

Divine Destiny and Decree and Human Free Will

DIVINE DESTINY AND DECREE
AND HUMAN FREE WILL

The Qur'anic word translated as "destiny" is *qadar*. In its derivations, this word also means "determination," "giving a certain measure and shape," "dividing," and "judging." Muslim scholars of Islam define it as "Divine measure," "determination," and "judgment in the creation of things."

As terms, *qadar* or Destiny means to predetermine or preordain within a certain measure, while Decree means to execute or put into effect. To be more precise, Destiny means that everything that exists, from subatomic particles to the universe as a whole, is known by God Almighty and measured, identified and established by Divine Eternal Will. His Knowledge includes all space and time, while He Himself is absolutely free of both of them. Everything exists in His Knowledge, and He assigns to each a certain shape, life span, function or mission, and certain characteristics:

> God knows what any female bears and what the wombs diminish and what they increase; and everything with Him is by a determined measure. (13:8)

> The sun and the moon are by an exact calculation . And the stars and the trees both prostrate (before God in perfect submission to His laws). And the heaven—He has made it high, and He has set up the Balance; so you must not go beyond (the limits with respect to) the Balance, and observe the Balance with full equity, and do not fall short in it. (55:5–9)

The universe's exact measure and balance, order and harmony, as well as that of all it contains, clearly show that everything is determined and measured, created and governed by God Almighty.

All seeds, measured and proportioned forms, and the universe's extraordinary order and harmony, which has continued for billions of years without any interruption or deviation, demonstrates that everything occurs according to God Almighty's absolute determination. Each seed or ovum is like a case formed by Divine Power into which Divine Destiny inserts the future life history of a plant or a living being. Divine Power employs atoms or particles, according to the measure established by Divine Destiny, to transform each seed into a specific plant, and each fertilized ovum into a specific living being. This means that the future life history of these entities, as well as the principles governing their lives, are pre-recorded in the seed or the fertilized ovum as determining factors and processes.

Plants and living beings are formed from the same basic materials. However, there is an almost infinite variety of species and individuals. Plants and living beings grow from the same constituent basic elements, and display great harmony and proportion. Yet there is such abundant diversity that we are forced to conclude that each entity receives a specific form and measure. This specific form and measure is established by Divine Destiny, that is, Divine measuring, determining, and establishing.

BELIEF IN DESTINY IS ONE OF THE ESSENTIALS OF FAITH[1]

Our conceit and weak devotion leads us to attribute our accomplishments and good deeds to ourselves and to feel proud of ourselves. But the Qur'an explicitly states: *God creates you and what you do* (37:96), meaning that Divine Compassion demands good deeds and the Power of the Lord creates them. If we analyze our lives, eventually we realize and admit that God directs us to good acts and usually prevents us from doing what is wrong.

In addition, by endowing us with sufficient capacity, power, and means to accomplish many things, He makes it possible for us to realize many accomplishments and good deeds. As God guides us to good deeds and causes us to will and then do them, the real cause of our good deeds is Divine Will. We can "own" our good deeds only through faith, sincere devotion, praying to be deserving of them, consciously believing in the need to do them, and being pleased with what God has ordained. Given this, there is no reason for us to boast or be proud of our good deeds and accomplishments; rather, we should remain always humble and thankful to God.

On the other hand, we like to deny responsibility for our sins and misdeeds by ascribing them to Destiny. But since God neither likes nor approves of any sin or wrong act, all such deeds clearly belong to us and are committed by acting upon our free will. God allows sins and gives them external forms, for if He did not, our free will would be pointless. Sins are the result of a decision on our part, through our free will, to sin. God calls and guides us to good deeds, even inspires them within us, but free will enables us to disobey our Creator. Therefore, we "own" our sins and misdeeds.

In short, because we have free will and are enjoined to follow religious obligations and refrain from sin and wrong deeds, we cannot ascribe our sins to God. Divine Destiny exists so that believers do not take pride in their "own" good deeds, instead of thanking God for them. We have free will so that the rebellious carnal soul does not escape the consequences of its sins:

> Whatever good happens to you, it is from God; and whatever evil befalls you, it is from yourself. We have sent you (O Messenger) to humankind as a Messenger, and God suffices for a witness. (4:79)

> If you disbelieve in Him (in ingratitude), yet surely God is absolutely independent of you. He is not pleased with ingratitude and unbelief from His servants; whereas if you give thanks (and believe), He is pleased with it from you. (39:7)

A second, important point is that we usually complain about past events and misfortunes. Even worse, we sometimes despair and abandon ourselves to a dissolute lifestyle, and might even begin to complain against God. However, Destiny allows us to relate past events and misfortunes to it so that we can receive relief, security, and consolation, and, without ever complaining about God,[2] we should derive lessons from what has happened to us and be careful about our acts. So, whatever happened in the past should be considered in the light of Destiny; what is to come, as well as sins and questions of responsibility, should be referred to human free will. In short, in one respect, Divine Destiny exists *so that we may not grieve for what has escaped us, nor exult because of what God has granted us: God does not love anyone proud and boastful* (57:23).

DIVINE DESTINY AND DECREE IN RELATION TO DIVINE WILL

God registers everything in His Knowledge in a record containing each thing's particular characteristics, life span, provision, time and place of birth and death, and all of its words and actions. All of this takes place by Divine Will, for it is through Divine Will that every thing and event, whether in the realm of Divine Knowledge or in this world, is known and given a certain course or direction. Nothing exists beyond the scope of the Divine Will.

For example, an embryo faces innumerable alternatives: whether it will be a live being, whether it will exist or not, when and where it will be born and die, and how long it will live, to mention just a few. All beings are completely unique in complexion and countenance, character, likes and dislikes, and so on, although they are formed from the same basic elements. A particle of food entering a body, whether an embryo or fully developed, also faces countless alternatives as to its final destination. If a single particle destined for the right eye's pupil were to go to the right ear, this might result in an anomaly.

Thus, the all-encompassing Divine Will orders everything according to a miraculously calculated plan, and is responsible for the universe's miraculous order and harmony. No leaf falls and no seed germinates unless God wills it to do so.

> With Him are the keys to the Unseen; none knows them but He. And He knows whatever is on land and in the sea; and

not a leaf falls but He knows it; and neither is there a grain in the dark layers of earth, nor anything green or dry, but is (recorded) in a Manifest Book. (6:59)

And no female carries or gives birth, save with His knowledge. No one long-lived has been granted a long life, nor another one not so long-lived has been appointed a shorter life, but it is recorded in a Book. Surely that is easy for God. (35:11)

Our relation with Divine Will differs from that of other beings, for only we (and the jinn) have the power of choice; in other words, free will. Based on His knowledge of how we will act and speak, God Almighty has recorded all details of our life. As He is not bound by the human, and therefore artificial, division of time into past, present, and future, what we consider "predetermination" exists in relation to us, not to God Himself. For Him, predetermination means His eternal knowledge of our acts.

In sum: Divine Will dominates creation, and nothing can exist or happen beyond Its scope. It is also responsible for the universe's miraculous order and harmony, and every thing and event is given a specific direction and characteristics. However, the existence of Divine Will does not mean that we do not have free will.

DESTINY AND HUMAN FREE WILL

We feel remorse when we do something wrong. We beg God's forgiveness for our sins. If we trouble or harm someone, we ask that person to excuse us. These actions show that we choose to act in a particular way. If we could not choose our actions and were compelled to do them by a superior power, why should we feel remorse and seek forgiveness for anything?

Obviously, we choose to move our hands, speak, or stand up to go somewhere. Nothing compels us to do or not to do something. We decide to read a book, watch television, or pray to God. We are not forced to do any of these things. We hesitate, reason, compare, assess, choose, and then decide to do something. For example, if our friends invite us to go somewhere or do something, we first hesitate, compare, and then decide whether we will accompany them or not. We repeat this very process maybe a hundred times a day before deciding to do or say something.

When we are wronged, we sometimes go to court to sue the one who wronged us. The court does not ascribe the wrong done to a compelling superior power like Destiny, and neither do we. The one accused does not excuse himself or herself by blaming that power. Virtuous and wicked people, those who are promoted to high social ranks and those who waste their time, those who are rewarded for their good acts or success and those who are punished for their crimes—all of this proves that each of us has free will.

Our free will is not visible and does not have material existence. However, such factors do not render its existence impossible. Everyone has two (physical) eyes, but we also can see with our third (spiritual) eye. We use the former to see things in this world; we use the latter to see things beyond events and this world. Our free will is like our third eye, which you may call insight. It is an inclination or inner force by which we prefer and decide.

Humanity wills and God creates. A project or a building's plan has no value or use unless you start to construct the building according to it, so that it becomes visible and serves many purposes. Our free will resembles that plan, for we decide and act according to it, and God creates our actions as a result of our decisions. Creation and acting or doing something are different things. God's creation means that He gives actual existence to our choices and actions in this world. Without God's creation, we can do nothing.

To illuminate a magnificent palace, we must install a lighting system. However, the palace cannot be illuminated until we flick the switch that turns on the lights. Until we do so, the palace will remain dark. Similarly, each man and woman is a magnificent palace of God. We are illuminated by belief in God, Who has supplied us with the necessary lighting system: intellect, reason, sense, and the abilities to learn, compare, and prefer.

Nature and events, as well as Divinely revealed religions, are like the source of electricity that illuminates this Divine palace of the human individual. If we do not use our free will to flick the switch, however, we will remain in darkness. Turning on the light means petitioning God to illuminate us with belief. In a manner befitting a servant at his or her lord's door, we must petition the Lord of the Universe to illuminate us and so make us a "king" in the universe. When we do this, the Lord of the Universe treats us in a way befitting Himself, and promotes us to the rank of kingship over other realms of creation.

God takes our free will into account when dealing with us and our acts, for He uses it to create our deeds. Thus we are never victims of Destiny or wronged by Fate. However insignificant our free will is when compared with God's creative acts, it is still the cause of our deeds. God makes large things out of minute particles, and creates many important results from simple means. For example, He makes a huge pine tree from a tiny seed, and uses our inclinations or free choice to prepare our eternal happiness or punishment.

To better understand our part and that of our willpower in our acts and accomplishments, consider the food we consume. Without soil and water, air and the sun's heat, none of which we can produce or create despite our advanced technology, we would have no food. We cannot produce a single seed of corn. We did not create our body and establish its relationship with food; we cannot even control a single part of our body. For example, if we had to wind our heart like a clock at a fixed time every morning, how long would we survive?

Obviously, almost all parts of the whole complex and harmonious universe, which is like a most developed organism, work together according to the most delicate measures to produce a single morsel of food. Thus, the price of a single morsel is almost as much as the price of the whole universe. How can we possibly pay such a price, when our part in producing that morsel is utterly negligible, consisting of no more than our own effort?

Can we ever thank God enough for even a morsel of food? If only a picture of grapes were shown to us, could all of us work together and produce it? No. God nourishes us with His bounty, asking in return very little. For example, if He told us to perform a thousand *rak'ats* (units) of prayer for a bushel of wheat, we would have to do so. If He sent a raindrop in return for one *rak'a*, we would have to spend our whole lives praying. If you were left in the scorching heat of a desert, would you not give anything for a single glass of water?

In sum: Almost everything we have is given to us for practically nothing, and our part in the bounty we enjoy here is therefore quite negligible. Similarly, our free will is equally negligible when compared with what God Almighty creates from our use of it. Despite our free will's weakness and our own inability to really understand its true nature, God creates our actions according to the choices and decisions we make through it.

Concluding points

- Divine Destiny, also called Divine determination and arrangement, dominates the universe but does not cancel our free will.
- Since God is beyond time and space, everything is included in His Knowledge, and He encompasses past, present and future as a single undivided point. For example, when you are in a room, your view is restricted to the room, but if you look from a higher point, you see the whole city. As you rise higher and higher, your vision continues to broaden. Earth, when seen from the moon, appears to be a small blue marble. It is the same with time. So, God encompasses all time and space as a single, undivided point, in which past, present, and future are united.
- Since all time and space are included in God's Knowledge as a single point, God recorded everything that will happen until the Day of Judgment. Angels use this record to prepare a smaller record for each individual.

- We do not do something because God recorded it; God knew beforehand that we would do it and so recorded it.
- There are not two destinies—one for the cause, one for the effect. Destiny is one and relates to the cause and the effect simultaneously. Our free will (our acts) is included in Destiny. That is, God Almighty pre-determined our acts by knowing beforehand in what direction we would use our free will how we would act.
- God guides us to good things and actions, and allows and advises us to use our willpower for good. In return, He promises us eternal happiness in Paradise.
- Our free will, if not used properly, can cause our destruction. Therefore we should use it to benefit ourselves by praying to God so that we may enjoy the blessings of Paradise, a fruit of the chain of good deeds, and attain eternal happiness. Furthermore, we should always seek God's forgiveness so that we might refrain from evil and be saved from the torments of Hell, a fruit of the accursed chain of evil deeds. Prayer and trusting in God greatly strengthen our inclination towards good, and repentance and seeking God's forgiveness greatly weaken, even destroy, our inclination toward evil and transgression.[3]

CHAPTER 5

The Resurrection and the Afterlife

THE RESURRECTION AND THE AFTERLIFE

THE VALUE OF HUMAN LIFE AND ITS PURPOSES[1]

A visible but oft-neglected difference between human and other types of life is instructive. Inanimate objects serve universal purposes in a complicated, amazing way, but do not know what they do or why they do it.

Plants and trees have some degree of life and serve animals and human beings as food. Also, addressing themselves to their senses by displaying spectacular scenes, spreading pleasant scents, and playing the most touching kind of music, they satisfy human senses (in particular, those of seeing, smelling and hearing) and decorate the earth. However, they do not know what kind of universal purposes they serve or what significant results they yield.

Animals perform tasks based on their abilities. Although they do not know why they are doing what they do, they derive some sort of pleasure from their work. A sheep, for example, gives milk, wool, and meat; a dog is a loyal friend; and birds are the loveliest singers in gardens or on mountains.

Of the earthly beings, only humans are conscious. They know what they are doing, why and for whom they are doing it, and why everybody else is working. People also can supervise and employ other people for their own advantage. However, human beings did not create themselves. Although of the same elements and living on the same substances, each individual is unique in countenance and character. Thus, each individual can be identified correctly by even his or her fingerprints.

People have no part in determining their physical features, family, race, color, birth date or place, and even their own nature. Their free will also is limited. For example, their role in producing bread is insignificant when compared with that of the One Who organizes the sun, rain, and soil; a wheat seed's germination, growth, and life; the seasons; and the mutual helping between these elements.

Besides, people did not establish the basic conditions of life—they cannot prevent hunger, thirst, and sleep. They have no authority over the cycle of day and night or their bodies; they function automatically. For example, if they had to "wind" their hearts at exactly the same hour every morning like a clock to continue living, they would certainly have forgotten to do so every day.

Another interesting fact is that from the very moment an animal is born, it seems to know what to do. As if trained in another realm, it comes (or rather is sent) into the world and acquires full possession of those functions and abilities that it needs to survive within several hours, days, or months. For example, a sparrow or a bee acquires (or rather is inspired with), in less than a month, the ability to integrate into its environment in a way that would take a human individual many years.

This reveals an important fact: Animals have no obligation or responsibility to seek perfection through learning, progress through scientific knowledge, or pursue prayer and supplication by displaying their impotence. They are obliged only to act within the bounds of their innate faculties, which is the mode of worship specified for them.

In contrast, people are born completely ignorant of life and their environment; we need to learn everything. Acquiring such knowledge requires our whole lifetime. We appear to have been sent here in such a state of weakness and inability that it takes us as long as two years even to learn how to walk, and almost a whole life to learn how to distinguish between good and evil, and what is beneficial for us and what is harmful.

Despite these basic differences, human life is the most valuable, for whatever exists was created to produce humanity. We are the fruit of the tree of creation. Just as a tree is grown for the sake of its fruit and its whole life is directed to yield this fruit, the whole universe serves humanity. Thus, each human being has the same value as the entire universe.

One might even say that its value is greater than the universe, for each individual is equipped with consciousness and other intellectual faculties that make him or her superior to all other life forms. In one instant, the human imagination can travel throughout and far beyond the universe. We can speak; experience very complicated feelings, desires, and goals; as well as learn, think, judge, reason, and employ other living beings. Therefore, our value lies not in our physical composition and material aspect, but in the metaphysical dimension of life.

The Hand of Power that created humanity made a great "expenditure" on each human being by attaching the greatest value to them. That is, in addition to their mental and spiritual faculties that no worldly scales can weigh, It included in their physical or biological composition almost all elements of the tree of creation. Each individual's physical or biological composition is so marvelous and expensive that if humanity joined together and built factories to produce a single cell, they would fail. When we consider only the neuron's structure and tasks and the thousands of cords extending from the brain to each of the more than 100 million cells in a human body, we can get a glimpse of what an amazing and miraculous creation we really are.

Despite this miraculous mechanism and the expenditure made on it, our earthly life is very short. Many people die soon after birth. However, the cost for and value of each individual, regardless of how long he or she lives, is the same. So short a life, despite such a vast expenditure and having the same essential value as a long one, cannot have been made for the life itself. Nor can it be limited to this world. It must have far-reaching aims, and there must be ways to eternalize it.

BENEFITS OF BELIEF IN THE RESURRECTION
AND THE AFTERLIFE[2]

Materialism was born in Europe in the middle of the eighteenth century. The British philosopher George Berkeley first used this term to mean an unjustified confidence in matter's existence. Later on, it was used to signify a philosophical movement or school attributing the origin of existence to matter and denying the existence of anything immaterial. Materialism also may be used to describe a way of life based on fulfilling material pleasures and bodily comforts and ignoring the satisfaction of spiritual needs.

The natural sciences deal only with the visible world, follow a sensory and experimental approach, and tend to accept only those conclusions resulting from their approach. Thus, the modern scientific worldview is quite similar to materialism. In other words, individual scientists may believe in God and the existence of immaterial entities like the spirit, whereas the modern scientific approach is by nature materialistic. For that reason, scientific materialism has the potential to be even more dangerous than materialistic philosophy. Philosophical ideas can be set aside as theories having little or no influence on one's daily life. In contrast, people must think, believe, and act in line with scientific conclusions.

Scientific materialism has a considerable effect on how we order our lives. For example, if people do not believe in a Day of Reckoning conducted by a Supreme Being Who knows everything about us and will call us to account, or believe that they are free to design their own laws and lives according to the requirements of a short, transient life, what should we expect? If being *scientific* means to deny or at least doubt the existence of anything metaphysical, and if *scientific* knowledge causes spiritual and metaphysical knowledge to be seen as superstitions, people have no alternative other than to live as materialists.

Given this, scientific materialism and the practical materialism it produces are responsible, along with philosophical materialism, for the global erosion of morals and spiritual values, increasing crime and drug addiction rates, and the unjust exploitation of the weak. They are also behind ongoing ruthless colonialism, now disguised, and other modern social and political crises.

Scientific materialism does not deny, theoretically, the existence of immaterial truths; rather, it says that anything immaterial cannot be known. You can discuss God's existence or any metaphysical topic with such people. But since scientific materialism argues that only material things can be known, it diverts our attention from immaterial truths. One result of this view is agnosticism, the belief that nothing can be known about God or of anything except material things. Scientific materialism, because it tends to explain immaterial truths in material terms and therefore reduces quality to quantity and spiritual to physical, is responsible for the rise of most modern false beliefs and "mystical" practices. This is seen most clearly in psychology, psychiatry, and psychoanalysis.

Practical materialism, to which scientific materialism gave birth, is now the dominant global worldview irrespective of one's religion or lack thereof. When development is mentioned, most people instantly think of economic development and the betterment of worldly life, and so give precedence to worldly life. Since material wealth and resources cause rivalry among peoples and countries, not a day passes without some clash occurring somewhere in the world.

Even if we leave out all human values, lofty truths and ideals, and spiritual happiness sacrificed for material development, scientific materialism has caused great harm. The products of science are usually exploited by the great powers to consolidate their dominion over the world. In addition, developments in genetics, biology, physics, and chemistry threaten the very existence of humanity.

Scientific materialism and the worldview based on it have, as pointed out by Said Nursi, given rise to five negative principles:[3]

- Power, which tends to be used to oppress others.

- Self-interest, the pursuit of which causes people to chase after what they want to possess. This gives rise to rivalry and competition.

- Life as struggle, a view that leads directly to internal and external conflict.

- Unity based on racial separatism. This is realized by swallowing up other people's resources and territories. Such racism also leads to terrible collisions between peoples.

- Satisfaction (whether real or not) of novel caprices or aroused desires. This brutalizes people.

The modern materialistic worldview stimulates consumption and so continually engenders and increases new, artificial needs. Its demands can be imposed via propaganda, advertisements, and their support of such undesirable human tendencies as "keeping up with the Jones." The resulting paradigm of "producing to consume and consuming to produce" destroys a person's delicate balance and causes extraordinary increases in mental and spiritual illness. Such a life has no place for spiritual profundity or true intellectual activity. In fact, it places intellect in the service of pragmatism and earning more money and other things (e.g., awards, recognition, and rewards).

It is highly questionable whether scientific and economic developments have brought true happiness to humanity, or whether developments in telecommunications and transportation have provided humanity with what it really needs. It is highly questionable whether modern people have found true satisfaction and solve their problems. Do their needs not increase day by day? While people in the past needed few things to lead a happy life, does not modern life make people feel the need of some new thing every day? To satisfy each new need requires more effort and production which, in turn, stimulates more consumption. This leads people to regard life as a course or process of struggle, and gives rise to cruel rivalry and competition. So it follows that because might is right in such a world, only the powerful have the "right" to survive.

Such attitudes lie behind such such philosophical attitudes or so-called scientific theories as Darwinian evolution and natural selection, historicism, and the like.

We do not belittle or condemn scientific study and accomplishment. On the contrary, we welcome them enthusiastically as signs and confirmation of humanity's superiority to angels. As the Qur'an states, God created humanity to rule on the earth in conscious, deliberate conformity with God's commands (2:30–31). Although humanity has been honored with free will, it is not compelled to do anything. Thus, to allow individuals to fulfil the reason for their creation, God gave them the knowledge of things and thereby made them superior to angels. However, if scientific study is to be directed toward humanity's real benefit, it must be pursued within the guidance of immaterial, metaphysical, and God-given rules.

BELIEF IN THE RESURRECTION MAKES DEATH LOVABLE

The All-Compassionate Creator has made this world in the form of a festival, a place of celebration and exhibition. He has decorated it with the most wonderful inscriptions of His Names, and clothed each spirit with a body possessing suitable and appropriate senses that allow the individual to benefit from the good things and bounties in the festival. He sends each spirit to this festival once only. As it is very extensive in time and space, He divided it into centuries and years, seasons and days, and various parts. His animal and plant creations promenade therein, especially during the spring and summer, when the earth's surface is transformed into a vast arena of successive festivals for all small creatures. This arena is so glittering and attractive that it draws the gaze of angels, other inhabitants of the heavens, and spirit beings in the higher abodes. For people who think and reflect, it is an arena for reflection, and one so wonderful that the mind cannot describe it.

The manifestations of Divine Grace, Mercy, and Munificence in this Divine festival are counterbalanced by the Names of All-

Overwhelming, All-Crushing, and the One Who Causes to Die through death and separation. This does not appear to be in line with the all-embracing Mercy expressed in *My Mercy encompasses all things* (7:156). However, consider the following points:

- After each group of creatures has served its purpose and produced the desired results, the All-Compassionate Creator causes most of them, by His Compassion, to feel weariness and distaste for the world. He then grants them a desire to rest and a longing to emigrate to another world. And so when they approach the time of discharge from their duties (through death), He arouses in them an enthusiastic inclination to return to their original home.

- The Most Merciful One bestows the rank of martyrdom on a soldier who dies in the line of duty (defending sacred values), and rewards a sheep sacrificed in His way with an eternal existence in the Hereafter. Given this, His infinite Mercy assigns a specific reward and wage, according to their nature and capacity, to other animate beings who perform their duties despite hardship and death. Thus, these beings are not sad when death comes; rather, they are pleased and look forward to it.

The world is continually enlivened through creation and predetermination, and ceaselessly stripped of life through other cycles of creation, determination, and wisdom. Death is not an extinction, but a door opening on a better, more developed, and more refined life.

The Qur'an presents death as something created and therefore having existence (67:2). When death enters a living body, life seems to depart. In reality, however, that organism is being elevated to a higher degree. The death of a plant, the simplest level of life, is a work of Divine artistry, just like its life, but one even more perfect and better designed. When a tree seed "dies," it appears to decompose into the soil. However, it actually undergoes a perfect chemical process, passes through predetermined states of re-formation, and grows into an elaborate, new tree. A "dead" seed represents the beginning of a new tree, and shows that death is something created (like life) and, accordingly, is as perfect as life.

Since fruit and animals, when consumed by people, cause them to rise to the degree of human life, their deaths can be regarded as more perfect than their lives. If this is true of plants, it must be true of people. As people are the pinnacle of creation, their deaths must be more perfect and serve a still greater purpose. Once individuals have died and been buried, they surely will be brought into eternal life.

Death is a blessing for human beings for several reasons, among them:[4]

- It discharges us from the hardships of life, which gradually become harder through old age. It also opens the gates to reunion with many of our friends who died before us.

- It releases us from a worldly life that is a turbulent, suffocating, narrow dungeon, and admits us into the wide circle of the Eternal Beloved One's Mercy. As a result, we enjoy a pleasant and everlasting life free from suffering.

- Old age and other unbearable conditions come to an end through death. Both the elderly and their families benefit from this. For example, if your elderly parents and grandparents were living in poverty and hardship, would you not consider their deaths to be blessings? The autumnal deaths of insects is a mercy for them, for otherwise they would have to endure winter's harshness and severity and be deprived of their lovers—lovely flowers.

- Sleep brings repose and relief, as well as mercy, especially for the sick and afflicted. Death, sleep's brother, is a blessing and mercy particularly for those afflicted with misfortunes that might make them suicidal. However, for the misguided, death and life are a torment within torment, and pain after pain.

- Just as death is a blessing for a believer, the grave is the door to illuminated worlds. This world, despite its glitter, is like a dungeon in comparison with the Hereafter. To be transferred from the dungeon of this world to the gardens of Paradise, to pass from the troublesome turmoil of bodily life to the world of rest and the realm where spirits soar, to be free of the distressing noise of creatures and go to the Presence of the Most Merciful—all of this is a journey, indeed a happiness, to be desired most earnestly.

- The All-Merciful One explains in His Scriptures, especially the Qur'an, the true nature of the world and the life therein, and warns us that love or attachment to either one are pointless.

THE WORLD WITH ITS THREE FACETS[5]

The world and things have three facets. These are the following:

- The first facet is turned to the Divine Names and Attributes. Each created thing is a manifestation of certain Divine Names and Attributes, such as Mercy, Creativity, Grace, Provision, Favoring, Hearing, Seeing, or Speaking. As this facet only mirrors those Names and Attributes, it does not experience decay and death, but is continually refreshed and renewed.

- The second facet is turned to the Hereafter—the world of permanence. Being like a field sown with the seeds of the Hereafter, seeds that will grow into permanent "trees" with permanent fruits, this facet serves the World of Permanence by causing transient things to acquire permanence. It also does not experience decay and death, but life and permanence.

- The third facet relates to our bodily desires. Many people love this facet, which is the marketplace of sensible conscious persons and a trial for the duty-bound. This facet is apparently the object of decay and death. However, in its inner dimension, there are manifestations of life and permanence to heal the sorrows brought by death, decay, and separation.

Why is love for this third facet not something to be approved? Consider the following:

- The world is a book of the Eternally-Besought-of-All. Its letters and words point not to themselves, but to their Author's Essence, Names, and Attributes. This being so, learn its meaning and adopt it; abandon its decorations and go.

- The world is a tillage for the Hereafter, so plant it to harvest in the Hereafter. Pay attention to the crop that you will receive in the Hereafter, and throw away the useless chaff.

- The world is a collection of "mirrors" that continually follow each other to reflect their Creator and then pass on. Therefore, know the One Who is manifested in them. See His lights, understand the manifestations of His Names appearing in them, and love the One they signify. Cease your attachment to "those fragments of glass" that are doomed to break and perish.

- The world is a moving place of trade. Do your business and leave. Do not tire yourself in useless pursuit of caravans that leave you behind and ignore you.

- The world is a temporary place of recreation. Study it to take lessons and warnings, but ignore its apparent, ugly face and pay attention to its hidden, beautiful face looking to the Eternal All-Gracious One. Go for a pleasant and beneficial recreation and then return. When the scenes displaying those fine views and beautiful things disappear, do not cry or be anxious.

- The world is a guesthouse. Eat and drink within the limits established by the Munificent Host Who built it, and offer thanks. Act and behave in accordance with His Law. Then depart from it without looking back. Do not interfere in it, or busy yourself in vain with things that one day will leave you and are no concern of yours.

Through such plain truths, He reveals the world's real character and makes death less painful. He makes death desirable for those awake to the truth, and shows that there is a trace of Mercy in all His actions.

DENEFITS OF BELIEF IN THE AFTERLIFE
FOR SOCIETY AND PEOPLE

Belief in the afterlife is the bedrock of social and individual human life, the foundation of all felicity and achievement, because after belief in God, belief in the Resurrection has the primary place in securing a peaceful social order. For if we act according to the conviction that whatever we do is seen and recorded and we will have to give an account for it, we will live a disciplined and upright life. The Qur'an declares:

> In whatever affair you may be, and whichever part of the Qur'an you recite, and whatever deed you do, We are witness over you when you are deeply engrossed therein. Not an atom's weight in the earth and in the heaven escapes your Master, nor is there anything smaller or greater, but it is in a Manifest Book. (10:61)

Whatever we do is recorded by angels entrusted with that task. In addition, God has complete knowledge of all our deeds, intentions, thoughts, and imaginings. An individual who lives in full consciousness of this will find true peace and happiness in both worlds; a family and community made up of such individuals will be as if living in Paradise.

Children are sensitive and delicate, very susceptible to misfortune, and easily affected by what befalls them and their families. When a family member dies or they are orphaned, their world darkens and they experience great distress and despair. So, what else other than belief in the Resurrection, in reunion with the loved ones who emigrated to the other world, can compensate for the loss of parents, siblings, and friends? Only when a child is convinced that his or her loved one has flown to Paradise, to a much better life than this, and that one day they will be reunited, will he or she find true consolation and begin to heal.

How can you compensate the elderly for their past years, their long-ago childhood and youth? How can you console them for the loss of their loved ones, friends, spouses, children or grand-children who went to the other world before them? How can you remove from their hearts the fear of death and the grave, which is coming closer every day? How can you make them forget death, which they feel so deeply? Can you console them with ever new pleasures of life? Only when they understand that the grave, an apparent open-mouthed dragon waiting for them, is really a door to another, much better world, or a lovely waiting room to that world, will they feel compensated and consoled for their losses.

Humanity is a unique part of creation, for people can use their free will to direct their lives. Free will is the manifestation of Divine Mercy. If our free will is used properly by doing good deeds, we will be rewarded with the fruits of Mercy. Belief in the Resurrection is a most important and compelling factor that urges us to use our free will in the right way and refrain from sin and from wronging and harming others.

Young people have a transforming energy. If you let them waste that energy in trivial things and self-indulgence, you undermine your nation's future. Belief in the Resurrection prevents young people from committing atrocities and wasting their energies on passing pleasures, and directs them to lead a disciplined, useful, and virtuous life.

Belief in the Resurrection is also a source of consolation for the ill. Suffering from an incurable illness, a believing patient thinks: "I am going. No one can make me live longer. Fortunately, I am going to a place where I will enjoy eternal health and youth. Everyone is doomed to die anyway." Such a belief has caused the beloved servants of God, primarily including the Prophets, to welcome death with a joyful smile.

The world is a mixture of good and evil, right and wrong, beauty and ugliness, oppressor and oppressed. Many wrongs go unnoticed, and numerous wronged people do not recover their rights. Only their belief in the Resurrection into a world of absolute justice consoles such people and prevents them from seeking vengeance.

The afflicted and those suffering misfortune also find consolation, for they believe that whatever befalls them erases some of their sins, and that what they have lost will be restored to them in the Hereafter as a blessing, just as if they had given these items as alms.

Belief in the Resurrection changes a house into a garden of Paradise. In a house where the young pursue their pleasures, children ignore religious sentiment and practices, parents are engrossed in procuring ever more possessions, and grandparents are sent to a poorhouse or a nursing home, or left to shower their love only on pets but not on their grandchildren, life is a heavy burden. Belief in the Resurrection reminds everyone of their responsibilities toward each other, and engenders a fragrance of mutual love, affection, and respect.

Belief in the Resurrection leads to mutual love and a deeper respect on the part of spouses. Love based on physical beauty is temporary, and therefore of little value. It usually disappears shortly after the marriage. But if the spouses love each other and believe that their marriage is eternal, and that in the other world they will be eternally young and beautiful, their love for each other will not disappear as they age and lose their good looks. If family life is based on belief in the Resurrection, family members will feel as if they are living in Paradise. If a country's social order is based on belief in the Resurrection and the Day of Judgment, life in that country will be far better than what Plato imagined in his *Republic* or al-Farabi (Alpharabios) in his *Al-Madinat al-Fadila* (The City of Virtues). It will be like Madina in the time of the Prophet, or the Muslim lands under the rule of Caliph 'Umar.

Arguments for the Resurrection and the afterlife

Although scientific findings like the second law of thermodynamics show that existence is gradually disappearing, even a collision of two planets could destroy the universe. If existence began with a big bang, why should it not end with another big bang or collision? Existence is an extremely delicately calculated "organism," a system with parts subtly dependent upon each other. A human body is made up of about a hundred million million cells. Just as a single deformed, cancerous cell can kill the entire body, any serious deformation anywhere in the universe also could "kill" it. Our death sometimes comes unexpectedly and without any visible, diagnosed reason. Do we know whether or not the universe might "die" all of a sudden, unexpectedly, from a "disease" or a "heart attack"? Maybe our old world has terminal cancer because we abuse it.

What follows comprises some other arguments for the Resurrection and the afterlife:

- God's Mercy and Munificence are, of course, eternal. An Eternal One Who manifests Himself eternally requires the existence of eternal beings. His eternal Mercy and Munificence demand eternal manifestation and thus eternal beings on whom to confer eternal bounties. But our world is only temporary, and millions of its living creatures die each day. What can such a fact indicate, other than this world's final and complete death?

  This world cannot receive the comprehensive manifestation of the Divine Names and Attributes. Nor can living beings, who experience great hardship and difficulty in maintaining themselves. For example, we cannot satisfy all our desires and appetites. Our youth, beauty, and strength, upon which we set our hearts, leave without a word and cause us great sorrow. Also, we have to exert ourselves even to obtain a cluster of grapes. If we were denied eternal nourishment after having tasted it, would this not be an insult and a mockery, a source of great pain? For a blessing to be real, it must be constant. Without an eternal life in which we can satisfy our desires eternally, all of God Almighty's bounties bestowed upon us would change into pain and sorrow. Therefore, after destroying this world, God will transform it into an eternal one that can receive the comprehensive manifestations of His Mercy and Munificence without obstruction, one in which we can satisfy all our desires eternally.

- Divine Pity and Caring heal wounds and wounded hearts and feelings, cause a patient to recover, end the pain of separation, and change pain and sorrow into joy and pleasure. They help human beings and animals throughout their lives, especially before and right after birth. Their mothers' wombs are well-protected homes in which human beings and animals are nourished directly without any effort on their part. After birth, Divine Pity and Caring provide them with breast-milk, the best possible food, and their parents' feelings of pity and caring. All of these are a single manifestation of Divine Pity and Caring.

  Although Divine Pity and Caring encompass the universe, here we encounter wounds, hurt feelings, incurable illness, hunger, thirst, and poverty. Why? As above, the answer is that this world cannot receive the comprehensive manifestation of Divine Attributes and Names such as Pity and Caring. Our inability to do so, as well as our injustice to others and abuse of our innate abilities, intervenes between beings and the manifestations of Divine Pity and Caring. Above all, every living thing dies. This arouses great sorrow in the heart, a sorrow that can only be compensated for by belief in another, eternal world. So, Divine Pity and Caring will be manifested fully in the other world, for that world allows no intervention, sorrow, and pain.

- God's Names and Attributes are absolute and eternal. Therefore, He is absolutely and eternally Merciful, Relenting, and Forgiving, as well as absolutely and eternally Mighty, Just, and Dignified. Although His *Mercy embraces all things* (7:156) and, as stated in a *hadith*, "exceeds His Wrath,"[6] some people's sins are so serious (e.g., unbelief and associating partners with God) that they deserve eternal punishment. Besides, the verse: *whoever kills a human being unjustly, it is as if he (or she) has killed humanity* (5:32) cannot be ignored. This is especially true today, where "might is right," thousands of innocent people are killed daily, and many others are wronged and deprived of their basic human rights. Even worse, many of the most serious sins and injustices go unpunished.

Death does not discriminate between the oppressed and oppressors, the innocent and the guilty, and the sinless and the sinful. This only can mean that just as in the world major crimes are deferred to supreme tribunals, so too, major sins (e.g., unbelief, associating partners with God, murder, and oppression) are referred to the Hereafter's Supreme Tribunal, where God will dispense absolute Justice. Even if God Almighty sometimes punishes them also here in the world, many injustices remain unpunished due to some instances of wisdom. Therefore, God's Justice will be fully implemented in the other world.

One day, those who thanked God will be welcomed with: *Eat and drink to your hearts content because of what you did in days gone by* (69:24) and *Peace be upon you! You have done well. Enter here to dwell forever* (39:73). In this place, God has prepared for us things we cannot even begin to imagine. Meanwhile, those who engaged in bloodshed, sin, and other prohibited activities will be thrown into Hell with the shout: *Enter (through) the gates of Hell to dwell therein forever: what an evil abode for the arrogant!* (39:72).

• A close examination of what goes on in the universe will show that it contains two opposed elements that have spread everywhere, become rooted, and clash with each other. This has resulted in the opposed elements of good and evil, benefit and harm, perfection and defect, light and darkness, guidance and misguidance, belief and unbelief, obedience and rebellion, and love and enmity. God kneaded these opposites together like dough, and made the universe subject to the law of alteration and the principle of perfection. The universe manifests, through such a continuous conflict of opposites, unceasing alterations and transformations in order to produce the elements of a new world.

One day, the Pen of Divine Destiny will have written what it has to write. The Divine Power will have completed its work, all creatures will have fulfilled their duties and services, and the seeds will have been sown in the field of the afterlife. The earth will have displayed the miracles of Divine Power, and this transitory world will have hung all the eternal scenes upon the picture-rail of time. The Majestic Maker's eternal Wisdom and Favor will require that the truths of the Divine Beautiful Names' manifestations and the Pen of Divine Destiny's missives be unveiled.

It will be time for all creatures' actions to be repaid, for the truths of the meanings expressed by the Book of the Universe's words to be seen, and for the fruits of potentialities to be yielded. A Supreme Court will be established, and the veil of natural causes will be removed so that everything is submitted directly to the Divine Will and Power. On that day, the Majestic Creator will destroy the universe in order to eternalize it. He will separate the opposites, causing Paradise to appear with all its beauty and splendor, and Hell to appear with all its awfulness.

Paradise and Hell are the two opposite fruits growing on the tree of creation's two branches, the two results of the chain of creation, the two cisterns being filled by the two streams of things and events, and the two poles to which beings flow in waves. They are the places where Divine Grace and Divine Wrath manifest themselves, and will be full of inhabitants when Divine Power shakes up the universe.

• We are provided here with whatever we need for almost nothing. The more necessary for life an item is, the more abundant and cheaper it is in nature. Our most pressing need is air, which we receive free of charge. Then comes water, which is almost free. God sends both of these from His infinite Mercy, and we make absolutely no contribution. Then come heat and light, which we receive from the sun for nothing. When we look at the rest of His bounties, we see that they are extremely cheap. Yet we still demand that He perform a miracle so that we might believe in Him! Our effort to procure these blessings is minuscule when compared to how they were produced. However, if these bounties or blessings were only temporary and imperfect, our fear of death, which cuts their supply, would change them into poison.

Thanks to God's being eternal, He will provide for us eternal and ever better forms of bounties. As these will be eternal, they will not become a source of pain engendered by our fear of death, because there will no longer be death in the eternal world.

• The universal wisdom in existence requires the Resurrection. God is absolutely free to do what He wills, and no one can call Him to account. However, being All-Wise, He acts with absolute purposiveness and wisdom, and never does something that is in vain, futile, or pointless.

Nothing in existence is in vain; there is nothing superfluous, and no act in creation is futile. The entire process observed in a living being's coming to the world and growth manifests an absolute will and determination based on an all-encompassing knowledge. The observed order and arrangement are so perfect that it is as if directions were written on each particle's "forehead." This purposeful wisdom, will, and determination open our eyes to the fact that everything in existence has been created for certain purposes.

Consider what deliberate results are produced by unconscious trees' actions. Is it really conceivable that something completely ignorant and unconscious of its own existence, which has no power of choice, can do such comprehensive things that require an all-comprehensive knowledge, power, and choice? The Power that attaches such significant purposes to a tree and makes it the means of many deliberate results will certainly not abandon humanity (the fruit of the tree of creation) to its own devices or condemn it to eternal annihilation.

For when we analyze ourselves, as well as our nature, physical and spiritual identity, structure and body, we realize that we were created for certain important purposes. We are unique beings, for we contain some aspect of all that exists in the universe. Our mental and spiritual faculties represent angelic and other spiritual worlds, such as the world of symbols or immaterial forms. But due to our inborn capacity to learn and to our free will, we can excel even the angels. Our physical or biological being represents plants and animals. Although contained in time and space, our spiritual faculties and such other powers as imagination allow us to transcend them. So the Creator Who creates the simplest things for many purposes and never allows anything to go waste, and Who perpetuates its life through its numerous seeds, will certainly not condemn us to eternal non-existence under the soil. He will resurrect all of us in an eternal world.

- This world cannot judge our actual worth. Although we have a small physical body, our mental and spiritual faculties allow us to embrace the universe. Our acts are not restricted only to this world, and therefore cannot be bound by time and space. Our nature is so universal that even the first human being's acts affect the last one's life and character and all of existence. Restricting us to a physical entity, a very short lifespan, and a limited part of space, as materialists do, shows a complete misunderstanding and lack of appreciation of what each of us really is.

This world's scales cannot weigh the intellectual and spiritual value of Prophets and their achievements, or the destruction caused by such monsters as Pharaoh, Nero, Hitler, and Stalin. Nor can they weigh the true value of sincere belief and moral qualities. What is the proper reward for a martyr who has sacrificed everything for the sake of God, or for such universal human values as justice and truthfulness; or for a believing scientist whose dedicated research results in an invention that benefits all people until the Last Day?

Only the other world's delicate scales, which account for an atom's weight of good and evil, can weigh such deeds accurately: *We set up a just balance for the Day of Resurrection. Thus, no soul will be treated unjustly. Even though it be the weight of one mustard seed, We shall bring it forth to be weighed; and Our reckoning will suffice* (21:47). Even if nothing required the Resurrection, the necessity of weighing our deeds would require an infinitely just and sensitive balance to be established.

- Look at a flower, a word of God's Power. For a short time it smiles upon us, then hides behind the veil of annihilation. It departs in the way a word that leaves our mouth disappears. The word disappears but leaves its meaning in the minds of those who heard it. Likewise, a flower goes but leaves its visible form in the memory of those who saw it and its inner essence in its seeds. It is as if each memory and seed records the flower's adornment, or somehow perpetuates it.

  If this is true for an existent thing near the simplest level of life, it will readily be appreciated how closely the human being, the highest form of life and owner of an imperishable soul, is attached to eternity. Actually, we have a strong desire for eternity and eternal life. Some of our senses or feelings, in particular, cannot be satisfied with anything less. None of us are content with this brief life of the world. If we could choose between eternal life with severe hardship during this life and eternal nonexistence after a short luxurious life, we would certainly choose the former, never desiring eternal nonexistence. So, the All-Merciful and All-Wise, Who has implanted in us this fervent desire for eternity, will certainly not condemn us to eternal nonexistence.

- A plant dies in an animal's or a human being's stomach and rises to the degree of animal or human life; an animal is consumed by a person and rises to the degree of human life. So, the Lord of the Worlds, Who promotes plants and animals to higher degrees of life through death will certainly not leave His most precious creature—humanity—to rot under earth eternal-ly. Rather, a human being drops into earth (after death) to attain a much higher degree of life in an eternal world.

- Listen to a bird's singing on a spring morning, the murmur of a brook flowing through green fields or deep valleys. Look at the beauty of spectacular green plains and trees in blossom. Watch the sun rise or set, or the full moon on a cloudless, clear night. All of these events, and many more that God presents to our senses, are but a single gleam of His absolute and eternal Beauty manifested through many veils. By observing such manifestations, through which He makes Himself known, we are enraptured.

Temporary blessings leave unbearable pain in our heart when they disappear. If spring came only once, we would sigh over it until we die. So, a true blessing must necessarily be eternal. In this world, the Eternally Beautiful One shows us only shadows of His Beauty in order to arouse our desire to see Its eternal and perfect manifestation. Moreover, He will allow us to see Him in Paradise in a manner free of any qualitative and quantitative measure or dimension: *On that day there will be shining faces, gazing upon their Master* (75:22–23).

- There is a basic relation between humanity and this world. We are born into an amiable environment and equipped with the required senses. We have feelings like compassion and pity, as well as caring and love, for there are many things here to which we can apply them. We feel hunger and thirst, cold and heat. Fortunately, these feelings can be satisfied with that which was prepared before or with only a slight exertion on our part.

Consider an apple. Its color and beauty appeal to our eyes and our sense of beauty. Its taste addresses our sense of taste, and its vitamins nourish our bodies. Despite our need of its nutriments, we might refuse to eat it if it were ugly and taste-less, and thereby deprive ourselves of its nourishment. This, as well as many other natural facts, shows that One with infinite

Knowledge and Power created us and prepared a suitable environment for us. He knows all of our needs, capacities, and qualities, just as He knows nature down to its smallest building blocks.

Another example is reproduction, which depends on mutual love and attraction between a man and a woman. If our Creator had not placed such things in us, if He had not allowed us to enjoy the process of reproduction, and if He had not implanted a great love and caring for our resulting children, we would never have reproduced. The first and final members of our species would have been Adam and Eve.

Death ends all pleasure and makes everything as if it had never been. Given this, if there were no Resurrection, our life would be a meaningless existence of suffering and pain. However, this world is a shadowy miniature of the other, eternal one. The bounties God bestows here are only examples of their eternal and much better forms in the eternal world, and are displayed here to encourage us to act in order to deserve them:

> Give glad tidings to those who believe and do good deeds. For them there will be Gardens beneath which rivers flow. Every time they are served with the fruits therein, they will say: "This is what was given to us aforetime." They shall be given in perfect semblance. And there will be pure spouses for them, and they will abide there forever. (2:25)

All joy and beauty, reward and happiness in this world point to their perfect and eternal forms in Paradise; all pain and punishment, ugliness and unhappiness point to their likes in Hell. God will use the debris from this world, after He destroys it, to build the other world. Thus, the interrelations among things here and between this world and the other point to the Resurrection.

• The universe works according to a moving timeline. Just as seconds point to minutes, minutes to hours, and hours to today's end and tomorrow's coming, and days point to weeks, weeks to months, months to years, and years to the end of a whole lifespan, existence has its own days in every sphere and dimension. Its appointed lifespan will one day come to an end.

Also, time is cyclical and the life of existence has certain terms or cycles: our worldly life, the life of the grave, and the afterlife, which is the last cycle and has many cycles or terms of its own. The Qur'an calls each of these a day, for a day corresponds to our entire life: dawn, morning, noon, afternoon, and evening correspond to one's birth and infancy, childhood, youth, old age and death, respectively. Night resembles the intermediate life of the grave, and the next morning resembles the Resurrection.

- Everything is subject to the law of development up to a final end. Given this, everything must evolve to a final end. This means that everything has a limited lifespan and that it will die upon reaching its final end. Since a human being (a microcosm, a conscious miniature of the universe) eventually will die, the universe (a macro-human being) also must perish and be resurrected on the Last Day. Just as a living tree, an unconscious miniature of the universe, cannot save itself from annihilation, so "the branches of creatures" that have grown from "the tree of creation" will die.

  If the universe is not destroyed by an external event coming from the Eternal Will, then a day, also predicted by science, will come when it will begin to die. It will give a sharp cry, and the following events will occur: *When the sun is folded up (and darkened); and when the stars fall (losing their luster); and when the mountains are set moving* (81:1–3); and *When the heaven is cleft open; and when the stars fall in disorder and are scattered* (82:1–3).

- Nothing disappears completely from this world. While we can record and preserve our every word and act on tapes, why should we not be able to understand that God, Who is the All-Recording and All-Preserving, records all of humanity's words and deeds in a way unknown to us? For we see that He enfolds everything in small things like seeds. For example, each human being is enfolded in a sperm or in his or her forty-six chromosomes. If we had forty-four or forty-eight chromosomes, we would be something completely different. He also records and preserves the whole life of a tree in its seeds, each of which will grow into a new, almost identical, elaborate tree. A plant that dies in autumn or winter continues to live not only in its seeds but also in innumerable memories. Likewise, He preserves sounds and voices, as well as appearances and sights to display them in another world. When we die and disappear into the soil, our most essential part, which is like a nucleus or a seed and is called "the root of the tail" (in a Prophetic saying),[7] does not disappear, for God will use it rebuild us on the Day of Resurrection.

- Consider an atom. The way it is formed and the way it maintains its relationships with other atoms are astounding miracles. Creating a solar system or an atom, both of which have orbiting bodies, and then regulating their movements and establishing their relationships are equally easy for God. Similarly, a cell is like an autonomous government. It has its own departments, each of which is interrelated with others and ruled by a center, as well as a "ministry of finance" that manages its income and expenditure. It is as if each cell were as smart as the smartest person on the planet. In addition, there are very close and substantial relations between these cells, all of which are ruled by a center—the brain.

God created the world and humanity when nothing of either thing existed. He brought our body's building blocks together from soil, air, and water, and made them into a conscious, intelligent being. Is there any doubt that the person who made a machine can tear it apart and reassemble it, or that an army commander can gather his dispersed soldiers through a trumpet call?

Similarly, while reconstructing the world, God Almighty will gather our atoms and grant them a higher, eternal form of life; *Say: "Travel in the land and see how He originated creation, then God brings forth the later growth. Assuredly, God is able to do all things"* (29:20); and *Look at the imprints of God's mercy (in creation): how He gives life to the earth after its death. He surely is the reviver of the dead (in the same way), and He is able to do all things* (30:50). These are only a few examples of the Creator's Power. Everything is equally easy for Him. Creating and administering the universe is as easy as creating and administering an atom. If all people worked together, we could not create even one atom. So, if the absolutely Powerful One says He will destroy the universe and rebuild it in a different form, He will do so. As God does not lie and is without defect, His promises can be believed. As stated in the Qur'an: *The Day of Final Decision and Judgment is a fixed time, a day when the Trumpet is blown, and you come in multitudes, and the heaven is opened and becomes as gates* (78:17–19).

Furthermore, not all component parts of us need to be present for our re-creation. Rather, only the fundamental part or the essential particles, as mentioned earlier, may be sufficient for the second creation. The All-Wise Creator will rebuild the human body upon this foundation.

- An overall death and revival is repeated every year. In winter, a white "shroud" covers the soil, whose yearly life cycle ends in autumn. Nature has already turned pale and shows fewer traces of life. The shell has fallen in and, ultimately, trees become like lifeless, hard bones; grass has rotted away and flowers have withered; migrating birds have left; and insects and reptiles have disappeared.

Just as every night is followed by day, winter, which is only temporary, is followed by a general revival. Warm weather causes trees to bud and, wearing their finery, present themselves to the Eternal Witness. The soil swells, and grass and flowers start to bloom everywhere. Seeds that fell into ground during the previous autumn have germinated and, having annihilated themselves, are transformed into new forms of life. Migrating birds return, and the planet hosts countless insects and reptiles. In short, nature appears before us in all its splendor and finery.

- Consider the following analogy: Traveling upon a road, we come upon a caravanserai built by a great person. It is decorated at the greatest expense in order to delight and instruct the guests during their night's stay. We can see just a little, for we are staying for a very short time. Briefly tasting the joys of what is offered, we continue our journey unsatisfied. However, the great one's servants busily record each guest's conduct and preserve the record. We see, too, that most of the wonderful decorations are replaced daily with fresh ones for newly arriving guests.

Having seen all this, can any doubt remain that the caravanserai's builder must have permanent exalted dwellings, inexhaustible precious treasures, an uninterrupted flow of unlimited generosity? With his generosity shown here, he intends only to arouse his guests' appetite for what remains in his immediate presence, to awaken their desire for the gifts he has prepared for them.

If we reflect upon this world, we will understand that this world, just like the caravanserai, does not exist for itself. Neither could it have assumed this shape by itself. Rather, it is a well-constructed temporary place, wisely designed to receive those beings who constantly arrive, stay awhile, and then depart. Those inhabiting it for a transient, short time are guests, invited by their Generous Sustainer to the Abode of Peace.

This world's adornments and amusements are not here for our perpetual enjoyment, for such temporary pleasures result in long-lasting pain when they disappear. They give us a taste to rouse our appetite. But they do not satiate us, for they are too short-lived, or our life is too short. Such valuable and temporary adornments must be there to instruct us in wisdom, arouse gratitude, and encourage us to seek their permanent originals.

In short, the adornments we see are for exalted goals beyond themselves. They are like samples and forms of blessings stored in Paradise, by the Mercy of the All-Merciful, for people of faith and good conduct.

- Almost all previous people believed in the Resurrection.[8] Even the self-proclaimed divine Pharaohs of ancient Egypt believed in it, and so wanted to be buried with their most precious things and slaves. If we search through the tombs, epitaphs, documents, and art of bygone peoples, we hear humanity's sighs for eternity echoing throughout time. Despite the alterations and distortions that have crept in over time, we find clear evidence of a belief in eternity in ancient India, China, and Greece, as well as in most Western philosophies.

    In the Muslim world, almost all philosophers believed in eternal life. Even the irreligious Abu al-A'la al-Ma'arri tried to describe, in his *Risalat al-Ghufran*, the Day of the Resurrection according to Qur'anic verses. Dante appears to have adapted this scholar's writings for his descriptions of Paradise, Hell, and Purgatory.

    To sum up: Except for a few materialists, the long history of Eastern and Western philosophy witnesses to belief in the Resurrection and an afterlife.[9]

How the Qur'an deals with the Resurrection

All the arguments put forward above are derived from the Holy Qur'an. In addition, the Qur'an, which assigns much room to the Resurrection, introduces it by giving examples from the world or making analogies between it and God's universal acts in the world. Examples are given below:

God's universal acts point to the Resurrection. The Qur'an argues for the Resurrection. To impress upon our hearts the wonder of what the Almighty will accomplish in the Hereafter, and to prepare our minds to accept and understand it, the Qur'an presents the wonder of what He accomplishes here. It gives examples of God's comprehensive acts in the macro-cosmos and, at times, presents His overall disposal of the macro-, normo-, and micro-cosmoses (the universe, humanity, and atoms, respectively).

For example, the following Qur'anic verses stress God's Power and, by mentioning specific instances of It, call us to have conviction in our meeting with Him in the Hereafter:

> God is He Who raised the heavens without any pillars that you can see, then He established Himself upon the Throne (of authority; having shaped the universe and made it dependent upon certain laws, He exercises His absolute authority over it), and subjected the sun and the moon (to His command); each runs (its course) for an appointed term. He regulates all affairs, expounding the signs, that you may believe with certainty in the meeting with your Lord. (13:2)

> Have they not seen that God, Who created the heavens and the earth and was not wearied by their creation, is able to give life to the dead? Surely He is All-Powerful over everything. (46:33)

The first origination of the universe and humanity indicate their second origination. The Qur'an presents the phenomenon of the universe's creation, which it defines as the *first origination* (56:62), while describing the raising of the dead as the *second origination* (53:47), to prove the Resurrection. It also directs our attention to our own origin, arguing:

> You see how you progressed—from a drop of sperm to a drop of blood, to a blood clot suspended on the wall of the womb, from a suspended blood clot to a formless lump of flesh, and from a formless lump of flesh to human form—how, then, can you deny your second creation? It is just the same as the first, or even easier (for God to accomplish). (22:5; 23:13–16)

The Qur'an makes analogies between the Resurrection and God's deeds in this world, and sometimes alludes to His deeds in the future and in the Hereafter, in such a way that we can become convinced of that which we cannot fully understand. It also shows similar events here and compares them to the Resurrection. One example is as follows:

> Has man not considered that We have created him from (so slight a beginning as) a drop of (seminal) fluid? Yet, he turns into an open, fierce adversary (selfishly disputing against the truth). And he coins a comparison for Us, having forgotten his own origin and creation, saying, 'Who will give life to these bones when they have rotted away?" Say: "He Who produced them in the first instance will give them life. He has full knowledge of every (form and mode and possibility of) creation (and of everything He has created, He knows every detail in every dimension of time and space)." He Who has made for you fire from the green tree, and see, you kindle fire with it. Is not He Who has created the heavens and the earth able to create (from rotten bones) the like of them (whose bones have rotted under the ground)? Surely He is; He is the Supreme Creator, the All-Knowing. (36:77–81)

The Qur'an likens the universe to a book unfolded. At the end of time, its destruction will be as easy for God as rolling up a scroll. As He unfolded it at the beginning, He will roll it up and, manifesting His absolute Power without any material cause, will re-create it in a much better and different form:

> On that day We shall roll up the heavens like a scroll rolled up for books. As We originated the first creation, so We will bring it forth again. It is a promise (binding) upon Us. Truly We will fulfill it (as We promised it). (21:104)

The Qur'an likens the Resurrection to reviving soil in spring following its death in winter, and mentions how God disposes of atoms and molecules while creating us in stages. Dried-up pieces of wood blossom and yield leaves and fruits similar, but not identical, to those that existed in previous years. Innumerable seeds that have fallen into soil now begin to germinate and grow into different plants without confusion. God's raising the dead on the Day of Judgment will be like this:

Among His signs is that you see the soil dry and barren; and when We send down rain on it, it stirs to life and swells. Surely God Who gives the dead soil life will raise the dead also to life. Indeed, He has power over all things. (41:39)

.... You sometimes see the soil dry and barren. But when We pour down rain on it, it trembles, and swells, and grows of every pleasant pair. That is so because God is the Truth, and He it is Who gives life to the dead, and He is powerful over all things. (22:5-6)

Look at the prints of God's Mercy: how He gives life to the soil after its death. Lo! He verily is the Reviver of the dead (in the same way), and He is able to do all things. (30:50)

God has brought you forth from the soil like a plant. And to the soil He will restore you. Then He will bring you back fresh. (71:17–18)

Especially in *suras* 81, 82, and 84, *the All-Mighty alludes to the Resurrection and its attendant vast revolutions.* Due to what we have seen here, such as seasonal changes, we can formulate an analogy that will help us understand and then, with awe in our hearts, accept the Resurrection and the vast events that will follow it.

As giving even the general meaning of these three *suras* would take a great deal of time, let us take one verse: *When the pages are spread out* (81:10). This implies that during the Resurrection, everyone's deeds will be revealed in the form of a "book," which we call "the record of deeds."

At first, this strikes us as strange and incomprehensible. But as the *sura* indicates, just as the renewal of spring parallels another resurrection, "spreading out the pages" has a very clear parallel. Every fruit-bearing tree and flowering plant has its own properties, functions, and deeds. Its deeds and life record are inscribed in each seed that will emerge next spring. These new trees or flowers offer an eloquent exposition of the original tree's or flower's life and deeds. That is, every fully-grown tree or plant is the developed form of its seed, which exposes its full content. This is perfectly analogous with the Qur'an's declaration, *When the pages are spread out,* which denotes that everyone's deeds will be revealed to them in the Hereafter.

In many verses, the Qur'an warns us that we were created to achieve specific goals, not to do whatever we want. As we are responsible beings, whatever we do is recorded. Our creation from a drop of fluid through several stages, the utmost care shown for our creation and the importance attached to us, demonstrate that we have great responsibilities. After death, we will be called to account for our lives. In addition, our creation through stages is a manifest evidence for God's Power, Who raises the dead to life.

> Does man think he will be left to himself uncontrolled (without purpose)? Was he not a drop of fluid which gushed forth? Then he became a clinging clot; then He shaped and fashioned, and made of him a pair, the male and female. Is He then not able to raise the dead to life? (75:36–40)[10]

ESCHATOLOGY IN ISLAM

The main aspects of Islamic eschatology are similar to the Judeo-Christian tradition. Since they were derived from the same source and so originate from Divine Revelation, many common points can be found: for example, the invasion of the world shortly before the end of time by the barbarous Gog and Magog (*Ya'juj* and *Ma'juj*) tribes, the appearance of *Dajjal* (the Anti-Christ) and then a Messiah and/or *Mahdi* who will bring justice and order after global chaos, and before a global apostasy just before the world's destruction, Doomsday, Resurrection, the Supreme Judgment, the Bridge (*Sirat*), and Paradise and Hell as the final abode of conscious beings.

In this section, we will summarize the "last things" or the events to occur before the destruction of the world. Before analyzing this, it is necessary to explain the language of the main Islamic religious literature.

The Language of the Divine Books
and the Prophetic Traditions

The Qur'an decrees: *There is not a thing wet and dry but it is in a Manifest Book* (6:59). The Qur'an contains everything, but not to the same degree, in the form of seeds, nuclei, summaries, principles, or signs. Things are explicit, implicit, allusive, vague, or suggestive. Each form is used to meet the Qur'an's purposes and the context's requirements.

The Qur'an pursues four main purposes: To expose and establish in human minds and hearts God's Existence and Unity, Prophethood, bodily Resurrection, and the worship of God and justice.[11] To realize its purposes, the Qur'an draws our attention to God's acts in the universe, His matchless art displayed through creation, the manifestations of His Names and Attributes, and the magnificent, perfect order and harmony in existence. It explains how to worship and please the Creator, makes frequent mention of the other life, and explains how we can gain eternal happiness and be saved from eternal punishment. It mentions certain historical events, and lays down the rules for personal and social good conduct and morality as well as the principles of a happy, harmonious social life. It also gives news of important future events, especially those that will happen before the end of time. These have a prominent place in both the Qur'an and the Prophetic sayings.

The Qur'an is the last Divine Book and Prophet Muhammad, upon him be peace and blessings, is the final Prophet, upon him be peace and blessings. Thus, both address all times, places, and levels of understanding. As the vast majority of people always have an "average" level of understanding, the Qur'an and the Prophet use the appropriate style and language to guide them to the truth and the Qur'an's basic purposes. Thus symbols, metaphors, allegories, comparisons, and parables requiring interpretation are quite common. Those who are well-versed in knowledge (3:7) know how to approach and benefit from the Qur'an and the Prophetic Traditions.

Another reason why the Qur'an does not concentrate on future events explicitly is that the point of religion is to examine and test the individual so that elevated and base spirits may be distinguished. Just as raw materials are fired to separate diamonds and coal, as well as gold and soil, Divine obligations test conscious beings and encourage them to "compete" in doing good so that the precious "ore" in the "mine" of human potential may be separated from the "dross."

Since the Qur'an was sent in order to perfect humanity through trial in this abode of testing and competition, it can only allude to future events that everyone will witness one day, and only opens the door to reason to a degree that proves its argument. If it mentioned them explicitly, the test would be meaningless. If the truth of Divine injunctions and Qur'anic and Prophetic predictions were clearly evident, everyone would have to affirm them, thereby rendering our God-given mental and spiritual faculties meaningless.

After this note, we may continue with brief mention of the last things:

The Last Things

The *Dajjal* (Antichrist)

God's Messenger, upon him be peace and blessings, mentioned two Antichrists: the *Dajjal*, who will appear in the non-Muslim world and try to remove the religious belief and spread heresy, and the *Sufyan*, who will appear in the Muslim world and struggle against Islam, especially against its way of life.[12] Both beings are the worst of all the *Dajjal*s and *Sufyan*s to appear in the world after the Messenger. Islamic sources report from the Messenger that more than thirty *Dajjal*s will appear after him,[13] and that the one or ones to emerge before the end of time will be the most harmful and destructive.

Another important point to stress is that the narrations of such beings are not exclusively about their persons. Rather, they are about their ideologies and committees, and the systems they will establish in all aspects of life. There are many reports from Prophet Muhammad, upon him be peace and blessings, about the Antichrist, with different degrees of authenticity according to the principles of Hadith science. Some of them are as follows:

- "The hands of the Sufyan will be holed," meaning that the Sufyan will be a prodigal one and encourage prodigality and dissipation.

- "A terrible person will appear before the end of time. When he gets up one morning, he will find that on his forehead is inscribed: This is an infidel."[14] This means that the Sufyan will be an apostate and, in imitation of unbelievers, will compel people to wear the attire which is a symbol of unbelievers.

- "The dictators to appear before the end of time, including especially the *Dajjal* and *Sufyan*, will have a false Paradise and Hell."[15] This means that during their time, people will be addicted to amusement and worldly pleasures and the income disparity among social classes will increase. As a result, there will be rebellions against governments. Therefore, the places of pleasure and amusement, jails, and similar places of torture will stand side by side.

- "Before the end of time, there will be almost no people who worship God and mention His Names as an act of worship."[16] This implies that the places in which God is worshipped and His Names are mentioned will be closed, and that the number of believing worshippers will decrease considerably. Another meaning is that just before the world's destruction, God will take the believers' souls and the world will be destroyed upon the unbelievers' heads.

- "Certain terrible persons will emerge before the end of time, such as the *Dajjal*, and claim divinity and make people prostrate to them."[17] This means that such persons will derive their force mostly from atheistic and materialistic trends and suppose themselves to have godly power. Their statues will be built, and people will be forced to bow before them as a way of adoration.

- "The dissipation and dissension to appear before the end of time will be so widespread and powerful that no one will be able to control his or her carnal soul against them."[18] This means the dissipated life will seduce most people, and that they will indulge in it willingly. The frightening dimensions of the dissipation and pleasure-addiction that the *Dajjal* will cause at this time have caused almost all Muslims, upon the Prophet's order, to take refuge in God for fourteen centuries.

- "The Sufyan will be a knowledgeable one and fascinate many scholars."[19] This means that although devoid of such means of power and reliance as kingdom, tribe, wealth, and courage, the *Sufyan* will gain authority due to his intriguing capacity and political genius. He bans religious education. Mostly because of their attachment to this life, many religious scholars and educationists will support him and his regime.

- "The first day of the *Dajjal* is equal to a year, his second day to a month, his third day to a week, and his fourth day to an ordinary day."[20] This miraculous Prophetic tradition means that the *Dajjal* will appear in the north and proceed toward the south. As we know, in the places near the North Pole a whole year consists of a day and night, each of which lasts six ordinary months. Coming toward the south, there are places where a day lasts three months, a month, and a week, respectively.

  Another meaning is that both the *Dajjal* and the *Sufyan* will have four periods of rule: in the first period, they will cause such destruction that normally could occur only in three hundred years. During the second period, the destruction they will cause each year will be equal to thirty years' worth of destruction by others, and in one year of their third period they will cause seven years' worth of destruction. Their fourth period will be normalized.

- "When the *Dajjal* appears, everyone will hear him. He will have an extraordinary mount and travel throughout the world within forty days."[21] This means that the *Dajjal* will appear when the means of communication and transportation develop to such an extent that an event happening in one part of the world will be heard in other parts, and that traveling throughout the world within around forty days is possible.

Ya'juj and *Ma'juj* (Gog and Magog)

According to the Qur'an 18:94–98 and 21:96, these are two barbarous tribes. Once before, a world conqueror known in the Qur'an as Dhu'l-Qarnayn went as far as their lands and, to protect neighboring peoples from their attacks, built a formidable wall. When the time comes, they will surmount this wall and invade the civilized world.

The forces that invaded the Muslim world and went as far as central Europe in the thirteenth century were considered to be Gog and Magog by the Muslims and Christians of that time. Said Nursi adds that a new invasion will come from the same direction.[22] According to certain Prophetic Traditions, such great wars will break out that innumerable people will be killed in them.[23]

The *Mahdi* and the Messiah

This is perhaps the most important element of the last things. Both Jews and Christians expect a Messiah toward the end of time, and regard his coming as the sign of the final, worldwide triumph for each.

Islamic sources mention both individuals. Shi'a Muslims give particular importance to the *Mahdi*, who they say is named Muhammad. He is the twelfth (and last) Imam of a series that began with 'Ali ibn Abi Talib, the Prophet's cousin and fourth Caliph. The *Mahdi* disappeared when he was seventy-four years old, and will reappear when the world is full of injustice to restore justice.

The majority of Muslims regard the *Mahdi* as one who will come toward the end of time, when the Muslim world is defeated and all Islamic principles are under comprehensive attack. Together with the Messiah, the *Mahdi* will defend the principles of Islam against atheistic and materialistic trends and revive the religious life. He will end the dominion of both the *Dajjal* and the *Sufyan*.[24]

According to certain contemporary thinkers and scholars, including Said Nursi and M. Fethullah Gülen, the Mahdi is not a single person but rather the name of a global Islamic revival. It has three periods, each of which will be represented by a person and his group. Its leaders will be well-versed in religious sciences, have the highest moral standards, know the sociopolitical and economic conditions of their times, and be equipped with the necessary qualities of leadership. Together with his followers, the leader of the first period will defend Islamic principles against materialistic trends and expose them in an appropriate way. In the second period, the revived Islamic principles will gain ascendancy in many parts of the world, and Islamic life will experience a significant revival. The third period will see the global revival of religious life.[25]

The descent of Prophet Jesus as the Messiah

The third period of the *Mahdi* most probably will follow the invasion of Gog and Magog, which will interrupt the second period. During the periods, especially the third period, of the *Mahdi*, Prophet Jesus will descend to the world and cooperate with the *Mahdi* and follow him.[26] According to the commentators, the hadiths concerning Jesus' descent mean that before the end of time the basic problems of humanity will arise from rebelling against God and God-revealed Religion, from excessive worldliness, scientific materialism, and the ruthless exploitation of nature. The world will need peace more than at any time in history. Basic freedoms and rights of humanity will be violated, and especially the ties of family and society will be severed. Parents will no longer be given their due respect. Human life will be very cheap. People will pursue peace but they will not be able to know that peace lies in being at peace with the spiritual dimension of existence. So, during that time, Islamic faith, and spiritual and moral values, which constitute also the main aspects of Jesus' Prophethood, must be given prominence in preaching Islam. These aspects are the following:

- Jesus, upon him be peace, always traveled. He never stayed in one place, but preached his message on the move. Those who will preach Islam towards the end of time, when the distances will be narrowed and the world globalized, must travel or emigrate.

- They must be penitents, worshippers, travelers (in devotion to the cause of Islam and to conveying it), those who bow and prostrate (to God only), command good and forbid evil, and observe God's limits. For them there is glad tidings (9:112).

- Mercy, love, and forgiveness should have the primary place. Those who dedicate themselves to the cause of Islam must emphasize these characteristics and, never forgetting that Prophet Muhammad, upon him be peace and blessings, was sent as a mercy for all the worlds and the whole of existence, must convey glad tidings to every place and call people to the way of God with wisdom and fair exhortation. They must never repel others.

- In the Qur'an, Jesus introduces himself as follows: "*I am indeed a servant of God ... He has commanded me to pray and give alms as long as l live. He has made me dutiful to my mother, and has not made me oppressive, wicked (79:31–32)*." The Qur'an attaches extreme importance to observing the rights of parents (17:23–24). Therefore, Muslims, especially those who spread Islam in our age must strive to show due respect to their parents and elders, in addition to performing their prayers correctly and helping the poor and needy.

- In the face of the violation of basic human rights, these rights, including, particularly, life must be given due importance. The Qur'an attaches great importance to life: *One who kills another wrongly is regarded as having killed humanity; one who saves a life is regarded as having saved humanity* (5:32). Those dedicated to the cause of Islam must attach the utmost importance to life and try to prevent wars, find cures for illnesses, and know that reviving a person spiritually is also very important. The

Qur'an declares: *O you who believe! Respond to God and the Messenger, when the Messenger calls you to that which will give you life* (8:24).

The Muslim scholars who comment on Jesus' descent at the end of time also maintain that Christianity will be freed from its borrowings from certain ancient religions and philosophies and draw closer to Islam. Christianity and Islam will cooperate to repel the attacks of Gog and Magog and free the world from their invasion. Sciences will realize their full development. Cities will be built in the sky, and it will be easy to travel there. Probably as a result of developments in genetics, one pomegranate will suffice for as many as twenty people, and its rind will provide shade for them. Wheat produced on a small house balcony will be enough to feed a family for a year.[27]

The final, worldwide apostasy and the world's destruction

The unprecedented developments in science and technology will finally cause humanity to believe that it has so much knowledge and power that an authority above itself is no longer required or necessary. This will lead people to rebel against Heaven and indulge in debauchery to the extent that a worldwide apostasy will take place. Few believers will be left, and the unbelieving, rebellious forces will destroy the Ka'ba.[28] This will mark the end of the world. God Almighty will gently take the souls of the believers, and the world will be destroyed on the head of unbelievers.[29] Some Qur'anic verses which describe this destruction are as follows:

> When the sun is folded up (and darkened); and when the stars fall (losing their luster); and when the mountains are set moving; and when (highly prized) pregnant camels are left untended; and when the wild beasts (as also the domesticated ones) go forth from their places of rest (in terror of the destruction of the world); and when the seas rise up boiling... (81:1–6)

> When the heaven is cleft open; and when the stars fall in disorder and are scattered; and when the seas burst forth (spilling

over their bounds to intermingle); and when the graves are overturned (and pour out their contents); everyone will come to understand all (the good and evil) that he has forwarded (to his afterlife while in the world), and all (the good and evil) that he has left behind (undone). (82:1–5)

When the earth quakes with a violent quaking destined for it; and the earth yields up its burdens; and human cries out, "What is the matter with it?" On that day, she will recount all her tidings, as your Lord has inspired her to do so. On that day, all humans will come forth in different companies, to be shown their deeds (that they did in the world). And so, whoever does an atom's weight of good will see it; and whoever does an atom's weight of evil will see it. (99:1–8)

CHAPTER 6

The Qur'an:
The Holy Scripture of Islam

THE QUR'AN:
THE HOLY SCRIPTURE OF ISLAM

GENUINENESS OF THE QUR'AN

The Qur'an consists of the rhythmic verses, phrases, sentences, and chapters relayed by Prophet Muhammad, upon him be peace and blessings, as revealed to him by God over a twenty-three-year period, and which he proclaimed as his Prophethood's everlasting miracle. He challenged the Arabs of his time who doubted its Divine origin, as well as all unbelieving Arabs and non-Arabs who would come later to produce alike of its one verse.

God revealed His books, among them the Pages of Abraham, the Torah, the *Zabur* (the Psalms), and the *Injil* (the Gospel), to all earlier Prophets. We do not know the names of the books given to certain other Prophets.

These earlier Divine Books were sent down in now-dead languages that only a few people today claim to understand. Given this, it would be virtually impossible to understand these books correctly, or to interpret and implement their injunctions, even if they retained their original and unadulterated form. Furthermore, as the original texts of earlier Divine Books have been lost over time, only their translations exist today. Obviously a translation can never be the same as the original. Therefore even if they had not been corrupted, we still would not have them in their original form. The Qur'an, on the other hand, exists in its original Arabic, which is spoken and understood by millions of people.

The Qur'an was revealed to Prophet Muhammad, upon him be peace and blessings, in stages and mostly on different occasions.

This last "version" of the Divine Word, which was planted in the Last Prophet as a seed, grew swiftly and, once raised on its stem, put out its shoots and leaves, blossomed, and yielded fruit in all aspects of life. Almost one third of the world lived peacefully under its calm, serene shade for many centuries, and it continues to illuminate minds and hearts, conquering new hearts in increasing numbers, and grows younger and fresher as time grows older.

Defining the Qur'an

Literally, the *Qur'an* means the thing arranged or collected and established in the heart, and recited. As a term, the Qur'an is the name of God's miraculous or inimitable Word which was revealed to Prophet Muhammad, upon him be peace and blessings, written down and transmitted to succeeding generations by many reliable channels, and which collects and contains the "fruit" of all previous Scriptures and knowledge, and whose recitation is an act of worship and obligatory in the daily Prayers.[1] The Qur'an itself describes some of its features as follows:

> The month of Ramadan, in which the Qur'an was sent down as guidance for people, and as clear signs of Guidance and the Criterion (between truth and falsehood). (2:185)

> And this Qur'an is not such that it could possibly be fabricated by one in attribution to God, but it is a (Divine Book) confirming (the Divine origin of and the truths that are still contained by) the Revelations prior to it, and an explanation of the Essence of all Divine Books—wherein there is no doubt, from the Lord of the worlds. (10:37)

> We send it down as a *qur'an* (discourse) in Arabic so that you may reflect (on both its meaning and wording) and understand. (12:2)

> This Qur'an surely guides (in all matters) to that which is most just and right, and gives the believers who do good, righteous deeds the glad tidings that for them there is a great reward. (17:9)

And, indeed, (by revealing it through human language) We have made the Qur'an easy for remembrance (of God, and taking heed). Then is there any that remembers and takes heed? (54:17)

Most certainly it is a Qur'an (recited) most honorable, in a Book well-guarded. (56:77–78)

The Qur'an has other titles, each of which describes an aspect and so can be considered an attribute, such as: the Book, the Criterion, the Remembrance, the Advice, the Light, the Guidance, the Healer, the Noble, the Book in Pairs, the Mother of the Book, the Truth, the Admonishment, the Glad Tiding, the Book Gradually Revealed, the Knowledge, and the Clear.[2]

God's Messenger, upon him be peace and blessings, declares:

The Qur'an is more lovable to God than the heavens and earth and those in them.

The superiority of the Qur'an over all other words and speeches is like God's superiority over His creatures.[3]

The Qur'an is a definite decree distinguishing between truth and falsehood. It is not a pastime. Whoever rejects it because of his or her despotism, God punishes him harshly. It contains the history of previous peoples, the tiding of those to come after you, and the judgment on the disagreements among you. Whoever searches for guidance in something other than it, God leads him or her astray. It is God's strong rope. It is the wise instruction. It is the Straight Path. It is a book which desires cannot deviate and tongues cannot confuse, and which scholars do not tire of, never worn-out by repetition, and has uncountable admirable aspects. It is such a book that they could not help but say: "We have indeed heard a wonderful Qur'an, guiding to what is right in belief and action and so we have believed in it." Whoever speaks based on it speaks truth; whoever judges by it judges justly and whoever calls to it calls to truth.[4]

We close with Said Nursi's definition:

The Qur'an is an eternal translation of the great book of the universe and the everlasting translator of the various "languages" in which Divine laws of the creation and operation of the

136 An Introduction to Islamic Faith and Thought

universe are "inscribed"; the interpreter of the books of the visible, material world and the world of the Unseen; the discoverer of the immaterial treasuries of the Divine Names hidden on the earth and in the heavens; the key to the truths which lie beneath the lines of events; the tongue of the Unseen world in the visible, material one; the treasury of the favors of the All-Merciful One and the eternal addresses of the All-Glorified One coming from the world of the Unseen beyond the veil of this visible world; the sun of the spiritual and intellectual world of Islam and its foundation and plan; the sacred map of the worlds of the Hereafter; the expounder, the lucid interpreter, articulate proof, and clear translator of the Divine "Essence," Attributes, Names and acts; the educator and trainer of the world of humanity and the water and light of Islam, which is the true and greatest humanity; the true wisdom of humanity and their true guide leading them to happiness; and for human beings it is both a book of law, a book of prayer, a book of wisdom, a book of worship and servanthood to God, and a book of commands and invitation, a book of invocation, and a book of reflection, a holy book containing books for all the spiritual needs of humanity, and a heavenly book which, like a sacred library, contains nu-merous booklets from which all the saints and the eminently truthful, and all the purified and discerning scholars have derived their ways peculiar to each, and which illuminates each of these ways and answers the needs of all those with different tastes and temperaments who follow them.

Having come from the Supreme Throne of God, and originated in His Greatest Name, and issued forth from the most comprehensive rank of each Name, the Qur'an is both the word of God as regards His being the Lord of the worlds, and His decree in respect of His having the title of the Deity of all creatures, and a discourse in the name of the Creator of all the heavens and earth, and a speech from the perspective of the absolute Divine Lordship, and an eternal sermon on behalf of the universal Sovereignty of the All-Glorified One, and a register of the favors of the All-Merciful One from the viewpoint of the all-embracing Mercy, and a collection of messages some of which begin with a cipher, and a holy book which, having descended from the surrounding circle of the Divine Greatest

Name, looks over and surveys the circle surrounded by the Supreme Throne of God.

Because of this, the title of "Word of God" has been, and will always be, given to the Qur'an most deservedly. After the Qur'an come the Scriptures and Pages which were sent to some other Prophets. As for the other countless Divine words, some of them are conversations in the form of inspirations coming as the particular manifestations of a particular aspect of Divine Mercy, Sovereignty, and Lordship under a particular title with particular regard. The inspirations coming to angels, human beings and animals vary greatly with regard to their universality or particularity.

The Qur'an is a heavenly book, the six sides of which are bright and absolutely free of the darkness of doubts and whimsical thoughts; whose point of support is with certainty Divine Revelation and the Divine eternal Word, whose aim is manifestly eternal happiness, and whose inside is manifestly pure guidance.

And it is surrounded and supported: from above by the lights of faith, from below by proof and evidence, from the right by the submission of the heart and the conscience, and from the left by the admission of reason and other intellectual faculties. Its fruit is with absolute certainty the mercy of the All-Merciful One, and Paradise; and it has been accepted and promoted by angels and innumerable human beings and jinn through the centuries.[5]

APPROACHING THE QUR'AN

The Qur'an was conveyed by Prophet Muhammad, upon him be peace and blessings, to humanity as God's Word and testifies to his Prophethood. Being his greatest miracle, it challenges the Arabs of that time and all people to come until the Last Day to produce one chapter like it. It is unparalleled among Divine Scriptures, as regards its preservation and transmittal, for all copies of the Qur'an that have circulated since its first revelation are exactly the same.

As the Qur'an deals with all important theological issues and surpasses all scriptural records of pre- or post-Islamic ages in the abundant variety of its contents, its approach, presentation, and solutions are unique. Rather than dealing with a topic in the usual systematic method of theologians or apostolic writers, it expressly states that it has its own manifold method: *tasrifi*. This style shows variety, changes topics, shifts between subjects, reverts to the previous one, and deliberately and purposefully repeats the same subject in unique rhythmic and recitative forms in order to facilitate understanding, learning, and memorization: *See how We display the revelations and signs so that they may understand and discern* (6:65).

The Qur'an shows the universe's order. As almost all types or varieties of existing things present themselves to us side by side or mingled, the Qur'an links varieties together with a specific rhythm to display God's Unity. This style encourages people to reflect upon unity in variety and harmony in diversity. In fact, each chapter deals with many topics in various ways, a characteristic that adds to its unique beauty and matchless eloquence. Attentive reciters or intelligent listeners can so enjoy its rhythmical pitches that the Qur'an declares:

> God sends down in parts the best of the words as a Book fully consistent in itself, and whose statements corroborate, expound and refer to one another. The skins of those who stand in awe of their Lord tingle at (the hearing and understanding of) it. Then, their skins and their hearts come to rest in the Remembrance of God (the Qur'an). This is God's guidance, by which He guides whomever He wills. And whoever God leads astray, there is no guide for him. (39:23)

In addition, its verses and chapters are not arranged chronologically. Some verses revealed and placed together are preceded and followed by other verses. Some chapters and verses are lengthy; others are short. This arrangement is an aspect of its miraculousness, which many Orientalists and their Muslim imitators cannot understand.

The Qur'an exhibits the universe's order. Just as its contents have both a whole–part and holistic–partial (or universal–particular) relation, so does the Qur'an itself. In other words, a body (the whole) consists of various limbs and organs (the parts). A single part cannot wholly represent the body, although each part is a whole in itself, because the whole body cannot be found in any of its parts. But humanity and all species are holistic or universal, for each species is composed of members, each of which contains all of the species' features and so represents the species. Each person is an exact specimen of humanity in structure.

In the same way, each Qur'anic verse is a whole in itself and has an independent existence. In addition, an intrinsic relation exists among most of the verses. Said Nursi writes that:

> [T]he verses of the Qur'an are like stars in the sky among which there are visible and invisible ropes and relationships. It is as if each Qur'anic verse has an eye that sees most of the verses and a face that looks towards them, so that it extends to them the immaterial threads of relationship to weave a fabric of miraculousness. A single *sura* can contain the whole "ocean" of the Qur'an, in which the whole universe is contained. A single verse can comprehend the treasury of that sura. It is as if most verses are small *suras*, and most *suras* a little Qur'an. In fact, the whole Qur'an is contained in *Surat al-Fatiha*, which itself is contained in the *basmala*.[6]

At first glance, this unique *tasrifi* style sometimes seems to produce contradictory verses. But this is not the case, for the Qur'an is like an organism that consists of interlinking parts. As a result of this whole–part arrangement and the holistic–partial relationship among verses, although its outward meaning or aspect is open to everybody in respect of people's basic duties, a profound and comprehensive understanding of a verse often depends upon a complete understanding of the Qur'an. This is another unique characteristic, another aspect of its miraculousness, and another sign of its Divine authorship.

This characteristic is crucial to Qur'anic interpretation, for the Qur'an is the written counterpart of the universe and humanity. Moreover, the Qur'an, the universe, and humanity are three "copies" of the same book—the first being the "revealed and written universe and humanity" and the second and third each being a "created Qur'an." Given this, the Qur'an teaches us how to view hu-

manity and the universe. Thus any apparent contradiction among
its verses is due to the reader's misunderstanding. One whose being
is unified with the Qur'an sees no contradiction, as he or she is free
of all contradictions. If people view the Qur'an in light of their particular contradiction-filled worlds, of course they will see contradictions. This is why those approaching the Qur'an first have to be
free of all contradictions.

Arabic, the language of Revelation, is the Qur'an's outer body.
Religion, a method of unifying all of our being's dimensions, is far
more than philosophy or theology. Therefore Arabic, an essential
and inseparable element of the Qur'an, was chosen so that the Arabs of that time would understand it and because a universal religion requires a universal language.

The Qur'an views the world as the cradle of human unity. It
seeks to unite all races, colors, and beliefs as brothers and sisters
and worshippers of the One God. Its language is a basic factor that
helps people ponder religious realities and unite all dimensions of
their being according to Divine standards. Translations cannot be
recited in prescribed Prayers, for they cannot be identical to the
original language. Without Arabic, one can be a good Muslim but
cannot understand very much of the Qur'an.

The Qur'an is the source of all religious, spiritual, social, scientific, economic, political, moral, legal, philosophical, and other
knowledge in Islam. As the guide to all truth, it has four main
purposes: demonstrating God's Existence and Unity, establishing
Prophethood and the afterlife, promulgating the worship of God,
and setting forth the essentials of justice. Its verses, which mainly
dwell on these purposes, contain creedal principles, rules for human life, detailed information on the Resurrection and the afterlife, how to worship God, morality, various scientific facts, principles of civilizational formation and decay, historical outlines of
previous civilizations, and so on.

The Qur'an also is a source of healing, for applying it in daily
life cures almost all psychological and social illnesses, as well as a

cosmology, epistemology, ontology, sociology, psychology, and law revealed to regulate human life regardless of time or place.

MATCHLESS ELOQUENCE AND PROFOUND MEANING

Although this medium-sized book contains a certain amount of apparent repetition, it declares that *everything wet and dry is in a Manifest Book* (itself) (6:59). It addresses and satisfies all levels of understanding and knowledge, regardless of time and place.

Hundreds of interpreters have written commentaries on the Qur'an in the fourteen centuries of its existence, and none has claimed to understand all of its aspects and meanings. Thousands of jurists have inferred laws from it and based their reasoning upon it, but none has claimed to infer all of the laws contained therein or understand all reasons behind its injunctions and prohibitions. All pure and exacting scholars who "marry" mind and heart follow it, all revivers (the great saintly scholars who come when needed to revive and restore Islam) find their ways in it, all beloved friends of God derive their sources of inspiration and ways of purification from it, and all authentic spiritual paths depend upon it. Yet, like a source of water that increases as it flows, it remains as if untouched.

The Qur'an's miraculous or inimitable eloquence gives it this depth and richness of meaning. Its creative and artistically rich style is only one element on which its eloquence is based. It frequently speaks in parables and adopts a figurative, symbolic rhetoric consisting of metaphors and similes. This is natural, for the Qur'an contains knowledge of all things and addresses all levels of understanding and knowledge.

Its verses, linked with rhythm and symmetry of form to display Divine Unity, stir our emotions and intellect to reflect upon unity in variety and harmony in diversity. Each chapter has a particular rhythm and presents topics in various ways. This style discloses a unique beauty with matchless eloquence. Attentive reciters and intelligent listeners experience how the Qur'an is the fairest discourse fully consistent in itself and whose statements corroborate, expound, and refer to one another (39:23).

Although the Arabs of the Prophet's time were highly intelligent and well-versed in poetry and eloquence, they could not produce anything like the Qur'an. Likewise, none of the countless literary figures who have lived since has duplicated it. In fact, God Almighty challenged his contemporaries and humanity at large, regardless of time or place, to create even a chapter like those of the Qur'an. That all attempts failed proves the Qur'an's Divine origin.

> If you are in doubt about the Divine authorship of what We have been sending down on Our servant (Muhammad), then produce just a *sura* like it and call for help from all your supporters, all those (to whom you apply for help apart from God), if you are truthful in your doubt and claim. (2:23)

> And this Qur'an is not such that it could possibly be fabricated by one in attribution to God, but it is a (Divine Book) confirming (the Divine origin of and the truths that are still contained by) the Revelations prior to it, and an explanation of the Essence of all Divine Books—wherein there is no doubt, from the Lord of the worlds. Or do they say that he (the Messenger) has fabricated it? Say: "(If it is possible for a mortal to fabricate it) then produce a *sura* like it, and call for help on anyone you can, apart from God, if you are truthful (in your doubt and the claim you base upon it)." (10:37–38)

> Say: "(Even) if humanity and jinn united to produce the like of this Qur'an, they will never be able to do so, even though some of them help the others." (17:88)

No human composition has ever equalled even the Qur'an's smallest chapter (*Surat al-Kawthar*), and no one will ever be able to do so. Opponents have always taken up arms. But their attempts have never succeeded. As one Muslim scholar (Jahiz) points out, if people could defeat the Qur'an or Islam through argument, science, or eloquence, they would not have to resort to arms. The Qur'an becomes younger and fresher as time passes, for this process allows its unlimited hidden treasures to be disclosed one by one.

Said Nursi frequently draws our attention to its wording's miraculous depths of meaning. For example, Arabic's definite particle *al* adds inclusiveness to the word, and so he interprets *Surat al-Fatiha*'s initial *al-hamd* (the praise) as: "All praise and thanks that everyone has given and will give until the Last Day to others since the beginning of human life on the earth, for any reason and on any occasion, are for God."

Also, from the characteristics of the words used and their order in: *Out of what We have provided for them they give as livelihood* (2:3) he infers the following rules or conditions of giving alms:

> In order to make their alms-giving acceptable to God, believers must give out of their livelihood a certain amount that will not make it necessary for them to receive alms. *Out of* in *out of what* expresses this condition.
>
> Believers must not transfer another person's goods to the needy, but must give from their own belongings. The phrase *what We have provided for them* points to this condition. The meaning is: They give (to maintain life) out of what We have provided for them (to maintain their life).
>
> Believers must not remind those who receive their alms of the kindness they have received. *We* in *We have provided* indicates this condition, for it means: "I have provided for you the livelihood out of which you give to the poor. Therefore, you cannot put any of My servants under obligation, for you are giving out of My property."
>
> Believers must not fear that they may become poor through giving to others. *We* in *We have provided* points to this. Since God provides for us and commands us to give others, He will not cause us to become poor by giving to others.
>
> Believers must give to those who will spend it for their livelihood, and not to those who will waste it. The phrase *They give as livelihood* points to this condition.
>
> Believers must give for God's sake. *We have provided for them* states this condition. It means: "Essentially, you give out of My property and so you must give in My name."
>
> *What* in *out of what* signifies that whatever God provides for a person is included in the meaning of provision. Therefore, believers must give out of their goods and also out of whatever

they have, such as a good word, an act of help, a piece of advice, and teaching. All of these are included in the meaning of *rizq* (provision) and giving others as livelihood.

Along with these conditions, the meaning of the original three-word expression becomes: "Out of whatever We have provided for them as goods, money, power, knowledge, and intelligence, and so on, believing that it is We Who provide and therefore without feeling any fear that they may become poor because of giving and without putting under obligation those to whom they give, they give to the needy who are sensible enough not to waste what is given to them, such amount that they themselves will not be reduced to needing to receive alms themselves."[7]

THE RECORDING AND PRESERVATION OF THE QUR'AN

It is commonly accepted that in human history, God the Almighty has sent 124,000 prophets. According to the Islamic definition, a Prophet is one who comes with important tidings, "the tidings of the Religion," which are based on faith in the existence and Unity of God and His angels, the mission or office of Prophethood and Prophets, Revelation and Divine Scriptures, the Resurrection and afterlife and Divine Destiny, including human free will. The "tidings" also include offering a life to be based on this belief and promises and warning with respect to accepting this belief and offering or not. It frequently happened in the past that the Religion was considerably corrupted, which caused a Prophet to be chosen to revive and restore the Religion and make some amendments in its rules, or make new laws concerning daily life. This Prophet, who was usually given a Book, is called a Messenger, and his mission, Messengership. Five of the Messengers, namely Noah, Abraham, Moses, Jesus and Muhammad, upon them be peace, are mentioned in a verse in *Surat ash-Shura* (42:13) and accepted as the greatest of all Messengers.

The name of the Religion which God the Almighty sent to all the Messengers during history is Islam or, literally, absolute submission to God Almighty. Just as the laws in the order and operation of the universe are the same and constant, then similarly, there is no difference between the first human being on the earth and all the human beings of today with respect to their being human with the same peculiarities, essential needs, and final destination awaiting them. So too, it is natural that the Religion should be one and the same based on the same essentials of faith, worship and morality. As this Religion was corrupted or altered or contaminated with borrowings from false creeds, God sent different Messengers in different epochs of history. He sent Prophet Muhammad, upon him be peace and blessings, as the last of the Messengers, with the perfected and last form of the Religion, and "undertook" the preservation of the Book: *Indeed it is We, We Who send down the Reminder in parts, and it is indeed We Who are its Guardian* (15:9). After Prophet Moses, upon him be peace, the Religion he communicated came to be called Judaism; after Jesus, upon him be peace, came Christianity; and Islam has remained as the name of the perfected, preserved form of the Divine Religion which the Prophet Muhammad, upon him be peace and blessings, communicated.

Why did the Almighty undertake to preserve the Qur'an while allowing the previous Scriptures to be altered? First, He has pre-knowledge of everything and thus knew and predetermined that human well-being and happiness would require a final Prophet. He chose Prophet Muhammad, upon him be peace and blessings, as the final Prophet and through him perfected Islam so that it would address all levels of knowledge of understanding and solve all human problems until the Last Day. As this made sending another Prophet who would revive or restore the Religion unnecessary, He preserved the Qur'an. Second, preserving the Qur'an is not a sign of God's peculiar favor to the Muslims. Rather, as His predetermination includes human free will, He knew beforehand that the Community of Prophet Muhammad would be more devoted to their Book than any other people would be devoted to their own. So, as in this world He acts behind natural or material

causes and certain means, He has preserved the Qur'an by employ-
ing the necessary means for its preservation—the Companions of
the Prophet, may God be pleased with them, and the succeeding
Muslim generations, who were sincerely devoted to their Book. As
the first step to preserving the Qur'an, it was written down during
the life of Prophet Muhammad, upon him be peace and blessings,
under his direct supervision. It is due to this that not one word of
its text has been deleted, added or mutilated. There is not a single
difference among the copies of the Qur'an that have been circulat-
ing throughout the world during the fourteen centuries of Islam.

In considering the fact that, unlike other Scriptures preceding
it, the Qur'an has been preserved in its original form or text, without a single alteration, addition or deletion, the following points
are of considerable significance:

• The Qur'an was revealed in parts. God the Almighty undertook
  not only the preservation of the Qur'an but also its due recitation and the arrangement of its parts as a Book. He revealed to
  His Messenger where each verse and chapter revealed would be
  placed:

> Move not your tongue to hasten it (for safekeeping in your
> heart). Surely it is for Us to collect it (in your heart) and
> enable you to recite it (by heart). So when We recite it,
> follow its recitation; thereafter, it is for Us to explain it.
> (75:16–19)

> Absolutely Exalted is God, the Supreme Sovereign, the
> Absolute Truth and Ever-Constant. Do not show haste (O
> Messenger) with (the receiving and memorizing of any
> Revelation included in) the Qur'an before it has been
> revealed to you in full, but say: "My Lord, increase me in
> knowledge." (20:114)

• The Almighty emphasizes that no falsehood can approach the
  Qur'an, and there will be nothing to cause doubt about its authenticity as the Book of God:

> It is surely a glorious, unconquerable Book. Falsehood can never have access to it, whether from before it or from behind it (whether by arguments and attitudes based on philosophies to be invented or by attacks from the past based on earlier Scriptures; it is) the Book being sent down in parts from the One All-Wise, All-Praiseworthy (to Whom all praise and gratitude belong). (41:41–42)

- The Messenger of God, upon him be peace and blessings, once a year used to review with the Archangel Gabriel the portion of the Qur'an that had been revealed until that year. In the Messenger's last year, after the completion of the Qur'an's revelation, Gabriel came twice for this purpose. The Messenger concluded from this that his migration to the other world was near.[8]

- From the very beginning of its revelation, the Prophet's Companions, may God be pleased with them, paid the utmost attention to the Qur'an, and tried their best to understand, memorize and learn it. This was, in fact, the order of the Qur'an:

> And so, when the Qur'an is recited, give ear to it and listen in silence so that you may be shown mercy. (7:204)

- There were few who knew how to read and write in the starting period of the Qur'an's revelation. It was decreed after the Battle of Badr, which was the first encounter between the Muslims and the Makkan polytheists, that the prisoners of war would be emancipated on the condition that each should teach ten Muslims of Madinah how to read and write. Those who learned to read and write first attempted to memorize the Qur'an. They attempted to do so because the recitation of some portion of the Qur'an is obligatory in the prescribed Prayers; because the Qur'an was very original for them; and because it purified their minds of prejudices and wrong assertions, and their hearts of sins, and illuminated them; and because it built a society out of illuminated minds and purified hearts.

- In order to understand the extent of the efforts the Companions exerted to memorize the Qur'an and the number of those who memorized it, it suffices to mention that in the disaster of Bi'r al-Ma'una, which took place just a few years after the Emigration, seventy Companions who had memorized the Qur'an were martyred. Another seventy or so memorizers of the Qur'an were also martyred in other similar events and battles during the life of the Prophet, upon him be peace and blessings.[9] When the Prophet died, there were several Companions who knew the Qur'an by heart, such as 'Ali ibn Abi Talib, 'Abdullah ibn Mas'ud, 'Abdullah ibn 'Abbas, 'Abdullah ibn 'Amr, Hudayfah ibn al-Yaman, Salim, Mu'adh ibn Jabal, Abu ad-Darda, Ubayy ibn Ka'b, as well as 'A'ishah and Umm Salamah, wives of the Prophet, upon him be peace and blessings. When a person came into Islam or emigrated to Madinah, the Prophet, upon him be peace and blessings, sent him to a Companion to learn the Qur'an. Since a humming sound rose when the learners of the Qur'an began reciting, the Prophet asked them to lower their voices so as not to confuse one another.[10]

- The Qur'an was revealed in parts, mostly on specific occasions. Whenever a verse or chapter or a group of verses was revealed, it was memorized by many people, and God's Messenger, upon him be peace and blessings, also had it written down. He instructed where it would be placed in the Qur'an. (The Qur'an was revealed within twenty-three years. However, it was called the Qur'an from the beginning of its revelation.) Those whom the Messenger employed in the writing down of the Qur'an were called the Scribes of the Revelation. Histories give the names of forty or so among them. In addition to writing down the parts of the Qur'an revealed, the Scribes copied them for themselves and preserved them.[11]

- When God's Messenger, upon him be peace and blessings, died, several Companions, such as 'Ali ibn Abi Talib, Mu'adh ibn Jabal, Abu ad-Darda, and Ubayy ibn Ka'b, had already collected the portions of the Qur'an as a complete book. 'Ali had arranged them according to the revelation time of the chapters.[12] Following the death of the Prophet, when around seven hundred memorizers of the Qur'an were martyred in the Battle of Yamama, 'Umar ibn al-Khattab applied to the Caliph Abu Bakr with the request that they should have an "official" version of the Qur'an, since the memorizers of the Qur'an were being martyred in the battles. Zayd ibn Thabit, one of the leading scholars and memorizers of the Qur'an at that time, was chosen for the task. After a meticulous work, Zayd prepared the official collection, which was called *the Mushaf*.[13]

- The Almighty openly declares in *Surat al-Qiyamah*: "Surely it is for Us to collect it (in your heart) and enable you to recite it (by heart)." (75: 17) All the verses and chapters of the Qur'an were arranged and collected as a book on the instructions of the Prophet himself, upon him be peace and blessings, as guided by the Revelation. After the Battle of Yamama, as stated above, an official version was compiled and many copies of this version were produced and sent out to all cities during the time of the third caliph 'Uthman, may God be pleased with him.[14] These copies are still to be found in certain cities in the world. There is even one of the copies produced from the Imam Manuscript, which is the name used for the basic copy which Caliph 'Uthman kept for himself, in Columbia University Library (U.S.A.).[15]

- One of the foremost reasons for the Qur'an coming down to us through many centuries without a single distortion or change is that it has been preserved in its own original language. No one in the Muslim world has ever thought to supersede it with any translation of it, with the result that it has been protected from being exposed to what the previous Scriptures were.

In conclusion, the authenticity and genuineness of the copies of the Qur'an now in our hands, in the sense that it is in the very words which were conveyed by God's Messenger, upon him be peace and blessings, is so evident that no Muslim scholar of any standard has ever doubted its genuineness or the fact that each and every letter, word or sentence, verse or chapter was conveyed by the Messenger, as part of the Qur'an revealed to him by God Amighty. In other words, the version we have in our hands is undoubtedly the Qur'an as conveyed and recited by the Messenger, upon him be peace and blessings.

ARGUMENTS FOR THE DIVINE AUTHORSHIP OF THE QUR'AN[16]

Even a superficial study of the Qur'an's wording, styles, and meaning shows that it is unique. Thus, it must be either below or above all other books in rank and worth. Since it is above all of them, it must be the Word of God.

The Qur'an declares:

> You did not (O Messenger) read of any book before it (the revelation of this Qur'an), nor did you write one with your right (or left) hand. For then, those who have ever sought to disprove the truth might have a reason to doubt (it). (29:48)

- History records that Prophet Muhammad, upon him be peace and blessings, was unlettered. Yet the Qur'an, which he brought, has challenged all people to produce a similar book or even a chapter:

> If you are in doubt about the Divine authorship of what We have been sending down on Our servant (Muhammad), then produce just a *sura* like it and call for help from all your supporters, all those (to whom you apply for help apart from God), if you are truthful in your doubt and claim. (2:23)

No one has ever met this challenge successfully. Unable to duplicate even its shortest *suras* (e.g., *Surat al-Ikhlas* and *Surat al-Kawthar*), all who have tried have only opened themselves to ridicule. This proves the Qur'an's Divine authorship.
- No one has ever written a book having the same degree of accuracy with respect to religion, law, sociology, psychology, es-

chatology, morality, history, literature, and so on. However, the Qur'an was revealed in stages and on different occasions in twenty-three years, and it contains at least the principles of all branches of knowledge, either in summary or detail, and none of this knowledge has ever been contradicted. This book of Divine truths, metaphysics, religious beliefs and worship, prayer, law, and morality; a book fully describing the other life; a book of psychology, sociology, epistemology, and history; and a book containing scientific facts and the principles of a happy life contains no contradictions:

> Do they not contemplate the Qur'an (so that they may be convinced that it is from God)? Had it been from any other than God, they would surely have found in it much incoherence and inconsistency. (4:82)

Is it logical to say that a person can write such a book?

• The Qur'an's styles and eloquence are beyond compare. All of its sentences, words, and letters form a miraculous harmony. With respect to rhythm and music, geometric proportions and mathe-matical measures, and how many times each is used, each is in the exact place it must be and is interwoven and interrelated with others. No other literary masterpiece, including the Hadith,[17] can make this claim.

• At the time of the Qur'an's revelation, eloquence, poetry, oratory, and soothsaying enjoyed great prestige in the Arabian peninsula. The Arabs held poetry competitions and hung the winning poems, written in gold, on the Ka'ba wall. Although Prophet Muhammad, upon him be peace and blessings, was unlettered and never composed or recited poetry, the Qur'an challenged all poets and forced them to surrender. Many who refused to believe in the Qur'an were nevertheless captivated by it. Seeking to prevent Islam's spread, they said it was something magical (10:76; 21:3; 43:30) and advised people to ignore it (41:26). But such believing poets as Hansa and Labid abandoned poetry out of their respect for and awe at the Qur'an's styles and eloquence, and the unbelievers were no longer able to claim it was poetry, rhymed prose, or the words of a sooth-sayer. Even when they secretly listened to the Prophet's recita-tion during the night, they could not overcome their arrogance and believe in its Divine origin.[18]

The Qur'an gives news of the past. Although communicat-ed by an unlettered one, the wise Qur'an mentions in a sol-emn and powerful manner the important experiences of the greatest of the Prophets from the time of Adam to the Time of Happiness as well as the main aspects of their mission. The information it provides usually coincides with the commonly agreed descriptions of the previous Scriptures. It also corrects the points on which their corrupted forms disagree. Thus, the Qur'an has an all-seeing vision that knows the past better than the previous Scriptures. While the stories of previous Proph-ets are mentioned mainly in Makkan *suras*, no one in Makka knew about them.

The Qur'an is also full of predictions concerning the near and distant future. Some of these predictions have come true, and others are waiting for the time they will prove to be true. For example, *Surat al-Fath* contains about ten explicit predic-tions of the distant future, all of which proved to be true (i.e., see verses 1, 2, 11, 15, 19–21, 27–28). The scholars of the Qur'an's inner aspects and the meanings of creation, such as Imam al-Rabbani Ahmad Faruq as-Sarhandi[19] found many predictions in *Surat ar-Rum* and the individual, disjunct letters at the beginning of certain *suras* concerning the distant future. So, if a person who was subject to the severest criticisms and objections, in whom even one fault was certain to lead to his cause's failure, makes predictions so unhesitatingly and confi-dently, and in such a serious manner, it shows without doubt that he speaks not of himself but of what he receives from his Eternal Teacher.

The Qur'an also speaks about creation and the universe, Divine truths, and the Hereafter's realities. Its explanations in these areas are among the most important pieces of information about the Unseen. Humanity cannot advance in a straight direction amid paths of misguidance and reach the Unseen's truths or realities. The deep, endless disagreements between schools of philosophy and scientists show that even their greatest geniuses cannot discover even the least of these truths by unaided reasoning. They can discover the realities of creation only after centuries and endless controversies, and after numerous trials and errors.

No one can discover and perceive the Hereafter's events, states, conditions, and stages, including the life of the grave, by himself or herself. However, approximately one tenth of the Qur'an is about the Hereafter, and it is so certain about the information it gives that it uses the past tense while describing its events as if they have already happened.

- Arabic allowed the production of high-level poetry, but its vocabulary was not advanced to the same degree and so it could not express metaphysical ideas or scientific, religious, and philosophical concepts. Restricted to voicing the thoughts and feelings of simple desert people, the Qur'an so enriched and uplifted Arabic that it eventually became the Islamic world's *lingua franca*. At its height, the Islamic world was one of the most brilliant producers of scientific, religious, metaphysical, literary, economic, juridical, social, and political knowledge and texts. How could an unlettered person prepare the ground for such an unparalleled and unique philological revolution?

- Despite its apparent simplicity, the Qur'an has such depths of meaning that all people, regardless of education or age, can find what they need in it. The Qur'an illuminates the ways of poets, musicians, orators, sociologists, psychologists, scientists, economists, and jurists. The founders of all true spiritual orders and established schools of legal thought and conduct drew their principles from it. The Qur'an shows everybody how to solve their problems and satisfies their spiritual quests.

- History shows that the Qur'an does not bore people. Countless Muslims recite portions of it in their five daily Prayers, and many recite it completely at least once a year, if not once a month or even once a week, and many others memorize it. No text other than the Qur'an, sacred or non-sacred, has ever been memorized even by one hundredth of those who have memorized the Qur'an. In addition, a person of average memory can memorize it in a few months. Its frequent recitation brings benefits and an increased desire to continue reciting it. Moreover, it never loses its originality and freshness, for as time passes it breathes new truths and meanings into minds and souls, thus making them more active and lively. Compare this with an ordinary book, which we read maybe two or three times and then place on the shelf, never to look at again.

- The Qur'an describes humanity's physical and spiritual aspects and contains principles to solve all socio-economic, juridical, political, and administrative problems regardless of time or place. Furthermore, it simultaneously satisfies the mind and spirit and guarantees happiness in both worlds.

No person, regardless of his or her intelligence, can devise such a system. As we know, such human-devised systems undergo constant revision and adaptation to survive. Even more importantly, none of them can promise and then deliver eternal happiness, for all of their principles are restricted to this transient and short worldly life. By contrast, no Qur'anic principle has become obsolete or proven defective.

For example, the Qur'an enjoins that wealth should not circulate only among the rich (59:7); that government offices should be entrusted to qualified persons and that absolute justice should prevail (4:58); that one is entitled only to what he or she has earned (53:39); that no one can be accused of and called to account for another's crime (6:164); and that whoever kills a person unjustly is as if he or she killed humanity, and whoever saves a life is as if he or she saved the lives of all humankind (5:32). These and many other eternal golden principles (e.g., prohibiting usury, gambling, alcohol, illicit sexual relations, backbiting, wrongdoing), as well as injunctions (e.g., praying, fasting, charity, and good conduct), are another undeniable proof of its Divine authorship. These principles are strengthened through one's love and consciousness of God, the promise of an eternal happy life, and the fear of Hell's punishment.

• The Qur'an unveils the mystery of humanity, creation, and the universe. Humanity, the Qur'an, and the universe are the three "books" that make the Creator known to us, and therefore three versions or expressions of the same truth. As is known, the post-Renaissance history of the West is full of conflicts between science and religion, but the Qur'an presents itself, the universe, the subject matter of sciences, and humanity as three versions or expressions of the same truth and therefore never gives rise to a contradiction between science and religion. It clearly shows and proves that the One Who created humanity and the universe is the One Who revealed the Qur'an.

• Prophet Muhammad, upon him be peace and blessings, followed the Qur'an, which he conveyed, strictly and designed his life exactly according to it. Thus, Muslim scholars say that the Qur'an embodies Muhammad in words and that Muhammad embodies the Qur'an in belief and conduct. In short, they are the two perfect expressions of the same truth. When 'A'isha was asked about Prophet Muhammad's conduct, she replied: "Don't you read the Qur'an? His conduct is the Qur'an."[20] This shows that both the Qur'an and Muhammad, upon him be peace and blessings, are works of God Almighty.

• Authors are influenced by surrounding conditions, regardless of whether they are realists, idealists, or even science-fiction writers. However the Qur'an, although revealed in parts on certain occasions, is equally universal and objective when dealing with particular issues as it is exact and precise when dealing with universal matters. When describing creation's beginning or time's end or humanity's creation and future life in the other world, it uses precise expressions. Typically, it draws universal conclusions from particular events and moves from universal principles to particular events. Such a unique style, found in no other book, is another sign of its Divine origin.

- Which author can claim that his or her writings are absolutely correct and cannot be contradicted until the Last Day? At a time when science's conclusions are quickly shown to be incorrect, and when even previous Divine Scriptures still suffer modifications, the Qur'an's truths retain their freshness. In the words of Said Nursi, "as time passes, the Qur'an grows ever younger." Despite all attempts to find mistakes and contradictions in it, the Qur'an remains unchanged and displays its uniqueness. Every day it conquers new hearts, and its hidden, unlimited treasures are discovered or bloom like a heavenly rose with countless petals.

- Can anyone, regardless of his or her reputation for truthfulness, speak on behalf of the president, prime minister, all ministers, associations of literary people, lawyers and craftsmen, and a board of university lecturers and scientists? If so, can he or she claim to represent each of them perfectly? If so, can he or she legislate all of the country's affairs? This is what Prophet Muhammad, upon him be peace and blessings, achieved through the Qur'an. Could he have done this at the age of forty, having had nothing to do with such things and being unlettered, without Divine inspiration and support?

- Many verses begin with: *They ask you* and continue with *Say (in answer)*. These were revealed to answer questions asked by Muslims and non-Muslims, especially the Jews of Madina. Topics ranged from what is lawful or unlawful, distributing war spoils, the moon's phases, Judgment Day, Dhu'l-Qarnayn (an ancient king who made great conquests in Asia and Africa), the spirit, and so on. How can someone without an all-encompassing knowledge answer such questions? But the unlettered Prophet's answers satisfied everybody. This shows that he was taught by God, the All-Knowing.

• If it is asked why the Qur'an is not extraordinary and resembles human speech despite being the Word of God, the reply will be as follows:

Our Prophet was a human being. All of his acts and attitudes, except for his miracles and states of Prophethood, originated in his humanity. Like all other human beings, he was subject to and dependent upon God's creational and operational laws. He suffered from cold, felt pain, and so on. He was not extraordinary in all his acts and attitudes, and set an example to humanity through his conduct. If he had been extraordinary, he could not have been an absolute guide in every aspect of life or a mercy for all through all his states.

In the same way, the Qur'an leads conscious beings, directs humanity and jinn, guides people of perfection, and instructs truth-seeking people. Thus it must follow the style of human speech and conversation. Humanity and jinn take their supplications and prayers from it, talk about their affairs in its terms, and derive their principles of good conduct from it. In short, every believer adopts it as the authorized reference for all their affairs. If, by contrast, it had been like the Word of God heard by Prophet Moses on Mount Sinai, no one could have borne it or used it as a reference, and it would have been restricted to Prophet Muhammad only.

• Calling the Qur'an a human work means that a most bright, true, and comprehensive criterion of the human world, miraculous of exposition and bringer of well-being to the world, is the product of an illiterate man. Moreover, his pretence and counterfeiting have appeared as earnestness, sincerity, and purity of intention for fourteen centuries even to great intellects and exalted geniuses. It is a most inconceivable allegation.

Further, accepting it would mean the following: A most il-
lustrious and virtuous being who spent his entire life displaying
and preaching conviction, truthfulness, trustworthiness, sincerity, earnestness, and uprightness in all his states, words, and actions, as well as raising many truthful persons, was—God forbid such a thought!—a mean and discreditable rascal, wholly
insincere, and the foremost in unbelief. Even Satan would be
ashamed to conceive of such a great lie.

People can imitate only those of nearly the same level. Only
those of the same species can take each other's form. Only those
of nearly the same level can aspire to each other's level. However it is very difficult, even in that case, for them to deceive
people for long, as their pretensions and false display eventually
unmask them to perceptive people. If, on the other hand, coun-
terfeiters are greatly inferior to those they try to imitate (e.g.,
an ordinary person claiming Ibn Sina's knowledge, or an ordinary official pretending to be the president), they would open
themselves to ridicule.

Could a firefly make itself appear as a star for a thousand
years, or a fly make itself appear as a peacock for a year? Could
a private pretend to be a famous marshal and occupy his chair
for a long time without giving himself away? Could a deceitful unbeliever sustain for a lifetime, before discerning people, a
false display of a most pious person's loyalty, truthfulness, and
conviction? If these "ifs" are inconceivable or unacceptable to
any intelligent person, considering the Qur'an a human work
would mean seeing that Manifest Book, which has been like
a star of truths or a sun of perfections radiating the lights of
truths in the sky of the Muslim world for centuries, as a collection of falsehoods invented by a counterfeiter. It would mean
that his Companions of twenty-three years, as well as all who
followed him during the next fourteen centuries, were unaware
of his real identity. This is beyond belief.

There is no third alternative. If the Qur'an were a human work, it would be so debased that it could be a source only of superstition. The rank of him who brought it also would be degraded from being a source of perfection to the greatest cheat. Thus, he could not be God's Messenger, for one who lies in His name is the worst of people. Such a supposition is as inconceivable as imagining a fly to have the qualities of a peacock. No normal person could regard such suppositions as possible.

Prophet Muhammad, upon him be peace and blessings, lived austerely and did not pursue fame, ruler, wealth, beautiful women, or any other worldly gains. Furthermore, he endured severe hardship and persecution. To claim that he wrote the Qur'an means this man, known among his own people as "the Trustworthy" (*al-Amin*), was—God forbid!—history's greatest liar. What could have caused him to falsely claim Prophethood despite the resulting severe deprivation and persecution? Such false claims are no more than the most groundless and extremely degrading accusations.

• The Qur'an directs the Muslim community, which contains some of history's greatest and most magnificent people. The Qur'an has enabled them to conquer this world and the next; has equipped them materially and spiritually; and has instructed and educated them in all rational, moral, and spiritual matters according to their particular level. It has purified them and used each bodily member, sense, and faculty in its most proper place.

The Prophet, who brought the Qur'an from God, used his life to exemplify His laws in his attitudes and actions. He instructed us via his actions and sincere practice of the principles of truth as long as he lived. He showed and established the ways of true guidance and well-being via his sincere and reasonable sayings. In addition, as his life and good conduct testify, he is the most knowledgeable of God and the most fearful of His punishment. He established his splendid rule of perfection over half the globe and one fifth of humanity. He truly became, through his well-known manners and actions as a Prophet, statesman, commander, spiritual and intellectual guide, father, husband, friend, and so on, the pride of humanity and of creation.

- The Qur'an is a book of pure truths and matchless value; a guide to God's beloved friends and scholars of truth and purity. It invites all people, regardless of time or place, as well as those seeking perfection, to truth and love of the truth, truthfulness and loyalty, trustworthiness and reliability. It secures happiness in both worlds through Islam's pillars of beliefs and fundamental principles. The Prophet, upon him be peace and blessings, is a most trustworthy being, the foremost and firmest in belief and conviction. This is testified to by Islam and its law, which he preached and showed by his acknowledged piety and sincere worship manifested throughout his life, as required by his laudable virtues, and confirmed by all people of truth and perfection.

- God's most beloved Prophet, upon him be peace and blessings, faced stiff resistance from Jews and Christians. He had to fight with the Jewish tribes of Madina because of their unending conspiracies and finally expelled them. Despite this, the Qur'an mentions the Prophets Moses and Jesus, upon them be peace, many times, and Prophet Muhammad, upon him be peace and blessings, only four times by name. Why would one who falsely claims Prophethood mention the Prophets of those who show him great hostility?

- Another argument is that the Qur'an refers to certain facts of creation only recently established by modern scientific methods. How else could it know such previously unknown things except by Divine authorship? For example, how could it state: *Do not the unbelievers realize that the heavens and the earth were one unit of creation before we split them asunder?* (21:20); and *We created humankind (in the very beginning) from a specially sifted extract of clay. Then We made it into a fertilized ovum in a safe lodging. Then we made the ovum into a leech-like, clinging struc-*

ture. Then We created of the fertilized ovum a clot clinging (to the womb wall), and (afterwards in sequence) We created of the clinging clot a (chew of) lump, and We created of (a chew of) lump bones, and We clothed the bones in flesh. Then We caused it to grow into another creation. So Blessed and Supreme is God, the Creator Who creates everything in the best and most appropriate form, and has the ultimate rank of creativity. (23:12–4) These are only two of innumerable examples.[21]

• Even those whose power of hearing allows them to appreciate the Qur'an's miraculousness acknowledge that it is not of the same kind and degree as all other books they have heard. Thus it is either inferior or superior to all other books. As not even a devil would assert the former, we must accept that it is superior and therefore a miracle. That being the case, based on the two decisive proofs of dichotomy and *reductio ad absurdum*, we openly declare:

The Qur'an is either God's Word or—God forbid!—the fabrication of an unbeliever who does not recognize or fear God. Even Satan could never say that this second alternative is true. Thus the Qur'an is, of necessity and undoubtedly, the Word of the Creator of the universe, given that there is no third alternative, as explained above.

Likewise Prophet Muhammad, upon him be peace and blessings, is either a Messenger of God, as well as the most perfect Messenger and superior to all other creatures, or—God forbid!—a man of unbelief and the lowest nature, since he lied against God and neither recognized Him nor His punishment. Not even unbelieving philosophers or hypocrites of the past and the present have alleged—nor will able to allege—such a thing, because no one will heed and accept such an allegation. Instead, even the most corrupt philosophers and unscrupulous hypocrites admit that Muhammad, upon him be peace and blessings, was a man of exemplary good conduct. So, there are only two alternatives. As with the Qur'an, the second option is inconceivable and unacceptable. Thus he is self-evidently and of necessity God's Messenger, the most perfect Messenger, and superior to all other creatures, upon him be blessings and peace to the number of angels, human beings, and jinn.

CONCLUSION

The Qur'an's six sides or aspects are luminous and demonstrate its truth. From below, it rests upon the pillars of proof and evidence (rational, scientific, historical, and those pertaining to conscience and sound judgment, and so on); above it are gleams of the seal of miraculousness or inimitability: it aims at happiness in both worlds; and behind it is another point of support: the truths of the Divine Revelation. To its right is the unanimous confirmation of guided reason based upon proof; and to its left are the intellectual and spiritual contentment of those with sound hearts and conscience, and their sincere attachment and submission to it. Together, these bear witness that the Qur'an is an extraordinary and unconquerable stronghold established upon the earth by "Heaven's Hand," and set their seal of admission upon it as God's faultless, true Word. The universe's Administrator, Who acts to manifest His Unity, protect virtue and goodness, and extirpate falsehood and slander, has given the Qur'an the most acceptable, high, and dominant rank of respect and success, and thereby confirmed its truth.

Also, its conveyor (Prophet Muhammad, upon him be peace and blessing,) believed in and respected it more than anybody else. He received it through Revelation, and confirmed and preached its decrees and commands with the utmost conviction and without exhibiting any deception or error to those seeking to discredit him. Despite being unlettered, he relayed the revealed news about the past and future, and about the universe's creation and operation, without hesitation. His own sayings (the Hadith) do not resemble the Qur'an and, in certain respects, are inferior to it. All of this proves that the Qur'an is the true, heavenly, and blessed Word of that person's All-Merciful Creator.

Most of the Qur'an's followers, about one fifth of humanity, have always had an enthusiastic and religious devotion to it. They have listened to it lovingly and adored its truth. Also, as testified to by numerous observations, signs, and events, angels, believing jinn, and other spirit beings gather around it during its recitation, just as moths are drawn to a flame. This also confirms that the Qur'an is accepted by almost all beings in the universe and is of the highest rank.

Also all people, from the most common to the most intelligent and learned, receive what they need from its teachings. All great scholars in such Islamic sciences as jurisprudence, theology, and religious methodology have found answers to their questions within it and so based their conclusions upon it. This is another evidence that the Qur'an is the source of truths, the mine of all true knowledge.

Furthermore, those unbelieving Arabs, considered the most advanced in literature, failed to match the Qur'an's eloquence, which is only one of its many major aspects of miraculousness, and could not produce even their own *sura*. Other geniuses of learning and eloquence who sought fame by trying to surpass its eloquence have been compelled to abandon this quest. This clearly shows that the miraculous Qur'an is not the result of human endeavor.

When judging a word's value, sublimity, and eloquence, one must ask: "Who has spoken it? To whom has it been spoken? Why has it been spoken?" When considered in this light, once again the Qur'an is shown to have no equal, for it is the Word of the Lord of all beings and the Speech of the universe's Creator. It bears no signs to suggest that it is a fabricated book of imitation falsely attributed to God.

God revealed the Qur'an to his chosen representative of all creatures, His most famous and renowned addressee. The extent and strength of the Prophet's faith embraced the comprehensive Religion of Islam and caused him to rise to the rank of the distance of "two bows' length" and be honored with the direct address of the Eternally Besought-of-All. After that honor, he returned to convey the principles of happiness in both worlds.

The Qur'an explains these principles, as well as the results of and the Divine purpose for creating the universe, and expounds upon the Prophet's most comprehensive faith, which sustains all of Islam's truths. It shows and describes the universe as a map, a clock, or a house, and teaches about its Creator. Such a work cannot be duplicated by any person.

In addition, numerous multi-volume Qur'anic commentaries written by meticulous scholars of the highest intelligence and learning relate proofs of the Qur'an's countless virtues, subtleties, and mysteries, and disclose and affirm its numerous predictions. Among them are the 130 treatises of the *Risale-i Nur,* which explain such Qur'anic virtues and subtleties as its allusions to modern civilization's scientific and technical wonders and its indirect references to future Muslim victories, the story of the Companions after the Prophet, and its letters' meaningful and mysterious design. All of this sets a seal on the Qur'an's unique and miraculous nature and the Word of the Knower of the Unseen, which is the Unseen World's tongue in this visible world of corporeality.

Such virtues have allowed the Qur'an's magnificent spiritual dominion and majestic sacred rule to continue, for more than fourteen centuries, to illuminate the earth, as well as time and space, and draw more people to it. These same virtues cause each of its letters to yield at least ten merits, rewards, and fruits pertaining to the eternal world; the letters of certain verses and *suras* to give hundreds or even thousands of merits, and, when recited on certain blessed occasions like the Night of Power and Destiny (*Laylat al-Qadr*) to have the light and merits of each letter multiplied by tens or hundreds. More and more people are thinking: "Based on the consensus of its lights and mysteries, and the concord of its fruits and results, this miraculous Qur'an proves and testifies to a single Necessarily Existent One's Existence, Unity, Attributes, and Names in such a manner that the testimonies of innumerable believers have their sources in it."

In a brief reference to the instruction contained within the Qur'an about faith and God's Unity, we say:

> There is no deity but God—the Necessarily Existent One, the One, the Single—the necessity of Whose Existence in His Oneness is proven decisively by the Qur'an of miraculous exposition, which is accepted and sought by angels, humanity, and jinn; whose verses are recited every minute with perfect respect by millions of people; whose sacred rule in the earth's regions and space's realms, and on the faces of ages and time; whose enlightened spiritual dominion has prevailed with perfect splendor over half the globe and a fifth of humanity for fourteen centuries... Likewise, with the consensus of its heavenly and sacred *suras*, the agreement of its luminous Divine verses, the correspondence of its mysteries and lights, the concord of its truths, and its results, it manifestly attests to and is a clear proof of this same truth.

CHAPTER 7

Prophethood and Prophet Muhammad ﷺ

PROPHETHOOD AND PROPHET MUHAMMAD ﷺ

PROPHETHOOD

G od creates every community of beings with a purpose and a guide or a leader. It is inconceivable that God Almighty, Who gave bees a queen, ants a leader, and birds and fish each a guide, would leave us without Prophets to guide us to spiritual, intellectual, and material perfection.

Although we can find God by reflecting upon natural phenomena, we need a Prophet to learn why we were created, where we came from, where we are going, and how to worship our Creator properly. God sent Prophets to teach their people the meaning of creation and the truth of things, to unveil the mysteries behind historical and natural events, and to inform us of our relationship, and that of Divine Scriptures, with the universe.

Without Prophets, we could not have made any scientific progress. While those who adopt evolutionary approaches to explain historical events tend to attribute everything to chance and deterministic evolution, Prophets guided humanity in intellectual—and thus scientific—illumination. Thus, farmers traditionally accept Prophet Adam as their first master, tailors accept Prophet Enoch, shipmakers and sailors accept Prophet Noah, and clock makers accept Prophet Joseph, upon them be peace. Also, the Prophets' miracles marked the final points in scientific and technological advances, and urged people to accomplish them.

Prophets guided people, through personal conduct and the heavenly Religion and Scriptures they conveyed, to develop their inborn capacities and directed them toward the purpose of their creation. Had it not been for them, humanity (the fruit of the tree

of creation) would have been left to decay. As humanity needs social justice as much as it needs private inner peace, Prophets taught
the laws of life and established the rules for a perfect social life
based on justice.

Whenever people fell into darkness after a Prophet, God sent
another one to enlighten them again. This continued until the
coming of the Last Prophet. The reason for sending Prophets Moses and Jesus required that Prophet Muhammad should be sent.
As his message was for everyone, regardless of time or place,
Prophethood ended with him.

Due to certain sociological and historical facts, which require
a lengthy explanation, Prophet Muhammad, upon him be peace
and blessings, was sent as "a mercy for all worlds." For this reason, Muslims believe in all of the Prophets and make no distinction among them in each being a Prophet sent by God Almighty:

> The Messenger believes in what has been sent down to him
> from his Lord, and so do the believers; each one believes in
> God, and His angels, and His Books, and His Messengers:
> "We make no distinction between any of His Messengers (in
> believing in them)." And they say: "We have heard (the call to
> faith in God) and obeyed. Our Lord, grant us Your forgive-
> ness, and to You is the homecoming." (2:285)

That is why Islam, revealed by God and conveyed to humanity by Prophet Muhammad, upon him be peace and blessings, is
universal and eternal.

Truthfulness, trustworthiness, exceptional intelligence and sagacity, communicating God's messages, sinlessness, and freedom
from mental and bodily defects are essential attributes of Prophethood. Describing Prophethood in further detail and narrating the
stories of all Prophets is beyond the scope of this book.[1] By focus-
ing on the Prophethood of the Seal of the Prophets who told us
about the other Prophets and Divine Scriptures and made our
Lord known to us, we will make the other Prophets known and
prove their Prophethood.

Prophet Muhammad's life before his Prophethood

Prophet Muhammad's life before his Prophethood foretold his Prophethood. Consider the following facts:

- The extraordinary events on the night of his birth, the unusual character he displayed even as a child, and the meaningful signs people of insight observed in him all meant that he would undertake a great mission. Many famous Jewish scholars and Christian monks abandoned their previous convictions and converted after seeing that Muhammad, upon him be peace and blessings, had the attributes mentioned in their Scriptures concerning the Last Prophet. They silenced some of their former co-religionist scholars by showing them the references in the Torah and the Gospels. Among them were the famous 'Abdullah ibn Salam, Wahb ibn Munabbih, Abu Yasir, Shamul, and Asid and Tha'laba (the two sons of Sa'ya), Ibn Bunyamin, Mukhayriq, and Ka'b al-Akhbar.[2]

  On the night of his birth, the Prophet's mother and the mothers of 'Uthman ibn al-'As and 'Abd al-Rahman ibn al-'Awf saw a magnificent light. Each woman said: "During his birth, we saw a light that illuminated the east and the west." On that night, idols within the Ka'ba toppled over; the palace of the Sassanid king shook and cracked, and its fourteen spires collapsed. The small lake of Sawa in Persia (sanctified by the Persians) sank into earth. The fire worshipped by the Magians at Istakhrabad, which had burned continually for a thousand years, went out. These incidents indicated that the person born on that night would abolish fire worship, destroy the palace of the Persian rulers, and prohibit the sanctification of things that God does not allow to be sanctified.[3]

- Prior to his Prophethood, he opposed injustice and joined organizations like the *Hilf al-Fudul*, which defended the helpless and restored usurped rights.[4]

- Although of honorable descent, he did not live in luxury; rather, he grew up as an orphan under the protection of his grandfather and then his uncle. Whatever money he may have earned by trading before and after his marriage went to support orphans, widows, and the poor.[5] Thus, he was never wealthy and had no powerful backers.

- Despite his community's moral corruption, he lived an extraordinarily chaste, disciplined, and morally upright life. He hated idols and idol worship. During his childhood, he intended only twice to attend wedding ceremonies, but was overpowered by sleep on both occasions. (Thus, he did not see improper things and practices that Islam would later outlaw.) When he was twenty-five years old, he married Khadija, a respected widow several years older than him. He only married again after her death twenty-five years later. Those who knew him said he was as shy as a young girl when marriage was proposed to him.[6]

- History records his moral commitment, trustworthiness, honesty, truthfulness, and integrity. He did not lie, an assertion proven by the fact that not even his worst enemies ever called him a liar. He talked politely and never used obscene or abusive language. His charming personality and excellent manners captivated the hearts of those who met him. He always followed the principles of justice, altruism, and fair play with others, and never deceived anyone or broke his promise.

Those who had business dealings with him had full confidence in his integrity. Everyone called him *al-Amin* (the Truthful and the Trustworthy). He was the embodiment of modesty in a society that was immodest to the core.[7] Once while the Quraysh were repairing the Ka'ba, a question of individual and clan honor arose over who would reinsert the sacred Black Stone. To prevent violence, they all agreed to let Muhammad decide. He asked them to bring a piece of cloth, which he then spread on the ground. Placing the Black Stone on it, he told each chief to raise his corner. When the Black Stone was raised to the required height, he set it in its place.[8]

- Born and raised among people who regarded drunkenness and gambling as virtues, he never drank alcohol or gambled. Surrounded by heartless people, his own heart overflowed with the milk of human kindness. He helped orphans, widows, and the poor, and was hospitable to travelers. Harming no one, he exposed himself to hardship for their sake. Avoiding tribal feuds, he was the foremost worker for reconciliation. He never bowed before any created thing or partook of offerings made to idols, even when he was a child, for he hated all worship devoted to that which was not God. In brief, his towering and radiant personality, when placed in the midst of such a benighted and dark environment, may be likened to a beacon of light illumining a pitch-dark night, to a diamond shining among a heap of stones.[9]

- Prophet Muhammad's enemies never accused him of lying or cheating either before or after his Prophethood. To prevent Islam's spread, they labeled him a poet, a sorcerer, a magician, or a lunatic. Sometimes they attempted to justify their rejection by such false pretexts as: "If only this Qur'an had been sent down to one of the great men of the two cities (Makka and Ta'if)," but never dared to accuse him of lying, deception, or any immorality.

- Muhammad, upon him be peace and blessings, did not know how to read and write. During his whole life, no one taught him and no written culture influenced him. Makka's ideas and customs were idolatrous and wholly untouched by Christian or Jewish religious thought. Even Makka's *hanif*s,[10] who rejected idolatry, were not influenced by Judaism or Christianity. No Jewish or Christian thought is reflected in these people's surviving poetic heritage. Moreover, Prophet Muhammad, upon him be peace and blessings, avoided the locally popular intellectual forms of poetry and rhetoric even before his Prophethood. He talked politely and never used obscene or abusive language.

His charming personality and excellent manners captivated the hearts of those who met him.

- Before his Prophethood, Prophet Muhammad, upon him be peace and blessings, was engaged in trade and commerce for years, but never entered into a dishonest transaction. Those who had business dealings with him had full confidence in his integrity. Even his enemies left their precious belongings with him for safe custody, and he scrupulously fulfilled their trust.[11]

- Until he was forty, no one had ever heard Muhammad, upon him be peace and blessing, give an eloquent speech, talk on religious or metaphysical issues, formulate laws, or handle a sword. Toward his fortieth year, he began retreating to the Hira cave. One day he emerged with a new, wholly authentic message to heal humanity's wounds, and challenged all literary geniuses to produce something like it.

And what was his message?

> The idols that you worship are mere shams, so stop worshipping them. No person, star, tree, stone, or spirit deserves your worship. Do not bow your heads before them in worship. The entire universe belongs to God Almighty. He alone is the Creator, Nourisher, Sustainer, and thus the real Sovereign before Whom all should bow down and Who is worthy of your prayers and obedience. So worship Him alone and obey His commands.
>
> The theft and plunder, murder and rapine, injustice and cruelty, and all the vices in which you indulge are sins in God's eyes. Leave your evil ways. Speak the truth. Be just. Do not kill anyone, for *whoever kills a person unjustly is like one who has killed all humanity, and whoever saves a person's life is like one who has saved all humanity* (5:32). Do not rob anyone, but take your lawful share and give that which is due to others in a just manner.
>
> Do not set up other deities with God, or you will be condemned and forsaken. If one or both of your parents reaches old age and lives with you, speak to them only with respect and, out of mercy, be humble with them. Give your relatives their due. Give to the needy and the traveler, and do not be wasteful. Do not kill your children because you

fear poverty or for other reasons. Avoid adultery and fornication, for they are indecent and evil. Leave the property of orphans and the weak intact.

Fulfill the covenant, because you will be questioned about it. Do not cheat when you measure and weigh items. Do not pursue that of which you have no knowledge, for your ears, eyes, and heart will be questioned about this. Do not walk around arrogantly, for you will never tear the earth open or attain the mountains in height. Speak kind words to each other, for Satan uses strong words to cause strife. Do not turn your cheek in scorn and anger toward others or walk with impudence in the land.

God does not love those who boast, so be modest in bearing and subdue your voice. Do not make fun of others, for they may be better than you. Do not find fault with each other or call each other by offensive nicknames. Avoid most suspicion, for some suspicion is a sin. Do not spy on or gossip about each other. Be staunch followers of justice and witnesses for God, even though it be against yourselves, or your parents and relatives, regardless if they are rich or poor. Do not deviate by following caprice. Be steadfast witnesses for God in equity, and do not let your hatred of others seduce you to be unjust toward them.

Restrain your rage and pardon the offences of others. Good and evil deeds are not alike, so repel the evil deed with a good one so that both of you can overcome your enmity and become loyal friends. The recompense for an intentional evil is a similar evil; but whoever pardons and amends the evildoer with kindness and love will be rewarded by God. Avoid alcohol and games of chance, for God has forbidden them.

You are human beings, and all human beings are equal in God's eyes. No one is born with the slur of shame on his or her face or the mantle of honor around his or her neck. The only high and honored people are the God-conscious and pious, true in words and deeds. Distinctions of birth and glory of race are no criteria of greatness and honor.

On a day after you die, you will appear before a Supreme Court and account for all your deeds, none of which can be hidden. Your life's record shall be an open book to God. Your fate shall be determined by your good or bad actions. In the court of the True Judge—the Omniscient God—

there can be no unfair recommendation and favoritism.
You cannot bribe Him, and your pedigree or parentage
will be ignored. True faith and good deeds alone will benefit you at that time. Those who have done them fully shall
reside in the Heaven of eternal happiness, while those who
did not shall reside in the fire of Hell.[12]

Prophet Muhammad's achievements

• Before Muhammad's Prophethood, darkness lay heavier and
thicker on one land than on any other. The neighboring countries of Persia, Byzantium, and Egypt possessed a glimmer of
civilization and a faint light of learning, but the Arab peninsula,
isolated and cut off by vast oceans of sand, was culturally and
intellectually one of the world's backward areas. Although their
highly developed language could express the finest shades of
meaning, a study of their literature's remnants reveals the limited extent of their knowledge. All of this shows their low cultural and civilizational standards, their deeply superstitious nature, their barbarous and ferocious customs, and their uncouth
and degraded moral standards and conceptions.

It was a land without a government, for every tribe claimed
sovereignty and considered itself independent. Robbery, arson,
and the murder of innocent and weak people was the norm.
Life, property, and honor were constantly at risk, and tribes
were always at daggers drawn with each other. A trivial inci-
dent could engulf them in ferocious warfare, which sometimes
developed into a decades-long and country-wide conflagration.
As one scholar writes:

> These struggles destroyed the sense of national unity and
> developed an incurable particularism; each tribe deeming
> itself self-sufficient and regarding the rest as its legitimate
> victims for murder, robbery and plunder.[13]

Barely able to discriminate between pure and impure, lawful and unlawful, their concepts of morals, culture, and civiliza-

tion were primitive and uncouth. They reveled in adultery, gambling, and drinking. They stood naked before each other without shame, and women circumambulated the Ka'ba in the nude.

Their prestige called for female infanticide rather than having someone "inferior" become their son-in-law and eventual heir. They married their widowed stepmothers and knew nothing of the manners associated eating, dressing, and cleanliness. Worshippers of stones, trees, idols, stars, and spirits, they had forgotten the earlier Prophets' teachings. They had an idea that Abraham and Isma'il were their forefathers, but almost all of these forefathers' religious knowledge and understanding of God had been lost.

Thus, in that benighted area, for forty years, Muhammad, upon him be peace and blessings, lived as an ordinary man among his people. He was not known as a statesman, preacher, or orator. No one had heard him impart wisdom and knowledge, or discuss principles of metaphysics, ethics, law, politics, economy, or sociology. He had no reputation as a soldier, not to mention as a great general. He had said nothing about God, angels, revealed Books, early Prophets, bygone nations, the Day of Judgment, life after death, or Heaven and Hell. No doubt he had an excellent character and charming manners and was well-behaved, yet nothing marked him out as one who would accomplish something great and revolutionary. His acquaintances knew him as a sober, calm, gentle, and trustworthy citizen of good nature. But when he left the Hira cave with a new message, he was completely transformed.

When he began preaching, his people stood in awe and wonder, bedazzled by his wonderful eloquence and oratory. It was so impressive and captivating that even his worst enemies were afraid to listen to it, lest it penetrate their hearts or very being and make them abandon their traditional religion and culture. It was so beyond compare that no Arab poet, preacher, or orator, no matter how good, could equal its beautiful language and splendid diction when he challenged them to do so.

Although they put their heads together, they could not produce even one line like the ones he recited.

- Just as the Prophets' consensus on the other pillars of belief is a very strong proof of their truth, it also is a firm testimony of the truthfulness and Messengership of Muhammad, upon him be peace and blessings. History confirms that all sacred attributes, miracles, and functions indicating the truthfulness and Messengership of Prophets, are found in Muhammad, upon him be peace and blessings, to the highest degree. Prophets predicted his coming by giving good tidings of him in the Torah, the Gospels, the Psalms, and other Scriptures (known as "Pages" in the Qur'an).[14] Through their missions and miracles, they affirmed and "sealed" the mission of Muhammad, the foremost and most perfect Prophet.

People usually consider their own occupations as more important, necessary, beneficial to social life, and more challenging than others. However, although every occupation has some degree of difficulty and social use, educating people is by far the most difficult and necessary for a healthy social life.

Raising really educated people requires true educators who have clear goals. But if such people are to succeed, they must embody what they teach and advise their students; they must intimately know their students' character and potential, as well as their desires and ambitions, shortcomings and strengths, and level of learning and understanding; they must know how to treat them in all circumstances, approach their problems, and persuade them to replace their bad qualities with good ones.

People may not live according to their asserted "strong" beliefs, have only superficial good moral qualities, or have weak spots (e.g., open to bribery, insensitivity, hoarding). How should we view educators who transform their students by completely replacing their bad qualities with good ones, and then proceed to establish a community to serve as a model for future generations; who transform the base rock, copper, iron, and coal in their hands into silver, gold, precious stones, and diamonds? Would such an educator not be considered extraordinary? What Prophet Muhammad, upon him be peace and blessings, achieved in his twenty-three years as the educator of his people is far more than what such educators do.

Not using force is another important dimension of a good education. Penal sanctions, coercion, and military and police forces can only succeed in "guiding" people for a short while. If a transformation is to be permanent, people must undertake it willingly, meaning that they must be convinced of its truth. No one has ever known people so comprehensively as Prophet Muhammad, nor has managed to transform such a pitiless, crude, war-mongering, ignorant, and unyielding people into a community that provides a perfect and complete life and moral example for all future generations.

His Family and Companions, whose insight, wisdom, and spiritual accomplishment make them the most renowned, respected, celebrated, pious, and intelligent people after the Prophets, declared that he was the most truthful, elevated, and honest person. This was their conclusion after having examined and scrutinized all of his thoughts and states, whether hidden or open, with the utmost attention to detail.

Thousands of God's beloved friends attained truth and perfection, performed wonders, gained insight into the reality of things, and made spiritual discoveries by following the Prophet's example. All of them assert the Prophet's truthfulness and Messengership, and his Message. Thousands of exacting scholars of purity, meticulous scholars of truthfulness, and believing sages have reached the highest station of learning through the sacred truths brought by this unlettered man. Many invincible commanders and most eminent statesmen of human history have appeared in his footsteps. I list only a few of countless such people: such saints and purified, meticulous scholars as Abu Hanifa, Shafi'i, Imam Malik, Ahmad ibn Hanbal, Imam al-Bukhari, Imam Muslim, Ibn Hajar al-Asqalani, Jalaluddin as-Suyuti, Bayazid al-Bistami, 'Abd al-Qadir al-Jilani,

Shah Naqshband, Hasan al-Shadhili, Imam al-Ghazzali, Imam Rabbani, and Bediüzzaman Said Nursi; innumerable scientists such as al-Biruni, az-Zahrawi, Ibn Sina (Avicenna), and Ibn Haytham; and hundreds of thousands of literary geniuses, commanders, statesmen, and other stars of humanity. All of them followed in the Prophet's footsteps.

In addition, such Western intellectuals and statesmen as Lamartine, William Muir, Edward Gibbon, John Davenport, L. A. Sedillot, Goethe, P. Bayle, Stanley Lane-Poole, A. J. Arberry, Thomas Carlyle, Rosenthal, Elisee Reclus, Andrew Miller, Bismarck, Leopold Weis, Marmaduke Pickthall, Martin Lings, and Roger Garaudy have admitted that he is the greatest person ever to have lived. Some of them even embraced Islam. This is another proof of his Prophethood. Sir William Muir, no friend of Islam, admits:

> The first peculiarity, then, which attracts our attention is the subdivision of the Arabs into innumerable bodies ... each independent of the others: restless and often at war amongst themselves; and even when united by blood or by interest, ever ready on some significant cause to separate and give way to an implacable hostility. Thus at the era of Islam the retrospect of Arabian history exhibits, as in the kaleidoscope, an ever-varying state of combination and repulsion, such as had hitherto rendered abortive any attempt at a general union ... The problem had yet to be solved, by what force these tribes could be subdued or drawn to one common center; and it was solved by Muhammad.[15]

- Prophet Muhammad, upon him be peace and blessings, blended many roles and his own personal excellences into one personality. He is a man of wisdom and foresight, a living embodiment of his own teachings, a great statesman and military genius, a legislator and teacher of morals, a spiritual luminary and religious guide. He sees life comprehensively, and all that he touches is improved and adorned. His teachings regulate everything from international relations to eating, drinking, sleeping, and personal hygiene. He used these teachings to establish a civilization and a culture that produced such a fine, sensitive, and perfect equilibrium in all aspects of life that no trace of a flaw, deficiency, or incompleteness has ever been found in it. What alleged shortcomings and imperfections deny him his rightful status as Prophet and Messenger of God?

Prophet Muhammad, upon him be peace and blessings, brought a law, a religion, a way of life, a code of worship, a way of prayer, a message, and a faith that was (and remains) unique. The law this unlettered man brought is matchless in that it has administered, both justly and precisely, one fifth of humanity for fourteen centuries. The daily practices of Islam, which originated in the Qur'an and his own sayings, precepts, and example, have served for centuries as a peerless guide and authority for billions of people. They have trained and refined their minds and souls, illumined and purified their hearts, and perfected their spirits.

What follows is the tribute of Lamartine, the French historian to the person of the Holy Prophet of Islam:

> Never did a man set himself, voluntarily or involuntarily, a more sublime aim, since this aim was superhuman: to subvert superstitions which had been interposed between man and his Creator, to render God unto man and man unto God; to restore the rational and sacred idea of divinity amidst the chaos of the material and disfigured gods of idolatry then existing. Never has a man undertaken a work so far beyond human power with so feeble means, for he had in the conception as well as in the execution of such a great design no other instrument than himself, and no other aid, except a handful of men living in a corner of desert. Finally, never has a man accomplished such a huge and lasting revolution in the world, because in less than two centuries after its appearance, Islam, in faith and arms, reigned over the whole of Arabia, and conquered in God's name Persia, Khorasan, Western India, Syria, Abyssinia, all the known continent of Northern Africa, numerous islands of the Mediterranean, Spain, and a part of Gaul.

If greatness of purpose, smallness of means, and astounding results are the three criteria of human genius, who could dare to compare any great men to Muhammad? The most famous men created arms, laws, and empires only. They founded, if anything at all, no more than material powers which often crumbled away before their eyes. This man moved not only armies, legislation, empires, peoples, and dynasties, but millions of men [and women] in one third of the then inhabited world; and more than that, he moved the altars, the gods, the religions, the ideas, the beliefs and the souls. On the basis of a Book, every letter of which has become law, he created a spiritual nationality which has blended together peoples of every tongue and of every race. He has left to us as the indelible characteristic of this Muslim nationality, the hatred of false gods and the passion for the One and immaterial God. This avenging patriotism against the profanation of Heaven formed the virtue of the followers of Muhammad: the conquest of one third of the earth to his creed was his miracle. The idea of the unity of God proclaimed amidst the exhaustion of fabulous theogenies, was in itself such a miracle that upon its utterance from his lips it destroyed all the ancient temples of idols and set on fire one third of the world. His life, his meditations, his heroic revilings against the superstitions of his country, and his boldness in defying the furies of idolatry; his firmness in enduring them for thirteen years at Mecca, his acceptance of the role of public scorn and almost of being a victim of his fellow-countrymen: all these and, finally his incessant preaching, his wars against odds, his faith in his success and his superhuman security in misfortune, his forbearance in victory, his ambition which was entirely devoted to one idea and in no manner striving for an empire; his endless prayer, his mystic conversations with God, his death and his triumph after death; all these attest not to an imposture but to a firm conviction. It was his conviction which gave him the power to restore a creed. This creed was two-fold, the unity of God and the immateriality of God; the former telling what God is; the latter telling what God is not. Philosopher, orator, apostle, legislator, warrior, conqueror of ideas, restorer of rational dogmas, of a cult without images; the founder of twenty terrestrial states and of one spiritual state, that is Muhammad. As regards all standards by which human greatness may be measured, we may well ask: Is there any man greater than he?[16]

• A leader must know his people thoroughly to educate them and lead them to realize a great cause. Alexis Carrel, a great twentieth-century French scientist and philosopher, still describes human beings as unknown, as the most complex and intricate of creatures.[17] However, Prophet Muhammad, upon him be peace and blessings, had such a comprehensive knowledge of his people that he could educate them in such a way that they transformed themselves willingly to realize his cause. Knowing how to act in every situation, his decisions never had to be changed or his appointments to office rescinded. He succeeded in bringing the most refined, well-mannered, and civilized society out of an extremely backward, uncivilized, and rough people.

Not only did he eradicate his people's savage customs and immoral qualities to which they were addicted, he also equipped and adorned these same desperate, wild, and unyielding peoples with all praiseworthy virtues and made them the teachers and masters of the world, including civilized nations. His domination was not outward; rather, he was the beloved of hearts, the teacher of minds, the trainer of souls, and the ruler of spirits.

Despite all the advanced techniques and methods, modern communities cannot remove permanently so small a vice as smoking. However, Prophet Muhammad, upon him be peace and blessings, quickly removed many ingrained bad habits with little effort, and replaced them with good habits in such a way that they became inherent in his people's very being. If people do not believe this, let them go to any part of the modern civilized world with hundreds of philosophers, sociologists, psychologists, pedagogues, and educators and see if they can achieve in one hundred years even one hundredth of what Prophet Muhammad, upon him be peace and blessings, achieved in a year in the uncivilized Arabia of fourteen centuries ago.

- The Prophet met all of his detractors with a smile. When the Qurayshi leaders told Abu Talib to make his nephew abandon his mission, the Prophet answered:

  > O uncle! Should they place the sun in my right hand and the moon in my left, so as to make me renounce this mission, I shall not do so. I will never give it up; either it will please God to make it triumph or I will perish in the attempt.[18]

  On another occasion, a deputation of the Qurayshi elite offered him all the worldly glory they could imagine if he would abandon his mission:

  > If you want wealth, we will amass for you as much as you wish; if you aspire to win honor and power, we are prepared to swear allegiance to you as our overlord and king; if you have a fancy for beauty, you shall have the hand of the most beautiful maiden of your own choice.

  The terms would be extremely tempting for anyone, but they had no significance in the eyes of the Prophet. He responded:

  > I want neither wealth nor power. God has commissioned me as a warner to humanity. I deliver His Message to you. Should you accept it, you shall have felicity in this life and eternal bliss in the life Hereafter. Should you reject the Word of God, surely God will decide between you and me.[19]

  The faith, perseverance, and resolution with which he carried his mission to ultimate success prove the supreme truth of his cause. Had there been the slightest doubt or uncertainty in his heart, he could not have withstood the opposition that continued for twenty-one long years.

- Prophet Muhammad, upon him be peace and blessings, was the foremost practitioner of all forms of Islamic worship, and the most God-conscious believer. He perfectly observed all details of worship, even when in danger. He never imitated anyone, and excellently combined the beginning and end of spiritual perfection. He is unparalleled in prayer and knowledge of God. In his supplications and prayers, he describes his Lord with such a degree of Divine knowledge that no believer has ever attained a similar degree of knowledge and description of God.

- His faith was so extraordinarily strong, certain, miraculous, elevated, and enlightened that no contemporary prevalent (and opposed) idea, belief, philosophy, or teaching ever caused him to doubt or hesitate. Moreover, all intellectually and spiritually elevated people of all times, primarily his Companions, benefited from his faith, which they admit to be of the highest degree. This fact proves that his faith is matchless.

- In spite of his unparalleled greatness and achievements, the Prophet, upon him be peace and blessings, behaved as an ordinary man with all people, and lived as the poorest of his community. All of his resources were used to spread Islam. He sought no reward or profit to compensate him for his life-long struggles and endeavors, and left no property for his heirs, for he lived to serve all humanity. He did not ask that anything be set aside for him or his descendants, and forbade his progeny from receiving *zakah* so that neither he nor his Family or progeny should benefit from his mission materially.

- No one in human history has ever been loved as much Prophet Muhammad, upon him be peace and blessings, has been loved by his Companions and Community. What follows is only one example to show how deeply he is loved:

  A group from the Adal and al-Qarah tribes, who were apparently from the same ancestral stock as the Quraysh and who lived near Makka, came to the Prophet during the third year of the Islamic era and said: "Some of us have chosen Islam, so send a group of Muslims to instruct us what Islam means, teach us the Qur'an, and inform us of Islam's principles and laws."

  The Messenger selected six Companions to go with them. Upon reaching the Hudhayl tribe's land, the group halted and the Companions settled down to rest. Suddenly, a group of Hudhayli tribesmen fell upon them like a thunderbolt with their swords drawn. Clearly, the mission either had been a ruse from the beginning or its members had changed their minds en route. At any rate, they sided with the attackers and sought to seize the six Muslims. As soon as the Companions were aware of what was happening, they grabbed their weapons and got ready to defend themselves. Three were martyred, and the rest were tied up and taken to Makka, where they were to be delivered to the Quraysh.

Near Makka, 'Abdullah ibn Tariq managed to free his hand and reach for his sword. However, his captors saw what he was doing and stoned him to death. Zayd ibn al-Dathina and Hubayb ibn Adiy were carried to Makka, where they were exchanged for two Hudhayli captives. Safwan ibn Umayya al-Qurayshi bought Zayd from the person to whom he had been sold so that he could avenge the blood of his father, who had been killed during the Battle of Badr. He took him outside Makka to kill him, and the Quraysh assembled to see what would happen.

Zayd came forward with a courageous gait and did not even tremble. Abu Sufyan, a spectator who wanted to use this chance to extract a statement of contrition and remorse or an avowal of hatred of the Prophet, stepped forward and said: "I adjure you by God, Zayd, don't you wish that Muhammad was with us now in your place so that we might cut off his head, and that you were with your family?" "By God," said Zayd, "let alone wishing that, I do not wish that even a thorn should hurt his foot." Abu Sufyan, astonished, turned to those present and said: "By God, I swear I have never seen a man so loved by his followers as Muhammad."

After a while, Hubayb was taken outside Makka for execution. Requesting the assembled people to let him perform two *rak'at* of prayer, to which they agreed, he did so in all humility, respect, and absorption. Then he spoke to them: "I swear by God that if I did not think that you might think that I was trying to delay my death out of fear, I would have prolonged my prayer."

After condemning Hubayb to crucifixion, his sweet voice was heard, with a perfect spirituality that held everyone in its spell, entreating God with these words: "O God! We have delivered the message of Your Messenger, so inform him of what has been done to us, and tell him my wish of peace and blessings upon him." Meanwhile, God's Messenger was returning his peace, saying: "Upon you be God's peace and blessings, O Hubayb!"[20]

• The following account shows the indelible mark that God's Messenger has imprinted on people of every age:

One of Ibn Sina's students told Ibn Sina that his extraordinary understanding and intelligence would cause people to gather around him if he claimed prophethood. Ibn Sina said nothing. When they were travelling together during winter, Ibn Sina woke up one morning at dawn, woke his student, and asked him to fetch some water because he was thirsty. The student procrastinated and made excuses. However much Ibn Sina persisted, the student would not leave his warm bed. At that moment, the cry of the muezzin (caller to prayer) called out from the minaret: "God is the greatest. I bear witness that Muhammad is the Messenger of God."

Ibn Sina considered this a good opportunity to answer his student, so he said:

> You, who averred that people would believe in me if I claimed to be a prophet, look now and see how the command I just gave you who have been my student for years and have benefited from my lessons, has not had the effect of making you leave your warm bed to fetch me some water. But this muezzin strictly obeys the 400-year-old command of the Prophet. He got up from his warm bed, as he does every morning together with hundreds of thousands of others, climbed up to this great height, and bore witness to God's Unity and His Prophet. Look and see how great the difference is!"[21]

The Prophet's name has been pronounced five times a day together with that of God for 1,400 years all over the world.[22]

HIS CHARACTER AND HIGH MORALITY

- If a man's universally admired accomplishments, wealth, and fame do not change him, and he remains as humble as he was at the beginning of his career, this shows an impressive strength of character, morality, and virtue. Despite his unparalleled achievements, which force even non-Muslims and atheists to consider him the greatest person of all times, Prophet Muhammad, upon him be peace and blessings, was poorer and more humble when he entered Makka victoriously than he was at the beginning of his mission.

- One's face reveals one's inner world and character. Those who saw Prophet Muhammad, upon him be peace and blessings, could not help but admire his appearance and, if unprejudiced, acknowledge his truthfulness. For example, 'Abdullah ibn Salam, the most renowned Jewish scholar of the time, believed in him at first sight, saying: "One with such a face cannot lie."

- If a firefly declares itself to be the sun, its lie lasts only until sunrise. Turkish people say that a liar's candle only burns till bedtime, meaning that a lie is short-lived. So, a deceitful person pretending to be a Prophet would soon be unmasked, and no one would accept his or her claim.

- Even an unimportant person in a small group cannot lie shamelessly and openly without somehow being discovered. Prophet Muhammad, upon him be peace and blessings, challenged everybody to come until the Last Day. He gave many important speeches to a large community concerning a great cause, all with great ease and freedom, without hesitation or anxiety, with pure sincerity and great solemnity, and in an intense and elevated manner that provoked his enemies.

- An unlettered person cannot speak on something requiring expert knowledge, especially to specialists in that area. However, Prophet Muhammad, upon him be peace and blessings, spoke on every issue from theology and metaphysics to medicine and history, physics and biology, and has never been contradicted. He challenged his people's strengths (literature, eloquence, and oratory), yet nothing they composed could compare with the Qur'an.

- People do not risk their life, wealth, and reputation, and bear hardship and persecution for a lie, unless they want even more wealth and higher worldly position. Before claiming Prophethood, Prophet Muhammad, upon him be peace and blessings, was well-off and respected. After Prophethood, he confronted great hardship and persecution, and spent all he had for his cause. His enemies slandered, mocked, and beat him. Finally forcing him out of his homeland, they took up arms against him. He bore all of this without complaint and asked God Almighty to forgive them, for all he wanted was to see everybody believing in and worshipping the One God exclusively, thereby prospering in both worlds and being saved from the torments of Hell.

- History is full of people who, saying one thing and doing another, never attained a large and devoted following. Their ideas did not change people permanently, nor did their systems outlive them for any length of time. However, Prophet Muhammad, upon him be peace and blessings, sincerely and honestly practiced what he taught, and was the most obedient worshipper of the Creator and follower of the religious law. This shows his full conviction in his cause and that he is a Messenger of God sent to guide humanity to the True Path.

- People's characters are usually well-established by the time they are thirty, and do not change significantly after that. To change one's character after forty is practically impossible. If, God forbid, there had been any imperfection and blemish in Prophet Muhammad's character, it certainly would have appeared before his Prophethood. Is it logical that a person recognized by his community as its most honest and upright member would suddenly, at the age of forty, assume the role of a great liar and fraud to his own people?

• Liars can neither acquire nor maintain a large group of dedicated followers eager to sacrifice themselves. Even though they were among the greatest Prophets, Moses and Jesus, upon them be peace, did not have such devoted followers. The Jews betrayed their Prophet—Moses—when he left them for forty days to receive the Torah on Mount Sinai, by worshipping a golden calf made by Samiri. Even after so many years of intellectual and spiritual training in the desert, only two God-fearing men obeyed when Moses ordered them to fight the Amalekites. As for Jesus, one of his most devoted twelve followers (Judas Iscariot) betrayed him and delivered him to his enemies.

The Companions were so devoted that they willingly sacrificed everything for the Prophet. Although brought up among a primitive, ignorant people without any positive idea of social life and administration or a Scripture, and immersed in spiritual and intellectual darkness, Prophet Muhammad, upon him be peace and blessings, soon transformed them into the masters, guides, and just rulers of the region's most civilized, socially, and politically advanced peoples and states. Their subsequent rule has been widely admired ever since—even by those who continue to oppose Islam and Muslims.

Also, innumerable universally acclaimed profound scholars, famous scientists, and pure, spiritual masters have been produced by the generations following the Companions. How could they establish a civilization, the most magnificent and advanced of all times, by following a liar? God forbid such a thought!

• Prophet Muhammad, upon him be peace and blessings, was the perfect exemplar of high moral conduct and virtue. He appeared among a desert people possessing only the most rudimentary level of civilization and devoted to immorality. Who brought him up as the most virtuous and moral person? His father died before he was born; his mother died when he was six years old. He was then raised by his grandfather and uncle, but how could they give these perfections to him when they did not embody them to such a degree? His teacher was God, as he himself said: "My Lord educated me and taught me good manners, and how well He educated me and how beautifully He taught me good manners."[23]

- History has seen many virtuous people. However, no one has ever combined all virtues and good qualities as perfectly as Prophet Muhammad, upon him be peace and blessings. Many generous people cannot show enough courage when and where necessary, and many courageous people cannot be so lenient and generous. But Prophet Muhammad, upon him be peace and blessings, combined in his person all virtues and laudable qualities at the highest level.

Virtue and good morality require balance. Excessive generosity becomes extravagance, excessive thrift becomes miserliness, courage is confused with rashness, and dialectics or demagogy with intelligence. Virtue requires knowing how to act in certain conditions. For instance, the respect of the weak for the strong, when assumed by the latter, becomes conceit; the humility shown by the strong to the weak, when assumed by the latter, becomes self-abasement. A person's voluntary forbearance and sacrifice (of his or her rights) is good and a virtue; when done on behalf of others, however, it is treason. People may bear their own conditions patiently, but they cannot do so for the nation. Pride and indignation on behalf of the nation are commendable, whereas they are not on behalf of oneself.

Prophet Muhammad, upon him be peace and blessings, was perfectly balanced in his virtues and good moral qualities; perfectly courageous when necessary; perfectly mild, forgiving, and humble among people; perfectly dignified but gracious;

and more generous than all others, but also thrifty and opposed to extravagance. In short, he was the most perfect balance of all virtues and good qualities.

- According to Muslim theologians, there are six essentials of Prophethood: truthfulness, trustworthiness, communication of God's commands, intelligence, infallibility, and freedom from any mental and physical defect. History records that Prophet Muhammad, upon him be peace and blessings, had these six essential attributes in the most perfect fashion.

- People often have to make quick decisions that might cause them problems in the future. Prophet Muhammad's great achievements, made during the relatively short time span of twenty-three years, are without parallel in human history. He never faltered, and his decisions always proved to be correct. Moreover, his actions and words were both for his own people and for all future generations regardless of time and place. As none of his statements have ever been contradicted, no one can criticize his actions, words, and decisions. Can one who is not a Prophet taught by God, the All-Knowing, have such intelligence, foresight, sagacity, insight, sound reasoning, and prudence?

- Prophet Muhammad, upon him be peace and blessings, was extremely merciful. In Makka, persistent persecution eventually forced him to emigrate to Madina. However, when he finally conquered Makka without bloodshed after eight years of warfare, he forgave all of his enemies, including the hypocrites and unbelievers. He knew who the hypocrites were, but concealed their identities so they could enjoy the rights of full citizenship to which their outward confession of faith and practice entitled them.

- Prophet Muhammad, upon him be peace and blessings, was particularly fond of children. Whenever he saw a child crying, he would sit beside him or her and share his or her feelings. He felt a mother's pain for her child more than the mother herself. Once he said: "I stand in prayer and wish to prolong it. However, I hear a child cry and shorten the prayer for the sake of its mother, who is praying in the congregation."[24] He took children in his arms and hugged them, sometimes carrying them on his shoulders. As for animals, he once said that a prostitute was guided to truth by God and ultimately went to Paradise for giving water to a dog dying of thirst, while another woman was condemned to Hell for letting a cat starve to death.[25]

- Prophet Muhammad, upon him be peace and blessings, was extremely mild and never became angry with anybody because of what they did to him personally. When people slandered his wife 'A'isha, he did not punish them after she was cleared. Bedouins often came to his presence and behaved impolitely; he did not even frown at them.

- He was the most generous of people, and liked to distribute whatever he had. After Prophethood had been bestowed upon him, he and his wealthy wife Khadija spent all they had in the cause of God. When Khadija died, they were so poor that he had to borrow money to buy a shroud in which to bury the first person to embrace Islam and his first supporter.[26]

- According to the Prophet, this world is like a tree whose shade is enjoyed by people on a long journey. No one lives forever, so people must prepare for the journey's second part: Paradise or Hell.[27] His mission was to guide people to truth by all permissible means, which he did. Once 'Umar saw him lying on a rough mat and wept, saying:

> O Messenger of God! While kings sleep in soft feather beds, you lie on a rough mat. You are the Messenger of God and therefore deserve an easy life more than any other person. The Messenger answered him: Do you not agree that [the luxuries of] the world be theirs but those of the Hereafter ours?[28]

Islam does not approve of a monastic life. It came to secure justice and humanity's well-being, and warns people against over-indulgence. For this reason, many Muslims chose an ascetic life. Although Muslims generally became rich after the death of the Messenger, caliphs Abu Bakr, 'Umar, and 'Ali preferred austerity partly because of their own inclination and partly to follow the Prophet's example strictly. Many other Muslims made this same choice.

- Prophet Muhammad, upon him be peace and blessings, was the most modest person. As he attained higher ranks, he increased in humility and servanthood to God. He preferred being a Prophet-slave to being a Prophet-king. While building the mosque in Madina, he carried two sun-dried bricks while everybody else carried one.[29] While digging the trench around Madina to defend it during the Battle of the Trench, the Companions bound a stone around their bellies because of hunger; the Messenger bound two.[30] When a man began to tremble because of his awe-inspiring appearance, the Messenger calmed him, saying: "Don't be afraid, brother. I am a man, like you, whose mother used to eat dry bread."[31] A mentally unbalanced woman once pulled him by the hand and said: "Come with me and do my housework." God's Messenger did as she asked.[32] 'A'isha said the Messenger patched his clothes, repaired his shoes, and helped his wives with the housework.[33]

'Ali describes the Prophet as follows:

> God's Messenger was the most generous of people in giving out and the mildest and foremost of them in patience and perseverance. He was the most truthful of people in speech, the most amiable and congenial in companionship and the noblest of them in family. Whoever sees him first is stricken by awe of him but whoever knows him closely is attracted to him deeply, and whoever attempts to describe him says: "I have, either before him or after him, never seen the like of him, upon him be peace and blessings."[34]

CHAPTER 8

Islam: The Universal Religion of Integrity and the Path to Perfection

ISLAM: THE UNIVERSAL RELIGION OF INTEGRITY AND THE PATH TO PERFECTION

Almost all moral or religious revival movements prior to Islam emerged or developed as either reactions against existing circumstances or were restricted to certain peoples and times. This explains why they lacked some principles and did not deal with every aspect of life and humanity. But Islam came as a religion that contains complete guidance for all aspects of life regardless of time and place; a faith-based system of life that combines action, intention, and faith and considers the totality of human life. In fact, the Qur'an mentions the basic qualities of Prophet Muhammad as a perfect guide to educate and lead humanity, and describes the foundations of a perfect community as follows: *As We have sent among you a Messenger of your own, reciting to you Our Revelations, and purifying you (of false beliefs and doctrines, and sins, and all kinds of uncleanness), and instructing you in the Book and the Wisdom, and instructing you in whatever you (must but) do not know* (2:151).

Unlike medieval Christianity which viewed nature as a veil between God and humanity, Islam sees it as a created book full of signs for the truth of God's messages or even full of these messages. Thus every thing and event in the universe and human life is a sign upon which we are to reflect and through which we can find ways to the Sublime Creator. By reflecting on these signs in the light of the Qur'an's guidance, we acquire knowledge of God and faith and lead a virtuous life based upon Islam, which purifies our soul from evil and sin. Such reflection enables us to "discover" modern science, all of which originates in the signs (commonly known as the Divine laws of nature).

However, we should note that only purified souls can use science and technology to benefit humanity. If this fact is ignored, such knowledge can lead to vast destruction and millions of deaths, widows and orphans, and homeless people, as we have witnessed in recent centuries. Only purified souls familiar with science and knowing how to use it can lead humanity toward true happiness and salvation.

Obviously, such purified individuals endowed with scientific knowledge and ability must live among people. Thus the Messenger was sent with the Qur'an, which contains the Divine principles of social life, and the Balance so that we could follow absolute justice.[1] Any religion or system that lacks the principles of spiritual purity or the conditions of a virtuous social life cannot provide true happiness. As witnessed by history, Islam provides complete guidance for our lives here and in the next world. Prophet Muhammad, upon him be peace and blessings, was sent as blessing for all the worlds, and so there is no need to renew the Divine message through another Prophet—we already have the eternal and uncorrputed Qur'an. All people have an innate inclination to know their origin, final destination, and purpose in life. Traditional people knew the answers to these questions, but today, under the heavy burden of modern life and the influence of modern concepts, we no longer know these answers. In fact, we know almost nothing about these essential problems arising from our very nature. Such ignorance does not change our situation, for all of us, whether traditional or modern, are born and die. Nothing, not even recent scientific and technological developments, can change these immutable facts. The only difference is that what was once a certainty has been replaced by doubt and fear.

PERENNIAL KNOWLEDGE

Our situation has not changed at all as regards birth and death. Although contained by an infinitude, we are still finite beings who cannot escape being stirred by our very nature to try and understand the Infinite and Absolute. With regard to the Absolute and all states of being constituting the universe, we are what we have always been and always will be: the fairest creatures and the highest point of creation, yet possessing the potential to fall to the lowest point.

The Qur'an states that the process of creation is circular: *As He initiated you (in existence), so to Him you are returning* (7:29). Thus creation ends at the point from which it started. Atheists believe this as well, but conceive of matter, space and time, or something presentable in terms of four dimensions as the process's starting and ending points. Matter has the least degree of perfection, and yet atheists hold it, in its most chaotic condition, to be the beginning and end of creation, which they consider accidental and purposeless. The Qur'an, however, says that existence starts with the highest state of perfection, proceeds downward to matter, and then turns upward to the point from which it started:

> He directs the affair from heaven to the earth; then the affair ascends to Him in a day, the measure of which is a thousand years of what you reckon. (32:5)

The Creative Will designs and administers this process, and Divine Love, Grace, Mercy, and Compassion are *a priori* factors in this Will's manifestation. Therefore Mercy or Compassion is the principle of the Infinite's manifestation. Each particle of existence is immersed in this Compassion, which endows it with a sympathy for and attraction to other beings, and above all with its source: Divine Compassion.

So each atom is regarded as the ground where the Divine Names and Attributes are manifested. Mahmud Shabstari, in his *Gulshan-i Raz* ("The Garden of the Roses of Secrets"), expresses how everything is a precious Divine work:

> Know the world is a mirror from head to foot,
> In every atom a hundred blazing suns.
> If you cleave the heart of one drop of water,

A hundred pure oceans emerge from it.
If you examine closely each grain of sand,
A thousand Adams may be seen in it.
In its members a gnat is like an elephant;
In its qualities a drop of rain is like the Nile.
The heart of a barley-corn equals a hundred harvests,
A world dwells in the heart of a millet seed.
In the wing of a gnat is the ocean of the life,
In the pupil of the eye a heaven;
What though the grain of the heart be small,
It is a station for the Lord of both worlds to "dwell" therein.[2]

Since existence manifests God's Grace or Compassion, creation's order and hierarchy begin with the highest and most comprehensive created entity. This being is the compassion unto all worlds or beings, the possessor of all excellences in their highest degree of perfection. This entity, the most comprehensive in perfection and embodiment of God's Compassion, is presented in various terms. However, the most appropriate ones are the *Muhammadan Light* or the *Muhammadan Reality*. Like sunshine radiating through everything that exists, the Muhammadan Light is actually the theater of the manifestation of all Divine Names and Attributes, as well as the archetype of the cosmos.

THE HIERARCHY OF CREATION

The hierarchy of creation unfolds itself in countless realms of certain invisible entities such as the Divine Supreme Seat (*Kursiyy*), Divine Supreme Throne (*'Arsh*), and the Supreme Preserved Tablet (*al-Lawh al-Mahfuz*), and in spheres of intellectual and angelic beings. Some of these realms are called by Muslim sages or scholars the Realm of the Transcendental Manifestation of Divinity (*'Alam Lahut*); the Realm of the Transcendental Manifestation of the Divine Mercy and Compassion (*'Alam Rahamut*); the Realm of the Transcendental Manifestation of Divine Attributes and Names (*'Alam Jabarut*); the Realm of the Transcendental Manifestation of Divine Commands (*'Alam Malakut*); the Realm of the (Initial Manifestation of) Divine Commands (*'Alam Amr*), and the Realm of Ideal Forms or Similitudes (*'Alam Mithal*). Each sphere is held by the one above it and holds the one below it, ending in the four-dimensional sphere known as the material or corporeal realm. Our world, the *'alam mulk* or *'alam shahada* (the visible or corporeal world), is the lowest sphere. It forms the hierarchy's base, from where the ascent of existence starts.[3]

In its upward course, matter or corporeality ranges from the simplest subatomic particles to gigantic nebulae and the solar system. These are then populated with such inanimate and animate things as plants, animals, humanity, and other conscious and intellectual beings, the nature and number of whom only the Creator knows. So far as the earth is concerned, the Creator causes inanimate elements to serve as the material for the existence of plants, thus elevating them to the simplest degree of life. Life, being the result of God's direct manifestation of His Attribute of Life and of His Name the Giver of Life without any cause, proceeds through plants and animals until it reaches perfection in humanity, the most complicated and highest intellectual entity. Thus, each hierarchy of existence contains the one below it and serves the one above it. That is, plants contain inanimate elements, while serving as food for animals and human beings. The animals consumed by human beings serve as food for them and rise to the level of human life in the human organism.

As human beings, we have in our existence the reflections or representations of both the heavenly and spiritual realms and entities, and the corporeal one. While our mental faculties such as intellect, reason, thought, reflection, recollection, deduction, and memory, and our spiritual faculties such as the heart, the spirit, conscience, and the innermost ones the Muslim sages or scholars call "the Secret" and "the Most Private," represent the heavenly and spiritual realms and entities, our body corresponds to or represents the corporeal realm.[4] In addition, we have been endowed with the power of discovery and invention, and have been taught "the names" (the keys to the knowledge of all things). We have been given the power to receive whatever is manifested by God's Will, whether in the terrestrial, celestial, or supercelestial spheres, through our external and internal senses, and to reflect and reproduce whatever we receive. Although our celestial origin places us at the summit of creation's hierarchy, we have to live upon the earth because of the vegetable and animal aspects of our existence. In other words, these contradictory features of our being—the angelic nature and the terrestrial crust hiding the spiritual core—cause us to live in this world and yet seek to transcend it.

The Qur'an defines our situation in a way that is at once perennial and universal: *Surely We have created human of the best stature, as the perfect pattern of creation; then We have reduced him to the lowest of the low.* (95:4–5). Created in the best stature, we nevertheless fall into separation and withdrawal from our celestial prototype—a condition the Qur'an calls the "lowest of the low." God created us as the most universal and all-embracing theater of Divine Names and Attributes, so that we might bear the Divine Trust and become the source of an unlimited effusion of light. The "lowest of the low" is identified with the world of natural passion and heedlessness. The grandeur of the human state, its great possibilities and perils, and the permanent nature of our quest for the Divine therefore lie at the very root of human existence.

Ibn Sina, a famous eleventh-century Muslim philosopher, expresses the idea that the human spirit feels constrained to leave this world and to return to the celestial world from whence it came:

> ... Now why from its perch on high was it cast like this
>   To the lowest Nadir's gloomy and dear abyss?
> Was it God who cast it forth for some purpose wise,
> Concealed from the keenest seeker's inquiring eyes?
>   Then is its descent a discipline wise but stern,
> That the things that it has not heard it thus may learn.
> So 'tis she whom Fate does plunder, while the star

> Sets at length in a place from its rising far,
> Like a gleam of lightning which over the meadows shone,
> And, as though it never had been, in a moment is gone.[5]

As a "book" created, the universe continually reveals the eternal message of the Ultimate Truth, and its finite forms reveal the traces of the Infinite. 'Ali ibn Ali Talib says: "I wonder about the person who observes the universe created by God and doubts His Existence." Those who have not lost their sight and darkened their hearts always see and experience the perennial truth in the universe. The Qur'an declares:

> And God's is the sovereignty (absolute ownership and dominion) of the heavens and the earth, and God has full power over everything. Surely in the creation of the heavens and the earth, and the alternation of night and day (with their periods shortening and lengthening), there are signs (manifesting the truth) for the people of discernment. They remember and mention God (with their tongues and hearts), standing and sitting and lying down on their sides (whether during the Prayer or not), and reflect on the creation of the heavens and the earth. (Having grasped the purpose of their creation and the meaning they contain, they conclude and say): "Our Lord, You have not created this (the universe) without meaning and purpose. All-Glorified You are (in that You are absolutely above doing anything meaningless and purposeless), so save us from (having wrong conceptions of Your acts, and acting against Your purpose for creation, and so deserving) the punishment of the Fire! Our Lord! Whomever You admit into the Fire, indeed You have brought him to disgrace. (Having concealed or rejected God's signs in the heavens and on the earth, and so denied God or fallen into associating partners with Him,) the wrongdoers will have no helpers (against the Fire). Our Lord! Indeed We have heard a caller calling to faith, saying: 'Believe in your Lord!', so we did believe. Our Lord, forgive us, then, our sins, and blot out from us our evil deeds, and take us to You in death in the company of the truly godly and virtuous. Our Lord! Grant us what You have promised us through Your Messengers. Do not disgrace us on the Day of Resurrection; indeed You never break Your promise." And thus does their

(All-Gracious and Generous) Lord answer them: "I do not
leave to waste the work of any of you (engaged in doing good),
whether male or female...." (3:189–195)

Humanity needs Revelation, which, like the universe itself,
comes from the Infinite and the Absolute. Hence, Revelation
serves as the key to unfolding the mysteries of our being and of
the universe. It is a gift from Divine Mercy that enables us to pass
beyond the finite to the Infinite, and enables the human soul to
move from the outward to the inward, from the periphery to the
center, and from form to meaning.

This journey is none other than the intellectual and spiritual
quest itself. Due to the soul's intimate relation with the cosmos,
this journey is at once a penetration to the center of human existence and a migration to the abode beyond the cosmos. By following Islam's outer form, we migrate to the inner and, by His Grace,
transcend the finite world to regain our primordial metaphysical
state and thereby complete creation's circle. The spiritual path of
Islam calls people to defeat their carnal souls so that they can be
reborn as their primordial selves.

> Those who find the Truth find Him in their souls;
> Those detained halfway are hindered by conjectures.
> Whoever truly seeks will truly find Him,
> while the indolent can do neither;
> For His servants on their spiritual journey,
> He is the final destination.
> Souls who do not recognize Him as a friend,
> who do not die to themselves to be raised again in Him,
> and who do not die for His sake
> are utterly bereft and destitute.
> Come, friends, let us set out to reach
> the realm of the Beloved;
> And let us see the rose of His Beauty
> for a moment in the light.
> The world is pitiless and cruel,
> all covered in fog and cloud.

It is but a loss and waste of time
to stay here even for a short while.
We are travelers, and our homecoming is with Him alone.
What an honor then to reach Him.
Faith is the only way to attain this aim
by His leave and grace.[6]

Islam is the religion of unity, and all aspects of its doctrine and practice reflect this central and cardinal principle. The Shari'a is a vast network of injunctions and regulations that inwardly relate the world of multiplicity to a single center and, conversely, is reflected in the multiplicity of the circumference. Islamic art seeks to relate the multiplicity of forms, shapes, and color to the One, to the center and Origin, and thereby reflect *tawhid* in its own way in the world of forms with which it is concerned.

THE PATH TO PERFECTION

Each person is composed of three parts—mind and spirit, carnal soul, and body. Each of these needs to be satisfied. They are so interrelated, and their needs are so different, that neglecting one results in our failing to attain perfection.

As we read in the Qur'an: *Fair in the eyes of humanity is the passionate love of women, children, stored-up heaps of gold and silver, horses of mark, cattle and tillage* (3:14). Our physical make-up and individual characteristics produce certain inclinations, and we can neither avoid satisfying these lusts implanted in us by the Creator nor be rid of them. This does not mean that people attempting to satisfy their lusts are free to do as they please or cannot overcome their inclinations. On the contrary, this means that we can change our inclinations by exercising our free will, and can control our lust, anger, and other emotions and then use them to propel ourselves along the path of perfection and wisdom.

Made of dust (our earthly element) and spirit (our heavenly element), we have to satisfy both our material, intellectual and spiritual needs. Just as we are subject to anger and passion, so can we exercise our intellect. We are not just plants or animals; rather, we are unique beings with both plant and animal aspects. Just as our physical body is subject to its own pleasures and diseases, our spirit has its own joys and ailments. Sickness harms the body, while the body's well-being, health, and whatever is in harmony with its nature gives it pleasure. As for the spirit, its pleasures and diseases depend on whether or not the carnal soul has been purified.

Our most important task, inseparable from existence and our life's ultimate aim, is to attain felicity and happiness. The most consummate happiness is to embody and manifest the attributes and characteristics that the Qur'an establishes and our Prophet represented in the perfect fashion. The soul of a truly happy person develops by knowing and loving God, and is illuminated by an effulgence emanating from Him. When that happens to a person, he or she radiates only beauty, for beauty can radiate only from that which is beautiful.

True happiness cannot be reached or retained unless all of the soul's faculties and powers are purified and reformed. Doing so either partially or temporarily will not result in true happiness. This is similar to physical health. Just as a body can be considered healthy only when all of its limbs and organs are eternally healthy, people can attain perfect happiness only when freed from all evil-commanding and animal forces preventing their ascension to higher realms.

Purifying our faculties and powers does not mean eliminating desire and anger or destroying our reproductive instincts and capacity for self-defense, for such abilities are necessary for our continued existence. For example, without intellect we could not distinguish between good and bad, right and wrong, true and false; without anger we could not defend ourselves; and without sexual attraction and desire humanity's continued existence would be threatened.

We must express our powers and faculties in a balanced and moderate way so that they can perform their functions properly. Doing so engenders a particular ability. For example, purifying and training the intellect brings knowledge and wisdom, purifying anger engenders courage and then forbearance, and purifying passion and desire develops chastity. The moral virtues acquired by those rising toward perfection and the realization of true happiness are wisdom, courage, and chastity.

If every virtue is considered the center of a circle, and any movement away from the center is considered a vice, each vice becomes greater the further it moves away from the center. Thus the number of vices is infinite, for there can be only one center. Moreover the direction of deviation does not matter, for *any* deviation from the center is a vice.

Each moral virtue has two extremes. For example, wisdom has stupidity and cunning, courage has cowardice and rashness, and chastity has lethargy and uncontrolled lust. Thus the purpose of our existence—perfection—lies in maintaining a balance and moderation between these two extremes. Concerning this, 'Ali ibn Abi Talib is reported to have said:

> God gave angels intellect without sexual desire and passions or anger, and gave animals anger and desire without intellect. He exalted humanity by bestowing all of these qualities upon it. Accordingly, if our intellect dominates our desire and ferocity, we rise above angels, because such a station is attained by people despite obstacles that do not vex angels.[7]

One important point related to our earthly existence is that since we are social, civilized beings coexisting with other people, our earthly life covers social, political, and economic aspects as well as spiritual ones. Our worldly nature makes it possible for us to be too obedient to our desires. History shows that when those who are interested only in power finally attain it, they light fires of oppression and enslave the poor and the weak. On the other hand, God is the All-Just and never approves of injustice and oppression. Thus the religion He revealed must—and does—cover all aspects of human life.

THE SPIRITUAL WAY AND *TAWHID*

Islam's inner dimension or the Islamic spiritual way is the best way to achieve *tawhid*. The Islamic creedal statement shows that all Muslims believe in absolute Divine Unity: *La illaha illa'llah* (there is no deity but God).

Islam seeks to free people from the prison of multiplicity, to remove any mental processes or physical actions that divert their ego-centers toward temporal and sensual desires, and to eradicate hypocrisy. In short, it seeks to make people whole, for only such people can become holy. People profess faith in God but live and act as if there were many deities, and so are guilty of polytheism and hypocrisy. As Islam seeks to bring such a condition into the open and cure the afflicted person, its goal is to integrate each person at every level of his or her existence.

Such integration is brought about by harmonizing all bodily, mental, and spiritual faculties, not by negating the intelligence, which so often occurs with modern religious movements. Islamic spiritual education bases its methods upon observing the Shari'a and, in particular, the daily Prayers, which are a most powerful means of integrating people's spiritual faculties and harmonizing them with their corporeal being.

Islamic spiritual education's main method is regular worship and refraining from forbidden things. Obligatory worship is combined or strengthened with invocation (*dhikr*), in which separation from the Divine is removed and *tawhid* is achieved. Invocation, when combined with the appropriate forms of reflection (*fikr - tafakkur*) as well, causes the emergence of an integrated, pure, and whole, gold-like soul. Islam seeks not only to purify the soul but also to enlighten the mind. It purifies the soul and illumines and enlivens the heart with religious knowledge, knowledge of God, regular worship, and invocation, and enlightens the mind with scientific knowledge. Bediüzzaman Said Nursi writes:

The human conscious nature, which we call conscience, and which distinguishes between what is good and evil, feeling pleasure and exhilaration in what is good, and suffering from, and grieved at, what is evil, has four basic elements, namely the spiritual intellect, willpower, the mind, and the power of perceptiveness. These four elements are also regarded as the senses of the spirit. In addition to their different duties and functions, each of these senses has an ultimate purpose for its existence. The ultimate purpose for willpower is worshipping God; for the mind, it is having knowledge of God; for the power of perceptiveness, love of God; and for the spiritual intellect, "vision" of God. What we call *taqwa* (piety and right-eousness), which is the perfect form or degree of worship, is the result of the functions of all of these four senses. The Divine Law, included in the Divine Religion, feeds them to develop, equips them with the necessary material, and directs them to the ultimate purpose for the existence of each.[8]

Those who achieve taqwa and integration with the essence of their existence possess certain characteristics that anyone can see, for it leaves its imprint even upon their outer appearance, which necessarily reflects their inner state. Such people are cured of all diseases of the heart by having their tensions and complexes removed, as their need for the transcendent has been met and satisfied, and not through modern psychoanalysis. Moreover, they do not compartmentalize their lives, for their thoughts and actions issue from a single center and are based on a series of immutable principles.

They realize the Islamic ideal of unifying reflective thought with the practical for their reflection is combined in the purest and most intense activity. As a result, they reflect Divine Unity and become bright mirrors to the Divine Names and Qualities. They act and live in such a manner that all of their actions and words exude a spiritual fragrance and beauty. They are somehow in touch with that Divine Grace running through the universe's arteries.

Such people have reached the goal of their lives and have no fear, which is so destructive to modern people. They see death not as total annihilation, but as a shift from a state of lesser sensitivity to a higher one. All of us belong to God, and the Qur'an states that each person and society moves towards God. Therefore death is only a shift and a change from one stage of existence to a higher one, and ultimately terminates with return to God.

Death does not destroy our internal or external sensory faculties, but rather refines and sharpens them. It only severs the conscious ego's direct relationship with the outer material world, to which it is connected through the external senses. As material life veils human senses and consciousness, death sharpens all human faculties by removing this veil. 'Ali ibn Abi Talib confirms this: "People are now in a state of sleep. They will awake when they die."[9]

So death is actually an ascension, a gate opening upon higher realities and pleasures of existence, not something to be feared by sincere Muslims. It is a transference from the dungeons of worldly life to the gardens of Paradise, from the world of labor and trouble to the abode of rewards. In a Prophetic Tradition, God says:

> My servant cannot draw near to Me with something more lovable to Me than fulfilling the things I have made incumbent on him. Then, My servant gets nearer and nearer to Me until I love him by fulfilling the supererogatory acts of worship. When I love him, I become his ears with which he hears, his eyes with which he sees, his hands with which he grasps, and his feet on which he walks. (His hearing, seeing, grasping, and walking take place in accordance with My will and commandments.) If he asks Me for something, I surely grant it to him, and if he seeks refuge from (something), I surely take him under My protection.[10]

A MOST ADVISABLE WAY TO GOD

Said Nursi sought to combine religious and scientific knowledge with spirituality to produce "complete" Muslims. In his terminology, these would be Muslims having minds enlightened by scientific knowledge and hearts illumined by religious knowledge and spirituality. He offers the following way:[11]

There are many ways to Almighty God. All true ways have been derived from the Qur'an, but some are safer and more comprehensive and direct than others. The way to be derived from the Qur'an as the most appropriate one in this age particularly depends upon our perception and confession of helplessness and poverty before God's Might and Riches, and upon affection or compassion, reflection and thankfulness.

This way is as sure as the way of loving God, or even safer, for it elevates us so as to be loved by God on account of our sincere devotion to Him. Our perception and acknowledgment of our poverty leads us to the Divine Name the All-Merciful. Affection or compassion is more effective than love, and leads to the Name the All-Compassionate. Reflection is brighter and more comprehensive than love, and leads to the Name the All-Wise. Thankfulness causes the Divine blessings to increase. This way does not resemble the way of those Sufi orders that have developed a ten-step method to purify and sharpen their members' ten outer and inner senses or faculties and that prefer to recite God's Names silently. Neither does it resemble those orders that practice public recitation and seek to purify their members from all defects contained in the soul's seven stations.

This way consists of four steps and is the Shari'a (or the truth) itself; it is not a Sufi order. Its fundamental principles consist of following the Sunna, performing the religious obligations, avoiding the major sins, performing the five daily Prayers properly, and praising, glorifying, and exalting God after every Prayer. The steps are as follows:

- The first step is expressed by: *Do not hold yourselves pure (sinless; it is vain self-justification)* (53:32).
- The second step is indicated by: *Be not as those who forgot God— and so He caused them to forget their own selves* (59:19).
- The third step is pointed to by: *Whatever good visits you is from God; whatever evil befalls you is from yourself* (4:79).

- The fourth step is shown by: *Everything is perishable (and so perishing) except His "Face" (His eternal Self, and what is done in seeking His good pleasure)* (28:88).

The following is a brief explanation of these four steps:

FIRST STEP: We should never regard ourselves as infallible and sinless. Since we love ourselves first on account of our evil-commanding soul, we will sacrifice anything to satisfy it. We praise ourselves as if we were a deity, and believe ourselves to be without defect. We strive so insistently to prove ourselves free of guilt that others consider us to be full of self-love. We exploit the faculties given to us for praising and thanking God by glorifying ourselves. Given this, we resemble those people mentioned in: *who takes as his [her] god his [her] own lusts and fancies* (25:43). We praise, rely on, and admire ourselves. To be purified of such attitudes, we should regard ourselves as fallible and liable—even susceptible—to error.

SECOND STEP: As the verse: *Be not as those who forgot God—and so He caused them to forget their own selves* teaches, we are oblivious and unaware of ourselves. We do not want to remember death, although we always consider others mortal. We hold back when confronting hardship and rendering service, but believe that we should be the first one rewarded when it is time to collect the wages. Purifying ourselves at this step involves carrying out our responsibilities, being prepared for death, and forgetting whatever reward we might obtain.

THIRD STEP: As the verse: *Whatever good visits you is from God; whatever evil befalls you is from yourself* teaches, our evil-commanding soul always ascribes good to itself and feels conceited. In reality, we should perceive our defects and insufficiency and then thank and praise God for whatever good we can do. According to the meaning of: *Prosperous is the one who purifies it* (91:9), our purification at this step consists of knowing that our perfection lies in confessing our imperfection, our power in perceiving our helplessness, and our wealth in accepting our essential poverty and inadequacy.

FOURTH STEP: As the verse: *Everything is perishable (and so perishing) except His "Face"* teaches, our evil-commanding soul causes us to consider ourselves as completely free and existent in our own right. Furthermore, we may claim "divinity" for ourselves and rebel against our Creator, Who alone deserves worship. We can save ourselves from this perilous situation only by perceiving the truth that everything, with respect to its own self, is essentially non-existent, contingent, ephemeral, and mortal. In addition, we must realize that we are existent, experiencing and experienced, only because we are a mirror reflecting the Majestic Maker's Names and entrusted with various duties.

Here, we can purify ourselves by perceiving that our existence lies in acknowledging our essential non-existence. Considering ourselves to be self-existent, we fall into the darkest pit of non-existence. In other words, relying on our personal existence and thus ignoring the Real Creator causes our ephemeral, fire-fly-like personal existence to be drowned in the infinite darkness of non-existence. But if we abandon pride and egoism and recognize that we are only a mirror in which the Real Creator manifests Himself with His Names and Attributes, we attain real existence. One who discovers the Necessary Being, the manifestations of Whose Names cause all things to come into existence, is counted as having found everything.

CONCLUSION

This way is the method of affection or compassion, reflection, and thankfulness, as well as that of recognizing our own incompetence and insufficiency. This four-stage way leads to its objective and is the easiest and most direct way. Recognizing our incompetence leads us to rely on God alone, for it means that we have freed ourselves from our evil-commanding soul's influence. This method is safer than other ways, for it obliges us to recognize our incompetence and ascribe all defects to ourselves.

This way is a main highway, one that is much broader and more universal, for it allows us to attain a constant awareness of God's Presence without denying or ignoring the universe's actual existence and being a "book" to study to have knowledge of God. It considers all things as mirrors reflecting the Divine Names' manifestations, and views creation as manifestations of His Names and thus devoted to His service, as opposed to being self-existent and self-perpetuating. It saves us from heedlessness by allowing us to travel to Him through everything, by making us always aware of His Presence.

In short, this way considers beings as neither existent nor working on their own behalf; rather, it states that beings function as signs and officials of God, the All-Mighty.

CHAPTER 9

Islam: The Religion of an Ideal Social Life

ISLAM: THE RELIGION OF
AN IDEAL SOCIAL LIFE

HUMAN INDIVIDUAL AND COLLECTIVE LIFE
FROM AN ISLAMIC PERSPECTIVE

In general terms, the Islamic view of life is the knowledge, discipline, and science of humanity's rights and obligations and of what is good and bad for humanity on the individual and collective levels. Thus the Islamic view of life consists of a set of rights and obligations by which Muslims are expected to live. Broadly speaking, Islamic law deals with our life in terms of our relationship with our Creator, ourselves (our rights over ourselves), other people, and our natural environment (the rights over the resources that God has given to us for our benefit).

Each person is an instinctive worshipper; only the nature of the deity worshipped or the way worship is offered differs. God's love abides in every person's heart. By the nature of their being created, all creatures have to submit to their Creator. Thus all creatures, including humanity in its biological life, are *muslim* (in submission to God) and have to obey the rules of creation. The Qur'an both establishes that God is the "natural Deity" for our worship and explains the right way to worship Him. It stipulates the uniformity of worship just as it stresses God's Unity, the unity of the worshipped, and the unity of worship.

There must be unity between our worship and our attitude towards life. The Deity to whom we pray is the same one we address while studying, earning a living, and improving conditions on the earth; the same one we remember while eating, drinking, interacting with family members and all other individuals or societies, regardless of time or place: *Say: "My Prayer, and all my (other) acts and forms of devotion and worship, and my living and my dying are for God alone, the Lord of the worlds. He has no partners; thus have I been commanded, and I am the first and foremost of the Muslims (who have submitted to Him exclusively)"* (6:162–163). Our constant reiteration of God's Name in our hearts makes us recall His Commands and our individual and social responsibilities.

When this happens, something very significant occurs in our life: our regular worship gives us an extraordinary spirit. For example, the prescribed daily Prayers (*salat*) allow us to repeat and refresh our faith five times a day. The prayer times—dawn, noon, afternoon, evening, and night—correspond with the five periods of our life: childhood and youth, maturity, old age, death, and life after death until the Resurrection. The next day's dawn signifies the Resurrection, so each day is a complete cycle of our life in parallel with that of the world.

While praying, Muslims dissociate themselves from their worldly engagements and even from all the world, turning to God with all their being. Reciting the Qur'an elevates us to a state as if we were receiving it directly from the Lord of the worlds. We request Divine help to enable us to follow His Chosen Path, refresh our belief, remind ourselves that one day we will have to account for our deeds, unburden ourselves, and ask Him to help us throughout our lives.

Thus the daily Prayers strengthen our faith, prepare us for a life of virtue and obedience to God, and refresh our belief, from which spring courage, sincerity, purposefulness, spiritual purity, and moral enrichment. The Qur'an states that: *Daily Prayers prevent a Muslim from committing vices of every kind* (29:45), and the Prayer is considered as the Muslims' (spiritual) ascension to God's holy Presence.

Muslims are urged to perform their daily Prayers in congregation, and men must do so for the Friday noon congregational Prayer. This creates a bond of love and mutual understanding, arouses a sense of collective unity, fosters a collective purpose, and inculcates a deep feeling of fellowship. Prayers are a symbol of equality, for poor and rich, low and high, rulers and ruled, educated and uneducated, black and white all stand in rows and prostrate before their Lord. Furthermore, this gives a strong sense of collective discipline and obedience to the community's leader. Prayers train Muslims in those virtues that engender the development of a rich individual and collective life.

Islam regards human beings as God's vicegerents and cannot tolerate the degradation brought on by their submission to humiliation or oppression, for Islam is the real way to freedom and liberation. It invites people to struggle against oppression and tyranny for their freedom and dignity. By prostrating before God, Muslims declare that they bow to no other power. Islam forbids serfdom; promises universal freedom, independence in thought, action, property, and religion; and safeguards a person's integrity, honor, and dignity.

Islam frees people from their lusts so that sensual pleasure does not tempt and corrupt them. Consuming intoxicants and engaging in sexual and moral permissiveness, gambling, immoral movies, fornication, adultery, extramarital sex, pornography, overspending, conspicuous consumption, arrogance, greed, and so on are all humiliating factors that destroy a person's honor and dignity. The daily Prayer and other forms of worship such as fasting and alms-giving (*zakah*), inculcate the will to struggle against self-degradation.

SOCIAL TURMOIL

There are two cardinal causes of social turmoil: the ideas of "let everyone work so I can eat," and "I don't care if others die of hunger so long as I am full." Islam eliminates the first by banning all interest-based and usurious transactions, and the second through *zakah*,[1] which serves as a bridge between a society's various economic levels.

Zakah must be paid by every Muslim whose financial situation is above a specified minimum amount, and must be given only to gain God's approval through serving people. God does not need or receive it, for He is above any need or desire. In His benign Mercy, He promises manifold rewards to those who pay it, provided that they do so only in His name. Those who pay it should not expect any worldly gain from the beneficiaries or an enhanced reputation as philanthropists, for:

> Those who spend their wealth in God's cause and then do not follow up what they have spent with putting (the receiver) under obligation and taunting, their reward is with their Lord, and they will have no fear, nor will they grieve. A kind word and forgiving (people's faults) are better than almsgiving followed by taunting. God is All-Wealthy and Self-Sufficient, (absolutely independent of the charity of people), All-Clement (Who shows no haste in punishing). (2:262–63)

Zakah is as basic to Islam as the five daily Prayers and the obligatory fasting during the holy month of Ramadan. Its fundamental importance, in addition to its socioeconomic functions, lies in fostering the Islamic qualities of sacrifice and ridding Muslims of selfishness and avarice.

Muslim society gains immensely from *zakah*, for every well-to-do Muslim must help those who are less fortunate. Devout Muslims realize that their share in their wealth is very small when all factors are taken into account, such as God's direct gifts of sun, rain, soil, and "natural" resources. Therefore they cannot use their wealth just for their own comfort and luxury, for others have just claims upon it: widows and orphans, the poor and sick, and those who for whatever reason cannot support themselves or become useful members of society. Islam regards it as a great injustice to fill one's own stomach and coffers while others die of hunger or are unemployed, and strongly condemns such selfishness and greed. Muslims share their wealth with others, and help them stand on their own and become productive members of society.

Dr. Laura Vaglieri, a well-known Orientalist, writes that:

> The spirit was liberated [through Islam] from prejudice, man's will was set free from the ties which had kept it bound to the

will of other men, or other so-called hidden powers, priests, false guardians of mysteries, brokers of salvation; all those who pretended to be mediators between God and man, and consequently believed that they had authority over other people's wills, fell from their pedestals.

Because the Unity of God embraces all other unities, this religion was born with the unique feature of amalgamating the secular with the religious, the worldly with the other-worldly, and with a clear approach to socio-economic affairs and with a well-defined administrative system.

Man became the servant of God alone and towards other men he had only the obligations of one free man towards another. While hitherto men had suffered from the injustices of social differences, Islam proclaimed equality among human beings. Each Muslim was distinguished from other Muslims only by his greater fear of God, his good deeds, and his moral and intellectual qualities.[2]

A GOOD SOCIAL ORDER

The foremost feature of a good social order from an Islamic perspective is twofold: All people are God's creatures and therefore no one enjoys any superiority coming from birth (race, family, and color, etc); and the authority's power is neither absolute nor designed to enslave people. Rather, its main objective is to establish and promote the virtues approved by God and to prevent and suppress vice. This is why all administrators in every rank should display righteousness and respect for God in their character, words, and actions. They should imbibe this spirit and infuse it into society.

M. Fethullah Gülen writes about a good social order envisaged by Islam as follows:[3]

> The main aim of Islam and its unchangeable dimensions affect its rules governing the changeable aspects of our lives. Islam does not propose a certain unchangeable form of government or attempt to shape it. Instead, Islam establishes fundamental principles that orient a government's general character, leaving it to the people to choose the type and form of government according to time and circumstances.

The Prophet, upon him be peace and blessings, says that all people are as equal as the teeth of a comb.[4] Islam does not discriminate based on race, color, age, nationality, or physical traits. The Prophet declared: "You are all from Adam, and Adam is from earth. O servants of God, be brothers [and sisters]."[5] Those who are born earlier, have more wealth and power than others, or belong to certain families or ethnic groups have no inherent right to rule others.

Islam also upholds the following fundamental principles:

1. Power lies in truth, a repudiation of the common idea that truth relies upon power.
2. Justice and the rule of law are essential.
3. Freedom of belief and rights to life, personal property, reproduction, and health (both mental and physical) cannot be violated.
4. The privacy and immunity of individual life must be maintained.
5. No one can be convicted of a crime without evidence, or accused and punished for someone else's crime.
6. An advisory system of administration is essential.

All rights are equally important, and an individual's right cannot be sacrificed for society's sake. Islam considers a society to be composed of conscious individuals equipped with free will and having responsibility towards both themselves and others. Islam goes a step further by adding a cosmic dimension. It sees humanity as the "motor" of history, contrary to fatalistic approaches of some of the nineteenth-century Western philosophies of history such as dialectical materialism and historicism.[6] Just as every individual's will and behavior determine the outcome of his or her life in this world and in the Hereafter, a society's progress or decline is determined by the will, worldview, and lifestyle of its inhabitants. The Qur'an (13:11) says: "God will not change the state of a people unless they change themselves (with respect to their beliefs, worldview, and lifestyle)." In other words, each society holds the reins of its fate in its own hands. The Prophetic Tradition emphasizes this idea: "You will be ruled according to how you are."[7]

As Islam holds individuals and societies responsible for their own fate, people must be responsible for governing themselves. The Qur'an addresses society with such phrases as: "O people!"

and "O believers!" The duties entrusted to modern democratic systems are those that Islam refers to society and classifies, in order of importance, as "absolutely necessary, relatively necessary, and commendable to carry out." The sacred text includes the following passages: "Establish, all of you, peace!" (2:208); "Spend in the cause of God and on the needy of the pure and good of what you have earned and of what We bring forth for you from earth!" (2:267); "If some among your women are accused of indecency, you must have four witnesses (to prove it)" (4:15); "God commands you to give over the public trusts to the charge of those having the required qualities and to judge with justice when you judge between people" (4:58); "Observe justice as witnesses respectful for God even if it is against yourselves, your parents and relatives!" (4:135); "If they (your enemies) incline to peace [when you are at war], you also incline to it!" (8:61); "If a corrupt, sinful one brings you news [about others], investigate it so that you should not strike a people without knowing!" (49:6); "If two parties among the believers fight between themselves, reconcile them!" (49:9). To sum up, the Qur'an addresses the whole community and assigns it almost all the duties entrusted to modern democratic systems.

People cooperate with one another by sharing these duties and establishing the essential foundations necessary to perform them. The government is composed of all of these foundations. Thus, Islam recommends a government based on a social contract. People elect the administrators and establish a council to debate common issues. Also, the society as a whole participates in auditing the administration. Especially during the rule of the first four caliphs (632–661), the fundamental principles of government mentioned above—including free election—were fully observed. The political system was transformed into a sultanate after the death of 'Ali, the fourth caliph, due to internal conflicts and to the global conditions at that time. Unlike under the caliphate, power in the sultanate was passed on through the sultan's family. However, even though free elections were no longer held, societies maintained the other principles mentioned.

Islam is an inclusive religion. It is based on the belief in one God as the Creator, Lord, Sustainer, and Administrator of the universe. Islam, [in the sense of submission to God,] is the religion of the whole universe. That is, the entire universe obeys the laws laid down by God, so everything in the universe is "Muslim" and obeys God by submitting to his laws. Even a person who refuses to believe in God or follows another religion has perforce to be a Muslim as far as his or her bodily existence is concerned. His or her entire life, from the embryonic stage to the body's dissolution into dust after death, every tissue of his or her muscles, and every limb of his or her body follows the course prescribed for each by God. Thus, in Islam, God, nature, and humanity are neither remote from each other nor are they alien to each other. It is God Who makes Himself known to humanity through nature and humanity itself, and nature and humanity are two books (of creation) through each word of which God is known. This leads humankind to look upon everything as belonging to the same Lord, to whom it itself belongs, so that it regards nothing in the universe as alien. His love and favors do not remain confined to the people of any particular race, color, or ethnicity. The Prophet summed this up with the command, "O servants of God, be brothers (and sisters)!"

A separate but equally important point is that Islam recognizes all religions previous to it. It accepts all the Prophets and Books sent to different peoples in different epochs of history. Not only does it accept them [in their pristine purity], but also regards belief in them as an essential principle of being Muslim. By doing so, it acknowledges the basic unity of all religions. A Muslim is at the same time a true follower of Abraham, Moses, David, Jesus, and of all other Hebrew prophets, upon them be peace. This belief explains why both Christians and Jews enjoyed their religious rights under the rule of Islamic governments throughout history.

The Islamic social system seeks to form a virtuous society and thereby gain God's approval. It recognizes right, not force, as the foundation of social life. Hostility is unacceptable. Relationships must be based on belief, love, mutual respect, assistance, and understanding instead of conflict and realization of personal interest. Social education encourages people to pursue lofty ideals and to strive for perfection, not just to run after their own desires. Right calls for unity, virtues bring mutual support and solidarity, and belief secures brotherhood and sisterhood. Encouraging the soul to attain perfection brings happiness in both worlds.

As justice and the rule of law are an Islamic constitution's foremost articles, people are to obey the authority so long as the authority does not order sinful acts, so that anarchy and social disorder can be avoided. Just as a Muslim individual is responsible and accountable for his or her happiness and salvation, so too, a Muslim community is responsible for its own felicity and salvation, for: *God does not change the state of a people unless they change themselves* (13:11). People make their own history and are responsible for their own individual and social conditions.

Essentially, the Religion is an extremely important barrier to wars, anarchy and terror in the world. Virtues like love, mercy, compassion and doing good to others have sprouted mostly in the "gardens" of the Religion and their standard was raised by the Religion. In addition, for example, the Holy Qur'an explains that killing a person unjustly is like killing all humanity, and saving one human being's life is like saving the lives of all humanity (5:32). Moreover, it is the goal of the Religion that anarchy and disorder not remain on this earth (2:193). Justice is as important a principle as religious faith.

As M. Fethullah Gülen mentions, the advisory system of administration is essential. Learned and pious people who possess sound judgment and expert knowledge, as well as enjoying the people's confidence, must be located and clarify their opinions based on the dictates of their conscience. This advisory system is so important that God praises the first, exemplary Muslim community as a *community whose affair is by counsel between them* (42:38).

This becomes even more explicit when we realize that this first community was led by the Prophet, who never spoke out of caprice or on his own authority, but only spoke what was revealed to him by God (53:2-3), and that God considers consultation so important that He orders His Messenger to practice it with his Companions (3:159). This order came after the Muslims' reverse at the Battle of Uhud (625) due to some of the Companions' disobedience to the Prophet. Informed of the Makkans' march upon

Madina, the Prophet, upon him be peace and blessings, had taken counsel with his Companions as to how best to resist the enemy. Although he had advised that they should defend themselves from within the boundaries of Madina, when the majority of the Muslims supported the view that it would be better to fight on the open ground outside the city, he had resigned himself to the opinion of the majority.[8] It was after the setback at the Battle of Uhud that God ordered His Messenger to take counsel with his Companions in affairs of public concern.

Freedom of opinion to promote virtue and prevent vice is also essential to Islamic public life. It is more than just a right for Muslims—it is their essential duty. Freedom of conscience and speech is the pivot that ensures the correct functioning of Islamic society and administration.

Another fundamental principle to mention for Muslim collective life is the public treasury, which is viewed as "God's property" and a trust. Everything should be received through lawful sources and spent only on lawful purposes. Administrators have no more control of the public treasury than trustees have over the property of minor orphans in their custody: *If he is rich, let him abstain altogether; if poor, let him consume it in a just and reasonable manner* (4:6). Administrators must account for the public treasury's income and expenditure, and Muslims have the right to demand a full account of these.

CHAPTER 10

The Spread of Islam and Its Main Dynamics

THE SPREAD OF ISLAM AND
ITS MAIN DYNAMICS

T hroughout the tenth century, Islam was the predominant religion of an area covering more than half of the then-known world. Its adherents inhabited three continents: from the Pyrenees and Siberia up to China and New Guinea, and from Morocco to the southern tip of Africa.

One of history's most striking facts is that Islam spread over such a vast area within three centuries. Most striking of all, within fifty years after the *Hijra*,[1] all of North Africa (from Egypt to Morocco) and the Middle East (from Yemen to Caucasia, and from Egypt to the lands beyond Transoxiana) had come under the sway of Islam. During 'Uthman's reign (644–56), Muslim envoys reached the Chinese royal court and were welcomed enthusiastically. According to historians, this important event marks the beginning of Islam's presence in China.

How Islam spread

Peoples of all eras have been ready to embrace Islam for a wide variety of reasons. But perhaps the foremost one, as pointed out by Muhammad Asad, a Jewish convert to Islam, is that:

> Islam appears to me like a perfect work of architecture. All its parts are harmoniously conceived to complement and support each other, nothing lacking, with the result of an absolute balance and solid composure. Everything in the teaching and postulate of Islam is in its proper place.[2]

Most Western writers continue to accuse Islam of spreading by the sword. One major cause of this prejudice is that Islam often spread at the expense of Christianity. For hundreds of years Christians have converted to Islam without much effort or organized missionary activity. Muslims, however, almost never convert to Christianity despite sophisticated means and well-organized missionary activities. This has caused its missionaries and most Orientalists to present Islam as a regressive and vulgar religion of uncivilized peoples.[3] Such negative attitudes also color their accounts of the Prophet. Some unbiased Western writers have admitted this:

> Muslims, according to the principles of their faith, are under an obligation to use force for the purpose of bringing other religions to ruin [probably he means *Jihad*, which is unfortunately misinterpreted and not for the purpose he claims]; yet, in spite of that, they have been tolerating other religions for some centuries past. The Christians have not been given orders to do anything but preach and instruct, yet, despite this, from time immemorial they have been exterminating by fire and sword all those who are not of their religion... We may feel certain that if Western Christians, instead of the Saracens and the Turks, had won the dominion over Asia, there would be today not a trace left of the Greek Church, and that they would never have tolerated Muhammadanism as the 'infidels' have tolerated Christianity there. We (Christians) enjoy the fine advantage of being far better versed than others in the art of killing, bombarding and exterminating the Human Race.[4]

WHY DID ISLAM SPREAD SO RAPIDLY?

Islam's rapid expansion, unequalled by any other religion, was due to its religious content and values, as many unbiased Western intellectuals state:

> Many have sought to answer the questions of why the triumph of Islam was so speedy and complete? Why have so many millions embraced the religion of Islam and scarcely a hundred ever recanted?.. Some have attempted to explain the first overwhelming success of Islam by the argument of the Sword. They forget

Carlyle's laconic reply. First, get your sword. You must win men's hearts before you can induce them to imperil their lives for you; and the first conquerors of Islam must have been made Muslims before they were made fighters on the Path of God. Others allege the low morality of the religion and the sensual paradise it promises as a sufficient cause for the zeal of its followers: but even were these admitted to the full, no religion has ever gained a lasting hold upon the souls of men by the force of its sensual permissions and fleshy promises...

In all these explanations the religion itself is left out of the question. Decidedly, Islam itself was the main cause for its triumph. Islam not only was at once accepted (by many peoples and races) by Arabia, Syria, Persia, Egypt, Northern Africa and Spain, at its first outburst; but, with the exception of Spain, it has never lost its vantage ground; it has been spreading ever since it came into being. Admitting the mixed causes that contributed to the rapidity of the first swift spread of Islam, they do not account for the duration of Islam. There must be something in the religion itself to explain its persistence and spread, and to account for its present hold over so large of a proportion of the dwellers on the earth... Islam has stirred an enthusiasm that has never been surpassed. Islam has had its martyrs, its recluses, who have renounced all that life offered and have accepted death with a smile for the sake of the faith that was in them.[5]

A. J. Arberry holds the same view:

The rapidity of the spread of Islam is a crucial fact of history... The sublime rhetoric of the Qur'an, that inimitable symphony, the very sounds of which move men to tears and ecstasy. (M. Pickthall, *The Meaning of the Glorious Qur'an*, p.vii) ...

This, and the urgency of the simple message carried, holds the key to the mystery of one of the greatest cataclysms in the history of religion. When all military, political and economic factors have been exhausted, the religious impulse must still be recognized as the most vital and enduring."[6]

Brockelman, usually very unsympathetic and partial, also recognizes Islam's religious values as the main factor for its spread.[7] Rosenthal writes: "The more important factor for the spread of Islam is the religious law of Islam which was designed to cover all manifestations of life."[8]

Along with many other reasons, Islam spread because of its followers' exemplary lifestyle and unceasing efforts to transmit its message throughout the world. These lie at the root of Islam's conquest of hearts. Islamic universalism is closely associated with the principle of *amr bi al-ma'ruf* (promoting and trying to spread the good), for this is how Muslims are to spread Islam. This principle seeks to convey whatever good to everyone without resorting to force, and to establish a model community that displays Islam to the world: *Thus We have made of you a Community justly balanced, that you might be witnesses for the peoples, and the Messenger has been a witness for you* (2:143).

Muslims, both as individuals and as a community, therefore, have certain goals to achieve: conveying the truth to everyone, striving to prevent oppression and tyranny, and establishing justice. To do this, they must live an exemplary life. Thus Islam's moral and ethical values usually have played an important part in its spread.

One nineteenth-century European writer recorded his impressions on how Islamic ethics influenced African tribes as follows:

> As to the effects of Islam when first embraced by a(n African) tribe, can there, when viewed as a whole, be any reasonable doubt? Polytheism disappears almost instantaneously; sorcery, with its attendant evils, gradually dies away; human sacrifice becomes a thing of the past. The general moral elevation is most marked; the natives begin for the first time in their history to dress, and that neatly. Squalid filth is replaced by some approach to personal cleanliness; hospitality becomes a religious duty; drunkenness, instead of the rule, becomes a comparatively rare exception... chastity is looked upon as one of the highest, and becomes, in fact, one of the commoner virtues. It is idleness that henceforward degrades, and industry that elevates, instead of the reverse. Offences are henceforward measured by a written code instead of the arbitrary caprice of a chieftain—a step, as everyone will admit, of vast importance in the progress of a tribe. The Mosque gives an idea of archi-

tecture at all events higher than any (tribe) has yet had. A thirst for literature is created and that for works of science and philosophy as well as for commentaries on the Qur'an.[9]

Islam also spread rapidly because of its tolerance. Toynbee praises the Muslims' tolerance toward the Peoples of the Book after comparing it with the Christians' attitude toward Muslims in their lands.[10] Link attributes Islam's spread to its credible principles and tolerance, persuasion, and other attractions.[11] Makarios, a seventeenth-century Orthodox Patriarch of Antioch, compared the Poles' harsh treatment of the Russian Orthodox to the Ottomans' tolerant attitude toward Orthodox Christians and prayed for the sultans.[12/13]

This is not the only example of non-Muslims' preference for Muslim rule over that of their own coreligionists. Byzantium's Orthodox Christian people openly expressed their preference for the Ottoman rule in Istanbul to their European coreligionists. Elisee Reclus, a nineteenth-century French traveller, wrote that the Muslim Turks allowed all non-Muslims to observe their religious duties and rituals, and that the sultan's Christian subjects were freer to live their own lives than those Christians whose lands were ruled by a member of a rival Christian sect.[14] Popescu Ciocanel pays tribute to the Muslim Turks by stating that the Romanians were lucky to have Turkish, instead of Russian and Austrian, rulers. Otherwise, he points out, "no trace of the Romanian nation would have remained."[15]

Here we should remember that some have criticized Islam because it recognizes war and even commands it in certain circumstances. The criticism is wholly unjust insofar as, though not in so many words, it seems to be arguing that Islam introduced war into human history. The criticism is particularly inappropriate when voiced by adherents of Christianity: for although there is not a specific commandment in the Gospels to permit or prohibit war—the Gospels are silent and present no rules for instigating war nor for its proper conduct and containment—western history is replete with examples of extremely bloody wars, wide in scope and ruthless in their intensity, which were conducted in the name of Christianity. Indeed, the religion of Christianity was often employed by Western powers in previous centuries to provide a cover and means for the colonization of two thirds of the world's peoples and resources. Furthermore, Graham Fuller and Ian O. Lesser record that the number of deaths of Muslims caused by Westerners in the twentieth century alone is much greater than the number of Christian deaths caused by Muslims throughout history.[16] The criticism is also entirely inappropriate when voiced by adherents of Judaism, for Jewish history, too, is largely a chronicle of religiously motivated conflicts and wars, and the Old Testament is explicit in sanctioning war. Especially the chapters Numbers 21 and 31, and Deuteronomy 2, 3, 20, and Joshua 8, and 10–11 are enough to see Judaism's position on war. As for modern cilivization, the driving forces behind the "modern, secularized world," which allow and even promote war in the service of individual rulers, nations, and even commercial interests—rather than God—have caused more bloodshed and destruction in the past one hundred years than all the wars throughout the whole of human history before it.

Part of the very meaning of the word *Islam* is peace; therefore, Islam prefers peace, desires it and seeks to establish it throughout the world. However, war is a reality of human history, a manifestation in the collective life of humankind resulting from the inner condition of those who have not been able to attain excellence in mind, heart (spirit) and conduct. Or, it is a manifestation of the war between the spirit and the carnal soul, or between Satan and the perfectibility of human nature. What is important and necessary, therefore, rather than denying the reality of war in a vainly idealistic manner, is to establish rules to make war just, in respect to both its motives and purposes, as well as its means and conduct, so that the harm of it is contained, and the good in it may benefit the people in general. War may then be, while not something in itself desirable, rather something capable of serving (versus perverting) a desirable end—like disciplining and training the body to improve its strength or skill, or doing a necessary operation to save someone's health, or administering upon a criminal the due punishment for the sake of deterrence and the health of the moral environment. Precisely such disciplining of the means and ends of war is what Islam has done.

The relevant verses of the Qur'an do not order war, but allow it on condition that it be in God's cause and for defensive purposes. It also enjoins that the limits set by God must not be exceeded. Those limits are related to both the intention and the practice. For example, Islam does not permit war for motives such as conquest or plunder, or to quench a lust for revenge, or for the sake of some material advantage, or to satisfy racist persuasions. Islam does not seek to compel anyone to change his or her faith. On the contrary, it seeks an environment where all are free to accept faith freely. Islam has also set limitations on the conduct of relations before, during, and after conflict. The Muslims' attitude towards war and the people they conquered is quite clear in the instructions given by the Caliphs:

> Always keep fear of God in your mind; remember that you cannot afford to do anything without His grace. Do not forget that Islam is a mission of peace and love. Keep the Holy Prophet (peace be upon him) before you as a model of bravery and piety. Do not destroy fruit trees or fertile fields in your paths. Be just, and spare the feelings of the vanquished. Respect all religious persons who live in hermitages or convents and spare their edifices. Do not kill civilians. Do not outrage the chastity of women and the honor of the conquered. Do not harm old people and children. Do not accept any gifts from the civilian population of any place. Do not billet your soldiers or officers in the houses of civilians. Do not forget to perform your daily prayers. Fear God. Remember that death will inevitably come to everyone of you at some time or other, even if you are thousands of miles away from a battlefield; therefore be always ready to face death.[17]

All followers of other religions have lived peacefully under the rule of Islam. The Jews especially lived their most blissful years of exile in the Ottoman State. The Ottoman expansion marked a very substantial change for the Jews of the Middle East and Europe. In complete contrast to their situation under the Byzantines, Jews entering the Ottoman dominions were allowed to practice whatever profession they wished, to engage in trade and commerce without restriction and to possess landed property and buildings in town and country.[18] After Sultan Mehmed II conquered Istanbul in 1453, he allowed Jews to settle in Istanbul and carry out their commerce. From the start, Sultan Mehmed II encouraged the emigration of Jews from Europe even more than the Jews already living in the expanding Ottoman State itself. Just as the Jews of England, France, Germany, Spain, and even Poland and Lithuania were being subjected to increasing persecution, blood libels, massacres, and deportations, the Turkish rulers of the expanding Ottoman state actively encouraged them to come and live under conditions of tolerance and freedom. Mehmed II himself is said to have issued a proclamation to all Jews:

> Who among you of all my people that is with me, may his God be with him, let him ascend to Istanbul, the site of my imperial throne. Let him dwell in the best of the land, each beneath his vine and beneath his fig tree, with silver and with gold, with wealth and with cattle. Let him dwell in the land, trade in it, and take possession of it.

As a result of these efforts, during the three decades following the Ottoman conquest, according to a Turkish register, Istanbul's population increased to 16,326 households including 1,647 Jewish households. By the mid-sixteenth century, according to a similar census in 1535, 8,070 Jewish households were listed in the capital city. The city's Jews numbered some 40,000—a tenth of the population. Salonica, which had no Jewish population represented in the census of 1478, had 2,645 Jewish households by 1535.[19]

Similar increases were to be found in many Ottoman centres in the Balkans and Asia Minor because the Turks trusted them. They preceded the Greeks and Armenians as bankers, physicians and interpreters, and eventually gathered most of the Empire's trade into their hands.[20]

The following quotes provide clear evidence that Jews of that time were happy with the Ottoman Empire as well. Rabbi Isaac Tzarfati invited the Jews who were suffering in Germany to the Turkish state:

> ...Listen my brethren, to the counsel I will give you. I, too, was born in Germany and studied Torah with the German rabbis. I was driven out of my native country and came into the Turkish land, which is blessed by God and filled with all good things. Here I found rest and happiness. Turkey can also become for you the land of peace... If you who live in Germany knew even a tenth of what God has blessed us with in this land, you would not consider any difficulties, you would set out to come to us... Here in the land of the Turks we have nothing to complain of. We possess great fortunes; much gold and silver are in our hands. We are not oppressed with heavy taxes, and our commerce is free and unhindered. Rich are the fruits of the earth. Everything is cheap, and every one of us lives in peace and freedom. Here the Jew is not compelled to wear a yellow hat as a badge of shame, as is the case in Germany... Arise my brethren, give up your lands, collect your forces, and come to us. Here you will be free of your enemies, here you will find rest... .[21]

The most significant example of tolerance the Ottomans displayed for the minorities, especially the Jews, is that they opened their land to those who were expelled from Portugal and Spain.[22]

An historical episode, recorded by the famous Muslim historian Baladhuri in his *Futuh al-Buldan*, tells how pleased the indigenous peoples were with their Muslim conquerors and is of great significance:

> When Heraclius, Emperor of the Eastern Roman Empire (610–41), massed his troops against the Muslims, and the

Muslims heard that they were coming to meet them, they refunded the tribute they had taken from the inhabitants of Hims, saying: "We are too busy to support and protect you. Take care of yourselves." But the people of Hims replied: "We like your rule and justice far better than our former state of oppression and tyranny. We shall indeed, with your help, repulse Heraclius' army from the city." The Jews rose and said: "We swear by the Torah, no governor of Heraclius shall enter Hims unless we are first vanquished and exhausted." Saying this, they closed and guarded the city gates. The Christians and Jews of cities that had capitulated did the same. When, by God's help, Heraclius' army was defeated and the Muslims won, they opened the gates of their cities, went out with singers and musicians, and paid the tribute.[23]

CHAPTER 11

Islam: From Past to Future

ISLAM: FROM PAST TO FUTURE

T he most striking feature of Islam and its history is that Islam completely changes those who accept it, no matter how ignorant, rude, and ill-mannered they were before, into embodiments of almost all virtues and human values. The intellectual, religious, cultural, and socio-economic decadence of the pre-Islamic nomadic Arabs is known. Islam alone elevated them to be humanity's guides and teachers for centuries, and models for every age. The manner displayed by the Muslim envoy and his speech to the Sassanid commander-in-chief at the Battle of Qadisiya (636) shows how Islam changed "stones" into "gold" or "diamonds," a point that by itself proves Islam's Divine origin.

HOW ISLAM TRANSFORMS PEOPLE

Rabi' Ibn 'Amir was brought up in pre-Islamic Arabia's dark polytheistic climate, where life was considered to consist of killing and plundering to eat. However, his embrace of Islam transformed him into one of the "immortal" guides of humanity. He entered the Sassanid commander's richly ornamented tent, dressed in a loose, white garment, and holding a spear. Not bowing before the commander, he began to roll up the carpet and then sat cross-legged on the ground. He did this to show Islam's dignity and how Muslims renounce their lives for the sake of their sublime cause and prefer the Hereafter to the worldly life.

When the bewildered commander asked about their cause, he replied:

> Our cause is to raise humanity from the dark pits of worldly life to the high, boundless realm of the spirit; from the humili-

ation of worshipping false and usually human-made divinities to the honor and dignity of worshipping the One God, the universe's sole Creator and Sustainer; and to free humanity from the oppression and depressions brought about by false religions into the luminous and peaceful climate of Islam.[1]

This is the testimony of one who experienced Islam's beauties and, as will be further elaborated in the following pages, how high Islam elevates its adherents culturally, intellectually, and spiritually.

Islam alone is responsible for major human developments, among them the following:

- Turning human thought away from superstition, love for the unnatural and inexplicable, and monasticism and towards a rational approach, a love for reality, and a pious and balanced worldly life.

- Inspiring the urge for rational and scientific research and proofs to verify the truth of established convictions.

- Opening the eyes of those accustomed to identifying God with natural phenomena, and saving people from such false notions of Deity as anthropomorphism, Incarnation, Union, and personification.

- Leading people away from the path of baseless speculation and towards that of a rational understanding and sound reasoning based on observation, experimentation, and research.

- Introducing nature or the universe, humanity, and the Divine Scripture as counterparts of one another and three universal books making known the Creator, the Lord of the Worlds, and thus leaving no room for any conflict or dichotomy between mind and heart, knowing and believing, and science and religion.

- Defining the limits and functions of sense-perception, reason, intuition, and spiritual experience.

- Engendering a rapprochement between spiritual and material values.

- Harmonizing faith with knowledge and action.

- Replacing idolatry, the worship of human beings, and all kinds of polytheism with a firm faith in God's absolute Unity.

- Showing the path of spiritual evolution, moral emancipation, and salvation through active participation in this world's daily affairs.

- Bringing home to all people their true worth and position. Those who acknowledged only a "God-incarnate" or a "child of God" as their moral preceptor or spiritual guide were told that a human being like themselves, one who has no pretensions to Godhead, can become God's vicegerent on the earth. Those who proclaimed and worshipped powerful personages realized that their false deities were people just like themselves.

- Emphasizing that no person could claim holiness, authority, or overlordship as a birthright, and that no one was born with the stigma of untouchability, slavery, or serfdom.

- Inspiring the thoughts of humanity's unity, human equality, and real freedom. Many principles of good behavior, culture and civilization, purity of thought and deed owe their origin to Islam. For example, Islam's social laws have infiltrated deep into human social life, its economic principles have ushered in many movements and continue to do so, its laws of governance continue to exert their influence, and its fundamental principles of law and justice continue to form a perpetual source of guidance for humanity.

- Establishing a practical framework for all aspects of international relations and regulating the laws of war and peace. This framework, the first of its kind in history, established an ethical code of war and foreign relations based on the ground of common humanity. Islam, as Arthur Leonard says, has left such an indelible mark on the pages of human history that it can never be effaced ... that only when the world grows will it be acknowledged in full.[2]

- Founding one of the most brilliant civilizations in history. This should come as no surprise, since the first revealed verse of the

Qur'an was: *Read: In the Name of your Lord Who creates* (96:1).
But why does the Qur'an order *read* when the local people have
almost nothing to read? Because they—and humanity—are to
"read" the universe itself as the Book of Creation, of which the
Qur'an is the counterpart in letters or words. We are to observe the universe and perceive its meaning and content so that
we can gain a deeper knowledge of the beauty and splendor
of the Creator's system and the infinitude of His Might. Thus
we must penetrate the universe's manifold meanings, discover
the Divine laws of nature, and establish a world in which science and faith complement each other so that humanity can attain true bliss in both worlds. Otherwise, as Bertrand Russell
says, "unless man increases in wisdom (and faith) as much as in
knowledge, increase of knowledge will be increase of sorrow,"[3]
and "Science teaches man to fly in the air like birds, and to
swim in the water like fishes, but man, without faith, cannot
know how to live on the earth."[4]

THE QUR'AN'S PURPOSES

The Qur'an contains everything that the Sublime Creator deems
necessary for us to make material and spiritual progress. Its most
important aims are to make God known to us, open the way to
faith and worship and establish in our minds and hearts the office
of Prophethood and the reality of the Hereafter, and organize our
individual and social life in such a way that we can realize perfect
happiness in both worlds. Thus it mentions things in proportion
to their significance and uses them to achieve these aims. Such
matters as the pillars of faith, which are the fundamentals of Islam,
as well as the foundations of human life and essentials of worship,
are explained elaborately, while other things are only hinted at
briefly. The meaning of a verse may be compared to a rosebud: It
is hidden by successive layers of petals, and a new meaning is perceived as each petal unfolds.

For example, the Qur'an hints at technological advances and marks their final development by mentioning the Prophets' miracles. It encourages us to fly by alluding implicitly to spaceships and aircrafts: *And to Solomon the wind; its morning course was a month's journey, and its evening course was a month's journey* (34:12). It invites us to search for cures to all illnesses: *(Jesus said:) I also heal the blind and the leper, and bring to life the dead, by the leave of God* (3:49), and hints that one day we will reach this goal and thus come to imagine that somehow we are immune to death. The verse: *Said he who possessed knowledge of the Book: "I will bring it (the Queen of Yemen's throne) to you (Solomon in Jerusalem) before your glance returns to you,"* (27:40) foretells that one day images or even actual things will be transmitted in a moment through knowledge of the Divine Book of the Universe, just as one with knowledge of the Book of Divine Revalation brings things from a great distance in the twinkling of an eye.

The Qur'an also symbolically informs us that a killer can be identified by some cells taken from the victim's corpse. Such a case took place during the time of Prophet Moses, upon him be peace. As recounted in 2:71–73, God told the Children of Israel to slaughter a cow and then place part of it on the corpse of a man who had been killed. When they did so, the corpse revealed the killer. These are just some of the examples of Qur'anic allusions to future scientific and technological advances.

The Qur'an, being the book for every age and person, has great depths of meaning. It is an infinite ocean into which all people with knowledge and ability can dive deeply and, according to their capacity, find its pearls and coral. The passage of time only rejuvenates its scientific wisdom. Every generation discovers its wisdom anew, and its secrets continue to be revealed over time.

In: *Then He turned to Heaven when it was smoke, and said to it and to the earth: "Come willingly or unwillingly." They said: "We come willingly"* (40:11), the Qur'an indicates that there is some difficulty in such cooperation. We know that the atmosphere's molecules and atoms try to escape into space, while the earth tries to attract and capture them. But for there to be an atmosphere, the motions leading to the molecules' escape must be counterbalanced by the the earth's gravitational attraction.

This is an almost impossible condition to fulfill. From the standpoint of geophysics, these conditions require that three important balances be preserved: atmospheric temperature, the earth's proportionate gravitational attraction, and the non-violation of this balance by various radiant energies arriving from space. The Qur'an expresses these facts in the verse mentioned above. That the almost impossible conditions are fulfilled only by God's power is indicated in: *They said: "We come willingly."*

Scientists interpret: *No, I swear by the positions of stars; and if you but knew, that is indeed a mighty oath* (56:75–76) as alluding to star locations, black holes, and white holes (quasars).[5] The verse: *Glory be to Him, Who created in pairs all things that the earth produces, as well as their own selves, and many other things of which they know nothing* (36:36), after beginning by proclaiming that God has no likeness or equal, proceeds to say that all things were created in pairs. This type of existence indicates opposition simultaneously with similarity. The scientific definition of creation in pairs implies "similar opposites." The Qur'an gives three examples:

- Pairs produced by the earth (positron–electron, antiproton–proton, antineutron–neutron), those with different physical and chemical characteristics (metals and nonmetals); biologically opposed pairs (male and female plants and animals), and physically opposed pairs.
- Pairs of their selves (man and woman; such personality traits as cruel–compassionate, generous–mean; and traits that are similar but subject to opposed value judgments, such as hypocrisy–consideration).
- Pairs about which we do not know. The discovery of the positron and "parity" (creation in pairs), mentioned by the Qur'an

fourteen centuries ago, may be regarded as a turning point in contemporary physics.

The planets' spherical shape and rotations are indicated in: *He is the Lord of the heavens and the earth, and all that lies between them; He is the Lord of the easts* (37:15), for the concept of the "easts" introduces infinite dimensions and differs for each location on the earth. A point on the earth is in the east with respect to its western regions. Therefore the concept of east differs at every point on the earth, and these form an ensemble of easts. Besides, there are 180 points of sunrise, which means that the sun rises at one place for only two days in the year and thus there are 180 easts. So this verse also indicates meridians, infinite dimensions, space's relativity, the planets' spherical shape, and the earth's rotation.

There are springs of sweet water at several locations in different seas where the sweet water remains separate from the salty water. Seydi Ali Reis, a Turkish admiral of the sixteenth century, mentions in his work, *Mir'at al-Mamalik*, one such place in the Persian Gulf. He writes that he found springs of sweet water under the salty water of the sea, and drew drinking water from them for his fellow sailors.[6] French scientist Jacques Cousteau discovered that the Mediterranean Sea and the Atlantic Ocean have different chemical and biological constitutions. After conducting undersea investigations at the Straits of Gibraltar to explain this phenomenon, he concluded that "unexpected fresh water springs issue from the southern and northern coasts of Gibraltar. These water spouts gush forth towards each other at an angle of forty-five degrees, forming a reciprocal dam like the teeth of a comb. Due to this fact, the Mediterranean and the Atlantic Ocean cannot intermingle." Afterwards, when shown the verse: *He has let forth the two seas, that meet together. Between them a barrier, they do not overpass* (55:19–20), Cousteau was amazed.

This verse further draws our attention to the plankton composition of the seas, and to the flora and fish distributions that change with variations in temperature.[7] Many other Qur'anic verses shed light upon scientific facts, and every person is invited to study them: *We made the Qur'an easy for reflection and study. Will anybody study and reflect?* (54:17).

THE TWO BOOKS

Obeying the Qur'an's injunctions, Muslims studied both the Book of Divine Revelation (the Qur'an) and the Book of Creation (the universe), and founded a magnificent civilization. Scholars from all over Europe and elsewhere benefited from the great Muslim centers of higher learning at Damascus, Bukhara, Baghdad, Cairo, Fez, Qairawan, Zaytuna, Cordoba, Sicily, Isfahan, and Delhi. Historians liken this Muslim golden age, in full flower when Europe was enduring its dark Middle Ages, to a beehive. Roads were full of students, scientists, and scholars travelling from one center of learning to another. Such "Renaissance" men and women as Jabir Ibn Hayyan, Ibn Ishaq al-Kindi, Muhammad Ibn Musa al-Khwarizmi, al-Farabi, Ibn Sina, Abu al-Hasan al-Mas'udi, Ibn al-Haytham, al-Biruni, al-Ghazzali, Nasirud-din at-Tusi, and Abu Bakr ar-Razi were shining like stars in the high sky of science.

In his monumental *Introduction to the History of Science*, George Sarton divided time into chronological chapters and named each chapter after that period's most eminent scientist. From the mid-eighth century to the mid-eleventh century, each of the seven fifty-year periods carries the name of a Muslim scientist: "The Time of al-Khwarizmi," "The Time of al-Biruni," and so on. Within these chapters we have the names of about a hundred important Islamic scientists and their main works.

John Davenport, a leading scientist observed:

> It must be owned that all the knowledge whether of Physics, Astronomy, Philosophy or Mathematics, which flourished in Europe from the tenth century was originally derived from the Arabian schools, and the Spanish Saracen may be looked upon as the father of European philosophy.[8]

Bertrand Russell, the famous British philosopher writes:

> The supremacy of the East was not only military. Science, philos-
> ophy, poetry, and the arts, all flourished... in the Muhammadan
> world at a time when Europe was sunk in barbarism. Europeans,
> with unpardonable insularity, call this period "The Dark Ages":
> but it was only in Europe that it was dark—indeed only in
> Christian Europe, for Spain, which was Mohammedan, had a
> brilliant culture.[9]

Robert Briffault, the renowned historian, acknowledges in his
The Making of Humanity:

> It is highly probable that but for the Arabs, modern European
> civilization would have never assumed that character which has
> enabled it to transcend all previous phases of evolution. For
> although there is not a single aspect of human growth in which
> the decisive influence of Islamic culture is not traceable,
> nowhere is it so clear and momentous as in the genesis of that
> power which constitutes the paramount distinctive force of the
> modern world and the supreme course of its victory—natural
> sciences and the scientific spirit... What we call science arose in
> Europe as a result of a new spirit of inquiry, of new methods
> of investigation, of the method of experiment, observation,
> measurement, of the development of Mathematics in a form
> unknown to the Greeks. That spirit and those methods were
> introduced into the European world by the Arabs.[10]

For the first eight hundred years of its existence, the realm of Islam was the most civilized and progressive portion of the world.
Studded with splendid cities, gracious mosques and quiet universi-
ties, the Muslim East offered a striking contrast to the Christian
West, which was sunk in the night of the Dark Ages. It retained its
vigor and remained ahead of Christian Europe for many centuries.[11]

During the tenth century, Muslim Cordoba was Europe's
most civilized city, the wonder and admiration of the time. Travelers from the north heard with something like fear of the city that
contained nine hundred public baths and seventy libraries with
hundreds of thousands of volumes. Whenever the rulers of Leon

and Navarre needed surgeons, architects, dressmakers, or musicians, they applied to Cordoba.[12] The Muslims' literary influence was so vast that, for example, the Bible and liturgy had to be translated into Arabic for the Christian community's use. The account given by Alvaro, a Christian zealot and writer, shows vividly how even non-Muslim Spaniards were attracted to Muslim literature:

> My fellow Christians delight in the poems and romances of the Arabs. They study the works of Muhammadan theologians and philosophers, not in order to refute them, but to acquire a correct and elegant Arabic style. Where today can a layman be found who reads the Latin commentaries on Holy Scriptures? Who is there that studies the Gospels, the Prophets, the Apostles? Alas, the young Christians who are most conspicuous for their talents have no knowledge of any literature or language save the Arabic; they read and study with avidity Arabian books; they amass whole libraries of them at a vast cost, and they everywhere sing the praises of the Arabian world..."[13]

If the purpose of education and civilization is to engender a sense of pride, dignity, and honor in individuals so that they improve their state and consequently that of society, Islamic education and civilization have done this. History records many instances when Islam realized this goal in far-flung lands. For example, Isaac Taylor delivered a speech at the Church Congress of England about Islam's effects and influence on people, at which he said:

> When Muhammadanism is embraced, paganism, fetishism, infanticide and witchcraft disappear. Filth is replaced by cleanliness and the new convert acquires personal dignity and self-respect. Immodest dances and promiscuous intercourse of the sexes cease; female chastity is rewarded as a virtue; industry replaces idleness; license gives place to law; order and sobriety prevail; blood feuds, cruelty to animals and slaves are eradicated... Islam swept away corruption and superstitions. Islam was a revolt against empty polemics... It gave hope to the slave, brotherhood to mankind, and recognition to the fundamental facts of human nature. The virtues which Islam inculcates are temperance, cleanliness, chastity, justice, fortitude, courage, benevo-

lence, hospitality, veracity and resignation... Islam preaches a practical brotherhood, the social equality of all Muslims. Slavery is not part of the creed of Islam. Polygamy is a more difficult question. Moses did not prohibit it. It was practiced by David and it is not directly forbidden in the New Testament. Muhammad limited the unbounded license of polygamy. It is the exception rather than the rule... In resignation to God's Will, temperance, chastity, veracity and in brotherhood of believers they (the Muslims) set us a pattern which we should do well to follow. Islam has abolished drunkenness, gambling and prostitution, the three curses of the Christian lands. Islam has done more for civilization than Christianity. The conquest of one third of the earth to his (Muhammad's) creed was a miracle.[14]

Although Islam ruled two thirds of the old civilized world for at least eleven centuries, the Muslims' laziness and negligence of what was going on around them caused their civilization to decline. However, Islam itself did not—and cannot—decline. Military victories and a superiority complex induced Muslims to rest on their laurels and neglect further scientific research. They abandoned themselves to living their own lives and reciting the Qur'an without studying its deeper meanings. Meanwhile, Europe was making great advances in science, which it had borrowed from Islamic civilization.

However, Islam, and only Islam is always alive and ever ready to satisfy humanity's perennial needs. It has been available to humanity for 1,400 years, and the luminous world of the future can be founded upon the firm foundation of its ethics and spirituality, as well as its socio-economic and administrative structures.

NOTES

_____

CHAPTER 1: ISLAM AS THE UNIVERSAL RELIGION
AND THE RELIGION OF PERFECT HARMONY

1   Said Nursi, *The Letters* (trans.), The Light, New Jersey 2007, p. 239. Said
    Nursi (1877–1960): One of the greatest contemporary Muslim scholars, re-
    nowned for his endeavors to prove the essentials of the Islamic faith and estab-
    lish them in minds and hearts.

2   Imam al-Malik, *al-Muwatta,* Book 47, Number 47.1.8.

3   Erich Fromm, *Escape from Freedom* ("Hürriyetten Kaçış" Trans. by Ayda Yörü-
    kan), Tur Yayınları, Istanbul, 1982.

4   Ibn Sina, Abu 'Ali (Avicenna) (980–1037): One of the foremost philosophers,
    mathematicians, and physicians of the golden age of Islamic tradition. In the
    West, he is also known as the "Prince of Physicians" for his famous medical text
    al-Qanun "The Canon." In Latin translations, his works influenced many Chris-
    tian philosophers, most notably Thomas Aquinas. Nasiruddin at-Tusi (1201–
    74): An outstanding Persian philosopher, scientist, and mathematician. In the
    East, al-Tusi is an example *par excellence* of the *hakim* (wise man). Jabir ibn al-
    Hayyan (721–815): Founder of algebra, chemist, and alchemist known as the
    "father of Arab chemistry."

5   Ibn Jarir at-Tabari (839–923): Muslim scholar, author of huge compendiums of
    early Islamic history and Qur'anic exegesis, who made a distinct contribution to
    the consolidation of Sunni thought during the ninth century. He condensed the
    vast wealth of exegetical and historical erudition of past generations of Muslim
    scholars and contributed to the development of Qur'anic and historical sciences.

CHAPTER 2: GOD'S EXISTENCE AND ONENESS

1   al-Bayhaqi, *Shu'ab al-Iman*, 1: 136.

2   at-Tirmidhi, *Sunan*, "Da'awat," 87 (3502).

3   Davenport, *An Apology for Mohamad and Quran*, London, 1869.

4   'Ali ibn Abi Talib (600–61) Son-in-law of Prophet Muhammad, fourth caliph
    (ruled: 656–61), one of the most outstanding figures of early Islam, and con-
    sidered to be a model of virtue, courage, and wisdom.

5   Sayyid Sharif ar-Radiyy, *Nahj al-Balagha, the Sermons, Letters, and Wise Sayings
    of Imam 'Ali*, [trans: Jafar Husayn], Qum, "1st Sermon," 120.

6   ad-Daylami, *al-Firdaws*, 2:376.

7   al-Bukhari, *Jami' as-Sahih*, Adab, 57, 58; Muslim, *Jami' as-Sahih*, Birr, 28–34.

8   C. E. M. Joad, *The Present and Future of Religion*, quoted in al-Mawdudi, *ibid.*, 101.

9   Phillip K. Hitti, *History of the Arabs*, 6th ed., New York, St. Martin's Press, 1956, p. 129, quoted in al-Mawdudi, *ibid.*, 101.

10 Vaglieri, Laura Veccia, *Apologia dell Islamismo*, (trans. by Aldo Caselli), *An Interpretation of Islam*. Beirut, 1957, pp. 30–33, quoted in Ulfat Aziz'us-Samad, *Islam and Christianity*, Tehran, 1997, p. 57.

CHAPTER 3: THE INVISIBLE REALM OF EXISTENCE

1   Nursi, *The Words* (trans.), The Light, New Jersey 2005, pp. 525–526.

2   Tunnicliffe, *Discover*, October, 1993.

3   Muslim, "Zuhd" 60.

4   The information given here about angels is summarized mainly from Said Nursi, *The Words* (trans.), "The Twenty-ninth Word," and M. Fethullah Gülen, *The Essentials of the Islamic Faith* (trans.,) and is based on the Qur'anic verses 2:30, 34; 7:206; 13:11; 15: 8; 16:28, 32; 21:18-20, 26-27; 34:40-42; 35:1; 36:28-29; 37:1-3, 6-10, 164-166; 40:7-9; 44:5-6; 47:27; 50:17-18; 51:1-4; 53:26; 66:6; 70:4; 74:30-31; 77:1-5; 79:1-5; 80:11-16; 81:23; 82:10-12; 86: 4, and the hadiths: al-Bukhari, "Qadar" 1, "Bad'u'l-Khalq" 6, "Anbiya" 1, "Da'awat" 66, "Zakah" 28; Muslim, "Masajid" 119 (600), "Zakah" 57 (1010), "Qadar" 1, 4 (2138, 2643), "Fitan" 119, (2942), "Dhikr" 25 (2689), 86, 88 (2732, 2783); at-Tirmidhi, "Qadar" 4, (2138), "Janaiz" 2, 24 (969, 1003), "Fitan" 66 (2254), "Da'awat" 140 (3595); Abu Davud, "'Aqdiya" 3 (3578), "Salat" 121 (763), 364 (1534), "Janaiz" 2 (969), "Malahim" 15 (4325).

5   Muslim, "Iman" 1 (8); at-Tirmidhi, "Iman" 4 (2613); Abu Dawud, "Sunna" 17.

6   Muslim, "Salah" 30 (903), "Salaam" 139 (1485); at-Tirmidhi, "Tahara" 14 (18), "Ahkam" 2 (1485); Abu Dawud, "Tahara" 20 (39), "Adab" 174 (5260).

7   Abu Dawud, "Tahara" 16 (29); an-Nasai, "Tahara" 30 (1, 33, 34).

8   al-Bukhari, "Ahkam" 2 (1485); Ibn Maja, "Siyam" 65.

9   This section is mainly based on M. Fethullah Gülen, *The Essentials of the Islamic Faith* (trans.), The Light, New Jersey 2005, pp. 69–74.

10 This section is mainly based on M. Fethullah Gülen, ibid, pp. 74–80; and Said Nursi, *The Letters* (trans), The Light, New Jersey 2007, pp. 70–72.

11 al-Bukhari, "Tibb" 36; Muslim, "Salaam" 58 (2188).

12 al-Bukhari, "Tibb" 39, "Da'awat" 12; Muslim, "Salaam" 43.

13 al-Bukhari, "Tibb" 39; Muslim, "Salaam" 50.

14 Abu Dawud, "Adab" 101; Ibn Maja, "Du'a" 14.

15 al-Bukhari, "Anbiya" 10; at-Tirmidhi, "Tibb" 18.

16 M. Fethullah Gülen, ibid, 194.

CHAPTER 4: DIVINE DESTINY AND DECREE AND HUMAN FREE WILL

1   This section is mainly based on M. Fethullah Gülen, *The Essentials of the Islamic Faith* (trans.), The Light, NJ, 2005, pp. 41–49.

2   al-Bukhari, "Qadar" 1; Muslim, "Qadar" 3 (2152).

3   Muslim, "Qadar" 34 (2664); at-Tirmidhi, "Qadar" 15 (2152).

CHAPTER 5: THE RESURRECTION AND THE AFTERLIFE

1   For deeper and detailed knowledge concerning Destiny and human free will, refer to Said Nursi, *The Words* (trans.), "The Twenty-Sixth and The Thirtieth Words," and M. Fethullah Gülen, *The Essentials of the Islamic Faith* (trans.), chapter 3.

2   Summarized from Said Nursi, *The Words*, "Twenty-Ninth Word."

3   Nursi, *The Words*, "Tenth Word" and the "Twelfth Word"; M. Fethullah Gülen, *The Essentials of the Islamic Faith* (Izmir: Kaynak Yayinlari, 1997). Also see Prof. Dr. Suat Yildirim, "Worldwide Corruption by Scientific Materialism," *Islamic Perspectives on Science*, The Light, New Jersey 2007, pp. 114–119.

4   Said Nursi, *The Letters* (trans.), The Light, NJ, 2007, 451–452.

5   Said Nursi, *The Letters* (trans.), "The First Letter," The Light, NJ, 2007, p. 6.

6   Said Nursi, *The Letters* (trans.), "The Twenty-Fourth Letter," The Light, NJ, 2007, p. 311.

7   al-Bukhari, "Tawhid" 15, 22; Muslim, "Tawba" 14; at-Tirmidhi, "Da'awat" 109.

8   This bone at the end of our spinal column cannot be consumed by the soil. It may contain our DNA.

9   For a detailed explanation of previous peoples' belief in the Resurrection, see Ali Ünal, *The Resurrection and the Afterlife*, The Light, New Jersey 2006, pp. 133–159.

10 This chapter up to this point was mainly summarized from Fethullah Gülen, *The Essentials of the Islamic Faith*, pp. 137–158; and Said Nursi, *The Words*, ("The Twenty-Fifth Word" and "The Twenty-Ninth Word"). For detailed scientific arguments for the Resurrection and its place in previous Divine religions, refer to Ali Ünal, ibid., pp. 70–86.

11 Said Nursi, *İşârâtü'l-İ'caz* ("Signs of the Qur'an's Miraculousness"), Tenvir Neşriyat, Istanbul, p. 11.

12 al-Hakim, *al-Mustadrak*, 4:520; Ibn Hajar al-Haythami, *al-Fatawa al-Hadithiyya*, 36.

13 Muslim, "Imara" 170; Abu Dawud, "Fitan" 1; at-Tirmidhi, "Fitan" 32.

14 al-Bukhari, "Tawhid" 17; Muslim, "Fitan" 101–103; at-Tirmidhi, "Fitan" 59.

15 al-Bukhari, "Anbiya" 3; Muslim, "Fitan" 104, 109; Ibn Maja, "Fitan" 33.

16 Muslim, "Iman" 234; at-Tirmidhi, "Fitan" 35; Ibn Hanbal, *al-Musnad*, 3:107.

17 Muslim, "Fitan" 112; al-Hakim, *al-Mustadrak*, 4:508; Ibn Maja, "Fitan" 33.

18 as-Suyuti, *al-Fath al-Kabir*, 1:315; ad-Daylami, *Musnad al-Firdaws*, 1:266.

19 Ahmad ibn Hanbal, *al-Musnad*, 4:216; at-Tabarani, *Mu'jam al-Awsat*, 5:156.

20 Muslim, "Fitan" 110; at-Tirmidhi, "Fitan" 59, 109; Ibn Maja, "Fitan" 33.

21 al-Hakim, *al-Mustadrak*, 4:573; ad-Daylami, *al-Musnad*, 2:237.

22 Said Nursi, *Şualar* (The Rays), "The Fifth Ray," 574.

23 at-Tirmidhi, "Fitan" 59.

24 Muslim, "Iman" 247; at-Tirmidhi, "Fitan" 53; Abu Dawud, "Mahdi" 4, 6, 7.

25 Said Nursi, *The Letters* (trans.), "The Fifteenth Letter," The Light, NJ, 2007;
    M. Fethullah Gülen, *Prizma* ("The Prism"), Nil Yayinlari, 4: 198–199.

26 al-Bukhari, "Anbiya" 49; Muslim, "Iman" 241, 247.

27 at-Tirmidhi, "Fitan" 59 (2240); Muslim, "Fitan" 20.

28 al-Bukhari, "Hajj" 47.

29 Muslim, "Iman" 234; at-Tirmidhi, "Fitan" 35.

Chapter 6: The Qur'an: The Holy Scripture of Islam

1 Abu al-Baqa', *Kulliyat*, 287; Raghib al-Isfahani, *Al-Mufradat fi Gharib al-Qur'an*
   (Beirut: n.d.) 402; Abdurrahman Çetin, *Kur'an İlimleri ve Kur'an-ı Kerim Tarihi*
   ("Sciences of the Qur'an and the History of the Holy Qur'an"), Istanbul, 1982,
   pp. 30–32.

2 Çetin, ibid, 32–36.

3 at-Tirmidhi, "Fadail al-Qur'an" 25.

4 Ibid, "Thawab al-Qur'an" 14.

5 Said Nursi, *The Words* (trans.), The Light, NJ, 2005, 388–389.

6 Said Nursi, *The Words* (trans.), The Light, NJ, 2005, 156–157, 394.

7 Said Nursi, Ibid., 392–393.

8 Suat Yıldırım, *Kur'an-ı Kerim ve Kur'an İlimlerine Giriş* ("The Holy Qur'an and
   an Introduction to the Qur'anic Sciences"), Istanbul, 1983, pp. 43, 62–63.

9 Subhi as-Salih, *Kur'an Ilimleri ve Kur'an-i Kerim Tarihi* (trans.) ("The Qur'anic
   Sciences and the History of the Holy Qur'an"), Konya, p. 55.

10 Ibid., 57 (reporting from az-Zarkani).

11 Ibid., 61 (reporting from *al-Burhan* by az-Zarkashi).

12 M. Mahdi Puye, *Genuineness of the Holy Qur'an*, Karachi, 1974, pp. 95–98 (re-
    porting from as-Suyuti's *al-Itqan*, and from at-Tabarani and Ibn al-Asakir).

13 Yıldırım, ibid., 62–66; as-Salih, ibid., 62–65.

14 Yıldırım, ibid., 66–70; as-Salih, ibid., 65–73.

15 For a more detailed explanation of these copies and what has happened them in Islamic history, see Ali Ünal, *The Qur'an with an Annotated Interpretation in Modern English,* The Light, NJ, 2007, xviii–xxii, 523–524.

16 This section is summarized and edited from Said Nursi, *The Words* ("The Fifteenth and Twenty-Fifth Words"), and M. Fethullah Gülen, *The Essentials of the Islamic Faith*, pp. 259–266.

17 The Arabic word *Hadith*, commonly translated into English as Tradition, means, as a term, "what was transmitted on the Prophet's authority, his deeds, sayings, tacit approvals, or descriptions of his physical appearance." Jurists do not include the last item in their definition of *Hadith*.

18 Ibn Hisham, *as-Sirat an-Nabawiyya*, 1:337–338; Ibn Jarir at-Tabari, *Tarikh al-Umam wa l-Muluk*, 2: 218–219.

19 Imam Rabbani (d. 1624): Accepted by many as the "reviver of the second millennium," especially in Islamic spirituality. Born in Sarhand (India) and well-versed in Islamic sciences, he removed many corrupt elements from Sufism. He also taught Shah Alamgir or Awrangzeb (d. 1707), who had a committee of scholars prepare the most comprehensive compendium of Hanafi Law called *Fatawa al-Hindiyya* or *Alamgiriyya*.

20 Muslim, "Musafirun" 139.

21 For many other examples of the Qur'an's reference to the scientific facts which have recently been discovered, see M. Fethullah Gülen, *The Essentials of the Islamic Faith*, 239–246.

CHAPTER 7: PROPHETHOOD AND PROPHET MUHAMMAD

1 For detailed knowledge about Prophethood, see M. Fethullah Gülen, *The Messenger of God*: *Muhammad*, The Light, New Jersey 2005, pp. 23–40.

2 Ibn Hisham, *as-Sirat an-Nabawiyya*, 3:49–51, 103; Ibn Sa'd, *at-Tabaqat al-Kubra*, 1:158–159, 164; Abu Nu'aym, *Dalail an-Nubuwwa*, 85–89.

3 Ibn Sa'd, *at-Tabaqat al-Kubra*, 1:102; Ibn Jarir at-Tabari, *Tarikh al-Umam wa'l-Muluk*, 2,128–132; al-Bayhaqi, *Dalail an-Nubuwwa*, 1:126–127.

4 Ibn Sa'd, ibid, 1:129; Ibn al-Kathir, *al-Bidaya wa'n-Nihaya*, 3:456.

5 al-Bukhari, "Bad'u'l-Wahy" 1:3; at-Tabari, ibid., 2:205; Ibn Sa'd, ibid., 1:195.

6 al-Bukhari, "Adab" 77; Muslim, "Fadail an-Nabiyy" 67.

7 Ibn Sa'd, ibid, 11:121; Ibn Hisham, ibid., 1:194.

8 Ibn Hisham, ibid., 1:209; Ibn Sa'd, ibid., 1:146; at-Tabari, ibid., 2:201; Abu Nu'aym, *Dalail an-Nubuwwa*, 1:176–177.

9 as-Suyuti, *al-Khasais al-Kubra*, 1:221; al-Bayhaqi, *Dalail an-Nubuwwa*, 2:32; Ibn Sa'd, ibid, 11:121; Ibn Hisham, ibid., 1:194; 2:43; Abu Nu'aym, *Da-*

lail an-Nubuwwa, 1:186–187; al-Bukhari, *Tarikh al-Kabir,* 1:130. Abu'l-A'la al-Mawdudi, *Towards Understanding Islam*, I.I.F.S.O. 1970, p. 57.

10   Those who followed some of Abraham's pure religion in an adulterated and unclear form.-

11   Abu'l-Faraj Ibn al-Jawzi, *al-Wafa*, 1:101; Abu Nu'aym, ibid., 1:173; Ibn Hisham, ibid., 1:199; al-Bayhaqi, ibid., 2:66.

12   al-Mawdudi, ibid., 59-60.

13   Joseph Hell, *The Arab Civilization*, 10, quoted in al-Mawdudi, ibid., 54.

14   For some of these good tidings, see Ali Ünal, *The Qur'an with Annotated Interpretation in Modern English*, 1261–1264.

15   Sir William Muir, *Life of Muhammad*, Osnabrück, 1988; quoted in al-Mawdudi, ibid., 66.

16   Lamartine, *Hisrorie de la Turquie*, 2:26–27; quoted in U. Azizu's-Samad, ibid., 22-24.

17   See *Man, This Unknown*.

18   Ibn Hisham, ibid., 1:220; at-Tabari, ibid., 2:220; adh-Dhahabi, *Tarikh al-Islam*, p. 149.

19   Ibn Hisham, ibid., 1:315–319; at-Tabari, *Jami' al-Bayan at-Tafsir 'Ayi'l-Qur'an,* 15: 164–166; al-Qurtubi, *al-Jami' li-Ahkam al-Qur'an*, 10:128–130.

20   Ibn Kathir, *al-Bidaya wa'n-Nihaya*, 4:76; Ibn Hisham, ibid, 3:182.

21   M. Mutahhari, *The Polarization around the Character of 'Ali ibn Abi Talib*, Tehran.

22   For further and detailed information on Prophet Muhammad with all the aspects of his life, character, mission, miracles, and his Sunna, see, M. Fethullah Gülen, *The Messenger of God: Muhammad* (trans.), The Light, New Jersey 2005.

23   al-Ajluni, *Kashf al-Khafa*, 1:70.

24   al-Bukhari, "Adhan" 65; Muslim, "Salat" 192.

25   al-Bukhari, "Anbiya" 54; Muslim, "Salaam" 153.

26   Ibn al-Kathir, *al-Bidaya wa'n-Nihaya*, 3:158-159.

27   al-Bukhari, "Riqaq" 3.

28   al-Bukhari, "Tafsir" 2; Muslim, "Talaq" 31.

29   Ibn Hanbal, *al-Musnad*, 2:381; Ibn Sa'd, ibid., 1: 240.

30   at-Tirmidhi, "Zuhd" 39.

31   Ibn Maja, "At'ima" 30.

32   Muslim, "Fada'il" 76; Abu Dawud, "Adab" 12.

33   Ibn Hanbal, 6:256.

34   at-Tirmidhi, "Manaqib" 8, "Shama'il" 33.

CHAPTER 8: ISLAM: THE UNIVERSAL RELIGION OF INTEGRITY AND THE PATH TO PERFECTION

1   The Balance is the Divine standard according to which the universe stands and the Qur'an's injunctions are implemented and practiced to secure justice.

2   Translated by E. H. Whinfield: Sayyid Hussein Nasr, *Science and Civilization in Islam*. Cambridge, MA: Harvard Un. Press, 1968, p. 345.

3   M. Fethullah Gülen, *Key Concepts in the Practice of Sufism: The Emerald Hills of the Heart*, NJ: Tughra Books, 2008, pp. 86–93.

4   Abdulkarim al-Jili, *İnsan-ı Kamil* (Turkish trans.) ("The Universal Man"), Üçdal Neşriyat, Istanbul, 1975, Vol.2, pp. 208–210.

5   Translated by E. G. Browne: Nasr, ibid., 298–299.

6   M. Fethullah Gülen, *Kırık Mızrap* ("The Broken Plectrum"), Istanbul: Nil Yayınları, 2000, pp. 63–64.

7   Sayyid Sharif ar-Radiyy, *Nahj al-Balagha, The Sermons, Letters, and Wise Sayings of Imam 'Ali*, [trans: Jafar Husayn], Qum.

8   Said Nursi, *Hutbe-i Şamiye* ("The Sermon of Damascus"), included in *Risale-i Nur Külliyatı* ("The Collection of the Risale-i Nur"), Nesil Yayınları, Istanbul 1996, p. 1980.

9   al-Ajluni, *Kashf al-Khafa'*, 2:312.

10 al-Bukhari, "Riqaq," 38; Ibn Hanbal, *al-Musnad*, 6:256.

11 Nursi, *The Words* (Trans.), The Light, NJ, 2005, "The Twenty-Sixth Word," 491–494.

CHAPTER 9: ISLAM: THE RELIGION OF AN IDEAL SOCIAL LIFE

1   Said Nursi, *The Letters* (Trans.) The Light, NJ, 2007, 450.

2   Laura Vaglieri, ibid, 33-34, quoted in U. Azizu's-Samad, ibid., 57.

3   M. Fethullah Gülen, "A Comparative Approach to Islam and Democracy," *SAIS Review*, vol. XXI, no. 2 (Summer-Fall 2001).

4   Abu Shuja' Shirawayh ibn Shahrdar ad-Daylami, *Al-Firdaws bi-Ma'thur al-Khitab* ("The Heavenly Garden Made Up of the Selections from the Prophet's Addresses"), Beirut: Dar al-Kutub al-'Ilmiya, 1986, 4:300.

5   al-Bukhari, "Adab" 132; Muslim, "Birr" 28-34; Abu Dawud, "Adab" 120.

6   See Karl R. Popper, *The Poverty of Historicism*, ("Tarihselciliğin Sefaleti"), (trans. Sabri Orman, Istanbul: İnsan Yayınları, 1985).

7   al-Muttaqi al-Hindi, *Kanz al-'Ummal fi Sunani'l-Aqwal wal-Af'al* ("A Treasure of the Laborers for the Sake of Prophet's Sayings and Deeds"), Beirut, 1985, 6:89.

8   Ibn Hisham, *as-Sira*, 3:67; at-Tabari, *Tarikh*, 3:11.

CHAPTER 10: THE SPREAD OF ISLAM AND ITS MAIN DYNAMICS

1   This chapter was mainly summarized from Abul-Fazl Ezzati, *An Introduction to the History of the Spread of Islam*, London: News and Media Ltd., 1976.

2   The *Hijra* commemorates the migration of the Prophet and most of the Makkan community of Muslims to Madina in 622. This event was chosen to mark the beginning of the Islamic lunar calendar.

3   Muhammad Asad, *Islam at the Crossroads* (New Era Pubs.: 1982), 5, quoted in Ezzati, ibid., 2.

4   John Cogley, *Religion in a Secular Age* (New York: Praeger, 1968); Muhammad Asad, *The Road to Makka*, 4th. ed. (Gibraltar: Dar Al-Andalus, 1980), quoted in Ezzati, ibid., 19–24. Karen Armstrong gives a history of how Islam and Prophet Muhammad were misrepresented in the West: See *Muhammad: A Biography of the Prophet*, New York 1993, pp. 21–54.

5   P. Bayle, *Dictionary,* "Mahomed," 1850, quoted in Ezzati, ibid., p. 15.

6   Stanley Lane-Poole, *Studies in a Mosque* (Beirut: Khayats, 1966), 86–89, quoted in Ezzati, ibid., p. 34.

7   A. J. Arberry, *Aspects of Islamic Civilization* (Westport, CN: Greenwood Press, 1977), 12, quoted in Ezzati, ibid., 35.

8   Carl Brockelman, *History of the Islamic Peoples* (London: Routledge & K. Paul, 1949), 37, quoted in Ezzati, ibid., 35.

9   Franz Rosenthal, *Political Thought in Medieval Islam* (Cambridge, UK: Cambridge Univ. Press, 1958), 21, quoted in Ezzati, ibid., 35.

10   B. Smith, *Muhammad and Muhammadanism*, 42–43 (quoting from Waitz), quoted in Ezzati, ibid., 105.

11   Arnold Toynbee, *A Historian's Approach to Religion*, New York: Oxford Univ. Press, 1956, p. 246, quoted in Ezzati, ibid., 7, 12.

12   T. Link, *A History of Religion*, 130–131, quoted in Ezzati, ibid., 6–7.

13   Ibid.

14   Hans Barth, *Le Droit du Croissant*, Paris 1898, pp. 143–157, quoted in Ahmad Djevad, *Yabancilara Göre Eski Türkler* (translated from its French origional: *Les Turcs d'après les auteurs célèbretes—Divers témoignages et opinions*), Istanbul: Yagmur Yayinlari, 1978, pp. 70–75.

15   Popescu Ciocanel, *La Crise de l'Orient*, quoted in Djevad, ibid., 91.

16   Graham E. Fuller, Ian O. Lesser, *Kusatilanlar-Islam ve Bati'nin Jeopolitigi* (trans.), Sabah Yayınları: Istanbul, 1996, pp. 41–42.

17   Ibn al-Athir, *al-Kamil fi't-Tarikh*, 3:227; Sayyid Sharif ar-Radiyy, ibid.

18   S.J. Shaw, *The Jews of the Ottoman Empire and The Turkish Republic*, Macmillan, 1991, 9, 26.

19 S. Kedourie, *Spain and the Jews*, Thomas and Hudson, London, p.165.

20 C. Thubron, *The Great Cities: Istanbul, Time-Life International*, Netherlands, 1978, p. 189.

21 Allister P, "Blissful Years of the Jews in the Ottoman State," *The Fountain*, July-September 1994, issue 7.

22 Ezzati, ibid., 144.

23 Shaw, ibid., p. 32.

CHAPTER 11: ISLAM: FROM PAST TO FUTURE

1   Ahmed Cevdet Paşa, *Kısas-ı Enbiya ve Tevarih-i Hulefa* ("The History of the Prophets and the Caliphs"), Bedir Yayınları, Istanbul, p. 357.

2   Quoted in al-Mawdudi, ibid., 69.

3   Bertrand Russell, *The Impact of Science on Society*, New York: Columbia Univ. Press, 1951, p. 121; quoted in al-Mawdudi, ibid., 15.

4   Quoted in C. E. M. Joad in *Counter Attack from the East*, 28; quoted in al-Mawdudi, ibid., 15.

5   *Black Hole*: An area of space–time with a gravitational field so intense that its escape velocity is equal to or exceeds the speed of light, a great void, an abyss. *White Hole*: A hypothetical hole in outer space from which energy, stars, and other celestial matter emerge or explode.

6   al-Mawdudi, *Understanding the Qur'an* (trans.), 7:32.

7   For examples of the Qur'an's reference to scientific facts and many others, see Haluk Nurbaki, *Verses from the Glorious Qur'an and the Facts of Science*, TDV Yayınları, Ankara 1989.

8   A. Karim, *Islam's Contribution to Science and Civilization*, quoted in al-Mawdudi, *Towards Understanding Islam*, 69.

9   Quoted in al-Mawdudi, ibid., 69.

10 Quoted in al-Mawdudi, ibid., 69-70.

11 Lothrop Stoddard, *The New World of Islam* London: Chapman and Hall, 1922, Introduction, quoted in Ezzati, ibid., 238.

12 Thomas Arnold, *The Legacy of Islam*, Oxford: The Clarendon Press, 1931, p. 9.

13 Dozy, Reinhart P. (tr.), *Indiculus Luminosus*, 268, quoted in Ezzati, ibid., 98–99.

14 Quoted in Ezzati, ibid., 235-237.

INDEX

A

'Abdullah ibn Salaam, 171, 188

Abraham (Prophet), 14, 60, 133, 144, 177, 224, 260

Abu Bakr, 149, 194, 248

Adam (Prophet), 169

'Ali ibn Abi Talib, 125, 148, 207, 210, 255, 260

angels, 5, 13, 27, 34, 47-59, 61, 63, 84, 95, 100, 108, 137, 144, 162-163, 165, 170, 177, 207, 256

B

Basmala, 3, 59

belief, x, 5-7, 13, 18, 23, 25, 28, 36-38, 40-44, 49, 56, 59, 62, 67, 69, 82-83, 92-93, 100-102, 104-105, 108, 116, 122, 135, 144, 155, 158, 160, 178, 185, 218, 222-224, 257; essentials of, 5, 62; certainty of, 6; in angels, 56; in Destiny, 78; in the afterlife, 100; in the Resurrection, 95, 101-102

Book; of Divine Revelation (the Qur'an), 17, 248; of Creation (the universe), 17, 248; Book of the Universe, 26, 106, 245

C

causality, 20, 24-25, 27; veil of causes and laws, 27

creation; hierarchy of; 200

D

Dajjal, 120, 122-124, 126

David (Prophet), 60

Decree, 5, 75, 77, 79-81, 83, 85, 257

deity; concept of, 29, 34-35

Destiny, 5, 13, 28, 75, 77-85, 106, 144, 164, 257; Pen of, 106

destruction; of the world, 120, 123, 128

Dhat (God's "Essence" as Divine Being), 29

Dhu'l-Qarnayn, 125, 156

din (religion), 3

Divine Names and Attributes (Beautiful Names of God), 5, 7, 30, 36-37, 39, 56, 104, 211; All-Compassionate, 3, 13, 33, 59, 65, 95-96, 211; All-Crushing, 96; Eternally-Besought-of-All, 33, 99; All-Generous, 13, 32; Giver of Life, 201; All-Harmonizing, 16; All-Healing, 16, 30, 33, 63; All-Hearing, 33, 36, 65; All-Just, 16, 31, 207; All-Knowing, 4, 30-31, 35, 63, 65, 118, 157, 192; All-Living, 30,